DATE DUE

JUSTICE

The Crisis of Law, Order, and Freedom
in America

JUSTICE

*The Crisis of Law, Order, and Freedom
in America*

RICHARD HARRIS

NEW YORK: E. P. DUTTON & COMPANY, INC.

Published simultaneously in Canada by
Clarke, Irwin & Company Limited, Toronto and Vancouver

Most of the contents of this book appeared originally in *The New
Yorker,* in somewhat different form.

Contents

I

Something Has Gone Terribly Wrong in America

American democracy has survived largely because it is a patchwork system. If one patch fades or is cut or burned out, another can usually be put in its place without much difficulty, and although the new piece may not fit exactly or may not carry out the surrounding pattern fully, no one seems to notice for long, because the complexity of the over-all design conceals changes in it. This is never more apparent than when the greatest change of all occurs—during the transfer of power over the executive branch of the government from one party to another. That the United States has peaceably, even placidly, undergone such a change seventeen times since 1789 marks it as a nation that believes in the rule of law. And that the process has been conducted each time with decency and purpose, even if sometimes none too cordially, marks the society as one that trusts itself. But part of the explanation for what may appear to be an extraordinary kind of public adaptability is that, despite the bitterness of any contest for the Presidency and the expectations which always accompany the transfer of authority from one President to another, not many patches in the quilt are actually changed. When Richard M. Nixon was sworn in as the nation's thirty-seventh President, he at once took command of the immense federal establishment, with 2,705,009 civilian employees and 3,489,922 people in the military services. Of nearly three million civilian jobs, however, fewer than three thousand were subject to change at his order, and of these perhaps three hundred were of enough significance to constitute a change where it counts—in determining policy. Although a couple of hundred vigorous policymakers may sound like a lot, a couple of million bureaucrats, vigorous or not, is a lot more, for most of them instinctively and adamantly resist *any* change—up, down, or sideways. While discussing the problems that would face General Eisenhower when he took over the Presidency, Harry Truman remarked, "He'll sit there, and he'll say, 'Do this! Do that!' And nothing will happen. Poor Ike—it won't be a bit like the Army. He'll find it very frustrating." Nor is this sort of frustration confined to a military man taking civil command. At the end of President Kennedy's second year in office, he was asked what had been his greatest surprise during his Presidency, and he replied unhesitatingly that it had been the gaping difference between the ease in giving an order and the difficulty in getting it carried out.

Of course, the two major political parties do not spend upward of fifty million dollars every four years just for the fun of it. The party that's out of power is determined to change the country's direction, and if it wins it usually does, though in a far slower and more arduous manner than anticipated. Once the power has symbolically changed hands, the reality of that change gradually appears in the way that issues—particularly the issues aired during the campaign —are dealt with. During the last Presidential campaign, the two principal issues were the Vietnam war and law and order. The first was not really discussed, because it had already been discussed to the point of national exhaustion, and because once President Johnson announced a limitation on the bombing of North Vietnam and his retirement, negotiations began on a peace settlement, which permitted all the candidates to gratefully set the issue of the war to one side, on the ground that imprecise and ill-informed remarks could only harm the prospects for a final peace.

Law and order, on the other hand, was discussed to a fare-thee-well. A precipitous rise in the crime rate and the accompanying fear of crime, which had become so infectious that President Johnson described it as "a public malady," provided a ready opportunity for demagoguery. It was not lost. George C. Wallace's entire campaign was based on the issue, and so was a large part of Richard M. Nixon's. By the time the election was over, the contention had created in some people more fear about the fear of crime than about crime itself, because they interpreted the fervent cry for law and order, without an equally fervent cry for justice, as heralding a move toward repression and tyranny. In their view, once the people were sufficiently aroused over the threat of being engulfed by criminality and public disorders, they might be persuaded to set aside their own Constitutional safeguards as the only way to preserve society, and thereby utterly destroy it.

On the night of August 8, 1968, Nixon rose before the delegates to the Republican National Convention, in Miami, and accepted their nomination to be the Party's candidate for President. His acceptance speech, which was heard by a radio-and-television audience estimated at better than sixty million people, was described beforehand by the nominee as "the most important speech of my life." When it was delivered, it seemed at first to be a rather uninspired example of the usual political fare, with the standard promises of peace with freedom, military strength to protect the nation's security, preservation of individual and local rights, and vigorous action to combat crime.

As the campaign unfolded, it became clear that the speech had contained one element that indeed made it the most important speech of his life, since it may well have won him the Presidency. Although the acceptance speeches of Presidential nominees not infrequently stretch the truth to meet political expediency, it is uncommon for them to contain outright lies, which can boomerang with disastrous consequences. Instead of lying to voters, it is far more effective to simply mislead them through inflammatory distortions that suggest how the problems they are most concerned about can be easily resolved. In this case, the problem was crime, and the candidate's solution was to say, "If we are to restore order and respect for law in this country, there's one place we're going to begin: We're going to have a new Attorney General of the United States of America."

The promise was questionable on several grounds. First, the task of controlling crime, both Constitutionally and historically, is primarily the responsibility not of the federal government but of the states, which guard their police powers more jealously than any others. Second, it suggested that a single official, Attorney General Ramsey Clark, was to blame for the rising crime rate. Third, it implied that the candidate was displaying notable courage and wisdom by promising to replace Clark, whereas, of course, all members of the incumbent Cabinet were expected to be replaced if Nixon won. And, finally, it could have politically useful results only if the voters could be trusted to be ignorant of the foregoing facts and if they could be kept ignorant through Election Day. In any event, the promise brought a great roar of approval from the audience in Convention Hall, and in all likelihood it brought Nixon a good deal of approbation from many of the millions who were watching and listening at home.

Nixon had repeatedly tested this approach during the Republican primaries the previous spring. It had drawn a surprising response there, and it seemed certain to be even more effective in the Presidential campaign against a Democratic opponent. To a large extent, the approach became the core of Republican strategy. As Mary McGrory observed in a column written shortly after the election, "At every rally, just before the balloons fell down and the candidate shot up his arms in his double-V sign, Nixon would assure his audience that respect for the law would begin at approximately the moment that the nation's chief law-enforcement officer quit the Department of Justice." And every audience, other reporters noted, clapped its hands, stomped its feet, whistled, and went hoarse shouting its delight.

Apparently, Nixon himself did not enjoy his attacks on the Attorney General. "Ramsey Clark is really a fine fellow," he said to his closest associates during the campaign. "And he's done a good job." In the view of one of the candidate's top advisers, the candidate had felt compelled to use this "simplistic approach" to stir up the voters. But in the view of a former official of the Eisenhower Administration that explanation did not go deep enough. "Whenever Dick finds himself in trouble, he always personalizes an issue," he explained. "In this case, crime was the issue and Clark was the person."

While Nixon was doing his utmost to personalize this issue, Clark, a man most of the electorate had scarcely heard of before the campaign, was doing his utmost to depersonalize it. Consistently throughout his term of office, he refused to popularize the causes he believed in by popularizing himself. As a result, most of his programs were generally unknown and he was generally misunderstood. "In the area of initiating new policies and carrying out his federal responsibility, Ramsey can't be faulted," Fred M. Vinson, Jr., who was Assistant Attorney General in charge of the Criminal Division under him, remarked shortly before the two men left office. "But in the area of getting his message across he has not been successful. That's been the problem for a long, long time." Clark himself once discussed the subject briefly on the "Today" show, and traced his problem back to the nature of his duties. "So many people want me to be only the chief law-enforcement officer in the United States," he explained. "They fail to recognize that, for instance, I head the Federal Bureau of Prisons. And if I don't speak for rehabilitation as the head of the Federal Bureau of Prisons, then who will? They fail to recognize that I have the responsibility for enforcement of the civil-rights laws—a responsibility, I might add, I cherish. I think it's essential to the future of this nation that we vigorously enforce those laws. And this creates animosity. In a sense, you might say that the job of the Attorney General isn't one where you're likely to make friends."

Although there was much truth to Clark's explanation, some of his closest associates and admirers have pointed out that it didn't go far enough, since Attorney General Robert F. Kennedy was equally concerned about and devoted to the causes of criminal rehabilitation and civil rights and yet had managed to create a reputation as an exceedingly tough Attorney General. One official who worked under both Kennedy and Clark has said he feels that Clark was the strongest and most able Attorney General in history but that he failed to come across that way because, wholly unlike anyone in the post before him, he was so deeply convinced the Department of Justice should be above politics that he refused to engage in them, even to the extent of defending himself by publicizing his record.

It is impossible to determine exactly when Clark got pinned with the tag "soft on crime," but several of his colleagues trace it back to a speech he delivered after the riots following the assassination of Dr. Martin Luther King, Jr., in which he demanded that the "loose talk of shooting looters . . . must stop." It may have been the first time in the history of the United States that a high government official publicly expressed the belief that one man's life was more important than another man's property. Clark's advisers unanimously urged him not to deliver the speech, or begged him to at least tone it down by stating that it was all right, say, to shoot someone who was about to put a torch to a bedridden old woman's house but not all right to shoot a youngster who was stealing a pair of shoes from a store's window display. Clark refused. "When everyone high and low kept saying that looters should be shot on sight, as Mayor Daley urged, I felt that a voice from someone in a high position *had* to be raised on the opposite side—no matter what effect it might have on him—to speak out for human life," he explained later.

The speech was delivered at the University of North Carolina, before a large and predictably unsympathetic assemblage of state trial judges—men whose experience with hoodlums and thieves, day in and day out, had tended to make them as hard-boiled as the toughest cop. "The need is to train adequate numbers of police to prevent riots and looting altogether," the Attorney General told them at the outset. "Where prevention fails, looters must be arrested, not shot. The first need in a civil disorder is to restore order. To say that when the looting starts the shooting starts means either that shooting is preferable to arrest or that there are not enough police present to arrest. By definition, adequate police manpower, adequately deployed, could prevent looting on any large scale from ever occurring. This failing, it is the clear and unquestioned duty of police to arrest looters, like all other law violators; arrest them immediately and present them for a speedy trial."

Clark's argument seemed persuasive, and many in the audience listened intently as he went on, "A reverence for life is the sure way of reducing violent death. There are few acts more likely to cause guerrilla warfare in our cities and division and hatred among our people than to encourage police to shoot looters or other persons caught committing property crimes. How many dead twelve-year-old boys will it take for us to learn this simple lesson? Far from being effective, shooting looters divides, angers, embitters, drives to violence. It creates the very problems its advocates claim it their purpose to avoid."

While this speech—or, at least, the "Don't Shoot Looters" headlines it produced—angered many people who feared that *their* homes and property would be next, some observers have felt that in the long run it was not nearly as damaging to Clark's reputation as his work on behalf of civil rights. One person inclined to this view is Warren Christopher, the Deputy Attorney General under Clark. "Ramsey sees this country as having enormous responsibility to Negroes, to the poor, to the young, and he sees an enormous need to extend to them sympathy, understanding, help," Christopher explained while he was still in office. "Of course, in the suburbs this at worst is anathema and at best is simply not shared." As it happened, Christopher added, suburbanites were the most responsive of all voters to political appeals for law and order, although they were also the least threatened by crime.

An incident that Christopher felt best demonstrated the effect of Clark's approach on the public mind occurred in the spring of 1968, when a crowd of angry Negroes from Resurrection City (which had been put up in the capital as a result of Clark's personal intercession with the President) marched on the Department of Justice to demand a fairer share of society's benefits. Some Cabinet officers would have summoned the police to disperse such a crowd, and certainly few of them would ever have faced it in person. Clark did, however, and stood on the stage of the Great Hall, the Department's main auditorium, and heard them out. "Finally, one woman came up to him and started screaming and shaking a fist in his face, and Ramsey stood there and took it," Christopher said. "Of course, it took courage and decency to behave as he did, but the public watching the encounter on television that night got the impression that he didn't respond because he was afraid to. *They* wouldn't have taken it, and, after all, *he* was the Attorney General of the United States. If they had seen him as I have—resisting fantastic pressures from Congress, from the military, and from the White House, and still never losing that infinite calm of his even in the worst crises—they would have known that he was tougher than the toughest of them. But Ramsey never would play it to the galleries."

One important reason for Clark's low standing with the public lay in his refusal to cater to the press. Many government officials—both high and low, elected and appointed—spend a good part of their time cooking up situations that will create headlines and "news" stories about themselves and their work. According to one Assistant Attorney General who worked with Clark for several years, "The media people have been very, very bad, because his philosophy is so quiet. They would much rather report the violent attacks than the soft response."

Shortly after Dr. King's death, Clark appeared on A.B.C.'s television program "Issues and Answers." There were two network correspondents on hand to interview him, and one of them, Bob Clark, started out the program by saying, "This is a rather jittery capital today, as I am sure you know, with the arrival of the first units of the Poor People's March," and went on to talk about the likelihood that violence would break out.

"I really hate to talk so much about violence at the beginning of a very hopeful campaign," the Attorney General said. "The poor people have an awfully important message for the country, and we have to hope that they will have a good opportunity to communicate it."

That point was soon lost as the interviewer continued to talk about the threat of violence and tried to lead the Attorney General to say whether he "would respond with mass arrests" in order to "prevent any disruption of the government."

The Attorney General would not be led. "It is an unhappy time to be talking about mass arrests, right at the beginning of a march that we can all be hopeful about," he replied mildly.

The first correspondent having failed, Irv Chapman, the second, took over and said that "some of the Negroes seem to be all ready to accept the fear that you are all preparing concentration camps for them, to arrest them en masse."

That was too much for Clark. "There are no concentration camps in this country," he said firmly. "There are no plans to prepare any concentration camps in this country. No concentration camps are needed in this country."

Having failed to get an inflammatory statement that would make a headline about the show for the next day's papers, Chapman yielded to his colleague, who asked whether there were plans to use "more tear gas or curfews or arrests."

The Attorney General sat forward and, with a note of impatience in his voice, said, "To dwell now on the riot potential and on law-enforcement capabilities and on the use of gas and mass arrests is to miss the major point, and that is that we have problems in this country that must be resolved, that one of them is the immense, the difficult plight of the poor in America today—and that it has to be addressed, and addressed courageously, by all of our people. We hope we will get some communication out of this opportunity that presents itself now."

Even when matters seemed to merit publicity, Clark was often hesitant to provide it. On one occasion, he was in Los Angeles to deliver a speech and afterward an old friend, Edwin Guthman, who had been Attorney General Kennedy's press officer and was now national-affairs editor of the Los Angeles *Times,* did his best to get a strong statement out of Clark about his efforts to counter organized crime. Guthman knew that in this area Clark had been remarkably effective—far more in a couple of years, in fact, than all his predecessors over the previous decade. Guthman also knew Clark well enough to realize that he would have to get any substance for a story that would justify headlines by the most indirect means. He kept pressing, but Clark politely avoided making any direct response. The Attorney General later remarked to an aide who had been present that he was well aware of what Guthman had in mind—"Clark the crimebuster," he said with a smile—but felt that a story of that kind might be misleading. "Organized crime is only one part of the general crime problem, and by no means the biggest part," he explained. "If I concentrated on playing it up, the public might get to think that everything was well in hand. It wouldn't help to give them the chance to ignore the more important crime problems they have to face."

That was one of the few times a newspaperman went out of his way to try and do Clark a favor. Not long after Clark was confirmed as Attorney General, on March 2, 1967, he accepted an invitation to speak before a meeting of the N.A.A.C.P.'s Legal Defense and Educational Fund, Inc., in New York. Always a close man with a dollar, especially if it belonged to the government, Clark decided to cut down on expenses by not taking along his newly appointed press aide, Cliff Sessions, who had formerly been a reporter with United Press International. After the speech, Clark held a press conference, and after that his hosts brought a man up to him and said that he was a friend of theirs and would like to join Clark for the taxi ride to LaGuardia Airport.

"Ramsey didn't know it, but the man happened to be Sidney E. Zion, of the *Times,* and he wanted an interview," one of Sessions' assistants said not long ago. "If Sessions had been along, he would have refused, because he wouldn't have allowed one reporter an exclusive interview right after a press conference. Anyway, during the ride Zion introduced himself and proceeded with an interview. He asked about the crime wave that was sweeping the country, and Ramsey answered that there was no crime wave as such, since a wave periodically recedes but crime didn't—it just kept increasing." The following day, May 19th, the *Times* ran an article by Zion under the headline "Clark Says Rise in Crime Is Small." The first paragraph read, "Attorney General Ramsey Clark said yesterday that he did not believe there was a crime wave in the nation. 'The level of crime has risen a little bit,' Mr. Clark said, 'but there is no wave of crime in the country.'" A couple of days later, the Washington *Evening Star* published a lead editorial entitled "Crime—What's That?," quoting the Zion story and charging that "our Attorney General, in all deference, is talking through his hat."

Sessions had tried to persuade Clark to respond to the *Times* piece the day it appeared, without success, and now he tried to persuade him to respond to the *Star* attack, again without success. The *Star* repeated its attack several times and ran a particularly vicious cartoon about the Attorney General, and then the issue was raised in Congress. At that point, Clark agreed to respond, but in a typically quiet way—by replying to a letter from Congressman Emanuel Celler, the chairman of the House Judiciary Committee and a good friend, who had written asking for clarification of his views on the subject. Clark wrote back and described what he had said to Zion in the taxi, and added, "Considerably more than half my time, indeed more than half the resources of this entire Department, are devoted to crime reduction. I deeply regret that the public might be led to believe that I do not think crime is a problem. It is a grave national problem." Of course, few people read the *Congressional Record*, where the letter was printed, but several million people read subsequent attacks, in the *Star* and elsewhere, that continued to misquote him.

One duty that falls to any Attorney General is to describe the problems that confront the Department of Justice and what it is doing to solve them before groups of people who have law-enforcement responsibilities or interests—policemen, district attorneys, judges, corrections officers, bar associations, and a large variety of private organizations. Clark found the duty distasteful, because he did not care for even this dim sort of limelight. But he also realized the value of getting his message across, so he accepted the more important invitations that could be fitted into his schedule, which usually involved working twelve to fourteen hours a day six days a week. Giving such speeches was especially burdensome for Clark since he insisted on writing them himself if he had any time available. More often than not, the only time available was the time spent in an airplane, away from telephones and secretaries, en route to an engagement. As a result, he rarely had a prepared text to give reporters, let alone that meat for the journalistic grinder, the press release. "One of the best speeches Ramsey ever gave was to a group of police chiefs in St. Louis in early 1968," one aide has recalled. "The audience was deeply impressed by it, but, as usual, he had no mimeographed text and no release. A lot of reporters were on hand at the start, but when they learned that, they simply walked out, to a man."

All of Clark's closest associates were frustrated and some were embittered by what they saw as his failure to put himself—and thereby the programs that he and all of them were working to make effective—across to the public. But it probably was not so much a failure as it was a personal resolution of one of the most difficult problems facing men in public life—how far one should go in playing politics to accomplish one's ends. Clark resolved it by deciding that in his job the best way to serve what he called "the mission of justice" was by not playing politics at all. It was not because he didn't know the game. Having been raised in a political family, he had heard little else during his youth as his father, Tom Clark, rose through Texas politics, the dirtiest and toughest kind of politics north of the Rio Grande, to serve as Attorney General in the Truman Administration and finally as a Justice of the Supreme Court.

That background offered young Clark a rare opportunity to learn the rules of political life, from the lowest gut-fighting to the loftiest pursuit of justice. Nor was there any doubt about his ability to absorb the lessons. After his discharge from the Marine Corps in 1946, at the age of nineteen, he managed to get a B.A. in less than two years, from the University of Texas, and both an M.A. in history and a law degree in another year and a half, from the University

of Chicago—a total of something under three and a half years for
the lot. "Everyone around here—and there are people in the Department who have brilliant scholastic and work backgrounds—stands in
awe of Ramsey's ability to take a law case or a legal problem and
sort it out," a colleague and friend observed while they were both
still in office. "All in all, I think the most important thing that happened to Ramsey is that he got out of Texas early enough to get a
fair perspective on the world. The second most important thing is
that he took his law degree and his Master's in history at the same
time, which gave him an unusual chance to balance the often harsh
needs of the law with the long-range needs of man. Ramsey's sense
of where history should lead him was worked out long ago, and that's
why the attacks on him now don't seem to bother him. I've never
seen him upset by even the most vicious attacks. About the only
way in which I could fault Ramsey after working with him for several years is that he is not what I would call a superb administrator.
He keeps people somewhat uncertain about where he will finally
come out on any given problem. He doesn't move things as crisply
as he might, and he doesn't delegate authority as much as he should.
But those faults, I think, are the reverse side of his strengths—that
is, he wants to think things through before acting, and he takes on
all the big issues himself where another man would let a subordinate
do them in case they blow up. Above all, though, his greatest fault
has been his refusal to permit publicity about his policies, because
he abhors the public-relations approach to public service. I do, too,
but sometimes it helps get the job done."

To this man and others who knew Clark well, his background
and experience made him uniquely qualified to be Attorney General. Besides what he learned from his father (who has called him
"a block off the old chip"), Clark learned a good deal by spending
half a dozen years in the Department of Justice before he reached
the top. Early in 1961, Attorney General Kennedy took him out of
a prosperous private law practice in Dallas and made him one of

his Assistant Attorneys General—the one in charge of the Lands Division. Before then, few people had considered that post a heady opportunity, but Clark applied himself to it diligently and acquired a reputation for efficiency, organizational grasp, and economy. The upshot was that in 1962 he was sent out to head the federal civilian forces that were present during the riots attending the integration of the University of Mississippi when James Meredith was enrolled there as a student; in 1963 Clark was sent to Birmingham and other parts of the South to oversee the desegregation of public schools and colleges; and in 1965 he was put in command of the federal forces at Selma and at Watts. At the beginning of 1965, he had been promoted to Deputy Attorney General, the second-ranking post in the Department and one of greater influence and responsibility than the similar post in most of the other departments. In October, 1966, he became Acting Attorney General when Nicholas deB. Katzenbach left the Attorney Generalship, and the following March President Johnson appointed him Attorney General.

Standing six feet three inches tall and weighing a hundred and seventy pounds, Clark made a rather frail-looking chief law-enforcement officer of the country. A retiring man, with a soft drawl and a mild manner that was made to seem even milder by the deceptively innocent look in his wide-set eyes under dark sandy hair, he often appeared even younger than he was—forty-one when he left office—and far from being a man used to command. "There's simply no side to Ramsey," a close friend remarked not long ago. "If you didn't know who he was and saw him in a roomful of people, you'd never ask, 'Who is *that?*'" Indeed, Clark often seemed to go out of his way not to impress anyone. While in office, he insisted on travelling tourist class—ostensibly to save the government money but perhaps also to preserve his anonymity.

His insistence on this point often caused some inconvenience. "We'd be on our way to or from the West Coast, with ten hours' work to do in five, and there we'd be, crammed in with some fat guy who would snore half the way and talk the other half," Sessions recalled not long ago. "Still, Ramsey absolutely refused to use the prerogatives of his office. He was almost never recognized—at least, not before the Republicans began roasting him. But one day we arrived at O'Hare Airport, in Chicago, to pick up our tickets before a flight and the clerk recognized his name. He insisted on putting us aboard before the other passengers. Ramsey didn't want to take any advantage, but the clerk forced it. Then when we were airborne, one of the stewardesses came up to Ramsey and asked who he was. She said he must be a movie star or somebody. He fumbled around and finally said that he was Attorney General. She said, 'Oh,' and went off. Half an hour later, she came back and asked what he was Attorney General of. He fumbled around some more and then told her of the United States. She said, 'Oh,' and went off again. When she came back, she said, 'You know, I checked with the pilot and the co-pilot and the other stewardesses, and none of them had ever heard of you.' I believe Ramsey was actually pleased."

On September 29, 1968, Nixon delivered his first major campaign speech on crime—a half-hour radio address over a national hookup. Although the speech seemed to ramble at times, it was actually adroitly fashioned to convey a single impression: that crime control was the job of the federal government. "Some have said that we are a sick society," Nixon told his radio audience. "We're sick, all right, but not in the way they mean. We are *sick* of what has been allowed to go on in this nation for too long. Under the stewardship of the present Administration, crime and violence . . . have increased ten times faster than population." He went on to list, category by category, the rise in the crime rate under the Democrats—an over-all rise of eighty-eight per cent. He did not mention that in the nineteen-fifties, during most of which the Eisenhower-Nixon Administration was in power, the rise had been ninety-eight per cent. "Now, by way of excuse, the present Administration places the blame on poverty," he continued. "But poverty is only one contributing factor. . . . The truth is that we will reduce crime and violence when we enforce our laws—when we make it less profitable, and a lot more risky, to break our laws. One lesson has not been lost on the criminal community. Today only one in every eight crimes results in conviction and punishment. Today an arrest is made in only one in every five burglaries. Today an arrest is made in less than a third of reported robberies. Today it is comparatively safe to break the law. Today all across the land guilty men walk free from hundreds of courtrooms. Something has gone terribly wrong in America."

Of course, the main thing that had gone wrong was that many local police forces were too inept, untrained, undermanned, or corrupt to do their job. Despite these drawbacks, Nixon neglected to say, the police were able to solve a large majority of the kinds of crimes that people were most worried about—eighty-eight per cent of all murders, sixty-nine per cent of all serious assaults, and sixty-one per cent of all rapes.

Although many criminologists and statisticians accept the figures Nixon cited as being reasonably sound, some of them believe that the F.B.I.'s reports of a rise in the nation's over-all crime rate are wholly unreliable. To support this contention, they point out that although nearly four million serious crimes were reported in 1968, probably an equal or greater number were committed but not reported. Since no one has the essential figures to base computations on—that is, the total number of crimes committed, unreported as well as reported, in past years—no one can say with certainty whether there has actually been an increase, let alone what it amounts to. In addition, they say, part of the apparent rise may well be the result of an increase in victims' willingness to report crimes that until recently were rarely brought to the attention of the police—particularly crimes committed in high-crime areas like slums, where the residents feared and mistrusted the police and preferred to accept criminal depredations as merely another unfortunate fact of life. And there has also been an increased willingness on the part of law-enforcement officials to keep more complete records. In the past, they were often reluctant to, because they feared that full disclosure might call attention to the kind of job they were doing; now, however, they are free to tell the worst, since the public has become convinced that the nation is in the grip of criminal forces that are beyond any normal police control. Finally, it has been suggested that some of our law-enforcement agencies' current preoccupation with statistics may be politically motivated, for the more crimes that are reported the more alarmed the public becomes, and the more alarmed the public becomes the more money legislatures are likely to vote for police departments.

Still, the widespread conviction that crime in this country is soaring uncontrollably has brought many people to the point where they live in terror. During the Presidential campaign, crime statistics were used by Nixon to frighten people into voting for him. And they were used by Wallace and others on the far right to create the kind of public mood in which a crackdown on *all* disruptive elements at home might someday be acceptable. But an analysis of the most reliable crime data demonstrates that much of the fear Nixon played on had no basis in reality. For example, of the four million serious crimes reported in 1968 only twelve per cent, or less than five hundred thousand of them, were the kind of crimes that the average citizen feared most—that is, violent or potentially violent crimes. In other words, one-quarter of one per cent of the two hundred million people in the country could expect to be the victims of such crimes in any given year. Although half a million crimes of this nature are too many, surely they are not enough to scare an entire nation out of its wits.

By far the greatest number of all crimes reported were committed by slum-dwellers upon slum-dwellers. For a resident of the black slums of Chicago, for instance, the chance of being physically assaulted, on the basis of reported crimes, was one in seventy-seven, whereas for the white resident of a nearby suburb the chance was one in ten thousand. Nixon did not campaign in the slums, but he campaigned intensively in the suburbs, where he repeatedly cited figures about the crime rate to suggest that audiences there were most threatened by it, rather than to ask them to help provide some measure of security for those who had none. This omission led Clark to say, "The most ironic and profound tragedy threatened by the prevailing fear of violent crime is that those who suffer least would deprive those who suffer most of the very programs that would attack the underlying causes of crime. Thus it is with fear, which crushes hope and opportunity."

Toward the end of Nixon's radio speech on crime, he got to his main point. "Now, what is the responsibility of the Administration of which Hubert Humphrey is a part?" he asked. "Well, it's time for an accounting. Its responsibility is large. It has failed. It has failed in energy, failed in will, failed in purpose. The Attorney General, Mr. Ramsey Clark, has the primary responsibility in this area. Just listen to him. 'The level of crime,' he said last year, 'has risen a little bit, but there is no wave of crime in this country.' . . . Is it any wonder that criminals in America are not losing much sleep over the efforts of the Department of Justice? Is it any wonder that the old saying 'Crime does not pay' is being laughed at by criminals?"

Clark felt compelled to respond, not because he was stung by these and earlier charges and hoped to refute them by placing his record before the public but because he believed that anyone who played upon the voters' deepest fears when, above all, they needed realistic evaluation was unfit to be President. The only way to demonstrate this, as Clark saw it, was to point out the candidate's misrepresentations and to show what they meant and what they could lead to. In other words, he had to become political at last. The opportunity arose a couple of weeks later, when he delivered the main address before a meeting of the Women's National Press Club, in the capital. "Politicians can lead or follow," he told his audience, which contained many of the leading journalists, male as well as female, in the Washington press corps. "They can appeal to the best in people or to the worst. They can divide, brutalize, and mislead, or they can unite, humanize, and give confidence. The great need of this moment is for unity, humanity, and truth." Moving on to the main issue of the campaign, he asked, "What of crime? How is it controlled and reduced?" and answered, "Not by exhortations to 'law and order,' which may mean many things but to most today signify force, order as an end in itself, repressiveness. It nurtures fear by conjuring terrible crimes. It fires anger by implying authoritarian power. It divides black from white, young from old, rich from poor, educated from ignorant. It speaks of the horror of the criminal act, overlooking the greater tragedy: the innate capability of our people to commit crime. It somehow calls for force to prevent the act of crime while ignoring the heart prepared to commit it. Besides dividing, the demagogic phrase misleads or leads not at all. . . . It states an end with the implication that it should be reached by any means."

Having addressed himself to the campaign issue, the Attorney General turned to the campaigner who had raised it. "If Mr. Nixon wants to serve the public interest, he will state his views on crime control rather than misstate mine," he said. Then he continued, "One reason Mr. Nixon resorts to trigger words and misstatements on the crime issue is that he doesn't know enough about the subject, for all his coaching, to talk at length on the merits. Another is that he finds it his style of politics to appeal to fear and hatred and emotionalism—the worst in us—rather than to build constructively with confidence, good will, and reason. We are *all* concerned about crime. Differences on the issues are the nutriment of the political process.

It is on these differences the public should judge. We must state positions on the issues clearly, not fabricate false issues. But the public never sees the issues when Mr. Nixon speaks. Can a man who deliberately misleads be trusted to lead?"

Clark reminded his listeners that the Republican candidate had charged the Administration with not having "much of a sense of urgency about the narcotics problem," and proceeded to say that the amount of opium and its derivatives seized by federal authorities in 1968 was a hundred and fifty per cent greater than the amount seized in 1967, and was an all-time high; that the amount of marijuana seized in 1968 was a hundred and sixty per cent greater than the amount seized in 1967, and was another all-time high; that new methods of treating addicts were being experimented with under the Narcotics Addiction Rehabilitation Act of 1966, which the Johnson Administration had drafted and sponsored; and that the new Bureau of Narcotics and Dangerous Drugs, which was set up early in 1968 on Clark's personal initiative, had doubled the government's enforcement power, educational efforts, and research capacity in the field. In refuting Nixon's charge that the Johnson Administration had done little to stem "a prodigious growth in organized crime," Clark said that in 1960—the last year of the Administration that Nixon served as Vice-President—nineteen members of criminal syndicates had been indicted by the Justice Department's Organized Crime and Racketeering Section, compared to a record high of eleven hundred and sixty-six in 1968. Nixon, he went on, had said nothing about the Department's Strike Forces (a combination of key federal agencies coöperating with local law-enforcement divisions to concentrate on organized-crime operations in specific localities, an innovation that Clark had put into effect a couple of years earlier with extraordinary success); nor had he mentioned that half of all the known members of La Cosa Nostra who had been convicted in federal prosecutions since 1955 had been convicted under Clark's direction—that is, eleven years equalled in two.

JUSTICE

"Was his voice heard when I pleaded time and again with the Congress for seventy-five additional specialists to increase our Strike Force capability and got none?" Clark asked. "While the Department of Justice fought through the years for gun control, did Mr. Nixon speak out? Guns are the principal weapon of the criminal. They are used in sixty-three per cent of all murders, twenty-five per cent of all violent crimes. When a major effort was made to secure meaningful controls following the assassinations of Dr. King and Senator Kennedy and the matter hung in the balance before the United States Senate—who was silent? Who was asked to help and gave none? Richard Nixon."

This time, Clark's speech was widely reported. By failing to fill in the record as the attacks on Clark were made and remade, the press itself had finally forced him to respond, thereby creating a story that was sensational enough to be reported. In this case, the failure of the press cannot be ascribed to the popular conception of harried reporters rushing to meet deadlines. Only at times of extreme crisis —during the riots following the assassination of Dr. King, for instance—was there any kind of "Front Page" activity in the Department of Justice press room. More often, that room was occupied by a few idle figures lolling about with their feet on the desks. About the only event that galvanized them into anything resembling action was the arrival of a release from the Public Information Office next door. Most of the reporters assigned to the Department seemed to consider that their task was not to look into the facts around and behind such releases but merely to rewrite parts of them, always being careful to cut out any of the implicit praise that publicity-minded press aides included in their handouts. The public thus informed and protected, the reporters considered their job done. Of course, there were also some diligent and capable members of the press corps at work there from time to time, but in the end few newspaper readers had any notion of what the Department of Justice's responsibilities were or how its staff and the Attorney General went about meeting them.

The Department of Justice, whose administration became a major issue in the last Presidential campaign, is one of the smallest of the twelve Cabinet-level departments in the federal government, with about thirty-five thousand employees (nearly half of whom are in the Federal Bureau of Investigation) and a budget of five hundred and fifty-five million dollars (about two-fifths of which goes to the F.B.I.). While Health, Education, and Welfare has three times the staff and fifty times the money, the Department of Justice's responsibilities today are staggering in their importance, variety, number, and complexity. A decade or so ago, the Department was known mainly as the agency that prosecuted violations of the Internal Revenue Code, instituted occasional anti-trust suits, kept an eye on subversives, and tracked down Public Enemies No. 1 through No. 10.

Since then, the Department has been given, or has taken on, a number of duties that have put it at the center of domestic controversy—the handling of racial discord, mass protests, riots, and draft resistance, along with an ever-increasing involvement in the problems of crime. To deal with these concerns and a dizzying array of more routine matters, the Department is divided into two hundred and eight separate units. There are five major offices (the Offices of the Attorney General, the Deputy Attorney General, and the Solicitor General, along with the Office of Legal Counsel and the Office of Public Information); eight divisions (the Criminal Division, the Civil Rights Division, the Antitrust Division, the Civil Division, the Tax Division, the Land and Natural Resources Division, the Internal Security Division, and the Administrative Division); three bureaus (the Federal Bureau of Investigation, the

Bureau of Prisons, and the Bureau of Narcotics and Dangerous Drugs); two services (the Immigration and Naturalization Service and the Community Relations Service); two boards (the Board of Parole and the Board of Immigration Appeals); the Law Enforcement Assistance Administration; the office of the Pardon Attorney; ninety-three offices of United States Attorneys; and ninety-three offices of United States Marshals. The Department is often referred to as "the biggest law firm in the world," and although most of its thirty-five thousand employees spend their time administering rather than practicing law, about two thousand lawyers are on duty at any given time, eleven hundred of whom work in Washington and the remainder in United States Attorneys' offices around the country.

As head of the Department, the Attorney General is, first of all, the government's chief legal officer. In that capacity, he is responsible for representing the United States in federal courts, providing both the government's criminal prosecution and its civil counsel. Second, he is responsible for the investigation of violations of federal law, ranging from income-tax evasion and draft dodging to the misdeeds of criminal syndicates and trespasses on citizens' civil rights. Third, he is responsible for the custody of those who are accused of federal crimes and of those who are convicted of them. Fourth, he is responsible for the procedure that aliens have to go through to become citizens. Fifth, he is responsible for the domestic security of the country when it is endangered by foreign subversion or internal dissension. Sixth, he is responsible for easing tension in the country's cities by preventing, or controlling, the kind of outbursts that have overcome many of them in recent years. Seventh, he is responsible for eliminating the booming business in narcotics and for supervising the less booming business of curing those who are the victims of it. Eighth, he is responsible for helping state and local governments beef up their police agencies, courts, and correctional systems through federal aid. Ninth, he is responsible for screening hundreds of candidates for appointment to the federal courts each year.

Tenth, he is responsible for giving legal advice to other Cabinet members and the President. Eleventh, he is responsible for drafting legislation to create a safer and more equitable nation. And, twelfth, he is responsible for assuring that at the same time the law is enforced justice is served.

The Department's specific responsibility for securing law and order—or, to put it in the sequence intended by those who used it most frequently during the Presidential campaign, order and law—is a limited one. It is limited primarily because the Constitution reserves the police power to the states, which, of course, are most directly afflicted by violations of their laws and most able to respond quickly, and secondarily because the federal government has only a small fraction of the manpower that is required to combat crime nationally. For instance, there are more local policemen in Los Angeles County than there are F.B.I. agents in the entire country. There are almost seven times as many deputy sheriffs in that county as there are Deputy United States Marshals in the country. And there are twice as many probation officers in that county as there are federal probation officers in the country. Taking California as a whole, half again as many convicts are in custody there as are held in all federal prisons. Limited as the federal role is, however, it can be critically significant. For one thing, it provides a model for every lesser jurisdiction, and the federal government's over-all approach to the violence and discord of the time will probably determine whether or not the nation's traditional freedoms are preserved.

The task of enforcing federal laws is divided among various parts of the Department of Justice. The most active of them, of course, is the Criminal Division, which supervises the enforcement of all federal criminal statutes except a few that are assigned by law to other agencies. More than sixty-five thousand federal crimes were reported last year, roughly half of which the division prosecuted in federal courts. The cases ranged from bank robbery and kidnapping to violations of the White Slave Traffic Act and of the Migratory Bird

Treaty Act. Except for the investigations conducted by the Strike Forces and trial work resulting from these, which the Criminal Division itself directs, much of the division's work load—more than thirty thousand court cases a year—is handled by United States Attorneys in the field, with supervision, advice, and, when needed, manpower from the Washington office. Not only are the ninety-three field offices closer to the crimes committed but they also are better staffed, with nearly nine hundred attorneys in all.

Even so, considering the case load and special duties of the Criminal Division, its task is prodigious. To perform it, the division, under Assistant Attorney General Vinson, had a staff of two hundred and ninety-three, a hundred and seventy-six of whom were lawyers, and a budget, for 1968, of $3,907,000. Clark had asked for $4,725,000, which was approved by the Bureau of the Budget, the President's watchdog over all government expenditures, but Congress reduced it by $818,000. Representative John Rooney, a Democrat from Brooklyn and chairman of the House appropriations subcommittee that determines the Department of Justice's annual budget, had long scoffed at what the Department claimed it needed to fight crime, and demanded that the appropriation be cut by that amount. (At the same time, he was happy to grant all of the F.B.I.'s request for $219,670,000 as well as the Internal Security Division's request for $2,518,000, even though the latter had so little to do that Clark and Katzenbach wanted to disband it, but couldn't because of political resistance on the Hill.) The Senate restored half the cut in the Criminal Division's budget, but Rooney got the addition thrown out in conference. Because of salary increases required by statute, the reduction meant that the division's resources were held at what they had been the year before, which compelled Clark to do without seventy-five additional men he had planned to add to the Strike Forces. According to a member of the division, "Nothing makes Rooney scream louder than the depredations wrought by criminals, unless it is our attempt to do something about them."

Of all the Criminal Division's operations, the Strike Forces have been the most successful. In January, 1967, Clark dispatched the first Strike Force, which consisted of a team of attorneys and investigators from key federal agencies moving in a closely coördinated manner with state and local agents to investigate, carry out raids, provide evidence for a grand jury, and conduct the prosecution of organized-crime operations in a single area—in this case, Buffalo. The purpose was to superimpose federal action on local law enforcement in order to find and prosecute members of crime rings and then to leave local authorities in control. The program worked so well in Buffalo that by the end of Clark's term in office other Strike Forces had been sent into Detroit, Brooklyn, Philadelphia, Chicago, Miami, and Newark, and ultimately resulted in indictments of close to two hundred racketeers, including some top members of La Cosa Nostra.

"The Strike Forces were Ramsey's idea, but he rarely gets credit for them," Vinson remarked toward the end of 1968. "His fight against organized crime has been extremely effective. His approach has been investigation, indictments, and prosecution—not press hoopla. But, unfortuntely, the absence of hoopla has made it more difficult to do the job. Congress is happy to give us new duties, but it doesn't want to pay for them." When asked how he felt about Nixon's charge that Clark had been remiss in the fight against organized crime, Vinson smiled. "Of course, that couldn't be further from the truth," he said. "Ramsey has been the most effective organized-crime buster in history. But the attack could have a beneficial effect. By generating all that publicity about organized crime, the Nixon Administration may pry more money out of Congress for the Department than we did."

In Nixon's campaign radio speech on crime, he asserted that "Congress has passed carefully considered and carefully drawn legislation authorizing wiretapping, with full Constitutional safeguards, for the investigation of serious crimes," that "three previous U.S. Attorneys General not only outlined the need but also sponsored legislation to authorize wiretapping," and that *"still* the present Attorney General opposes it." It was true that Clark, with the full support of the President, refused to enforce the wiretapping-and-bugging measure that had been enacted the previous summer as part of the Omnibus Crime Control and Safe Streets Act of 1968—on the grounds that it was probably un-Constitutional, that it was certainly an invasion of privacy, and that no one had ever proved it would be effective. It was also true that his three predecessors had advocated the use of electrical and electronic surveillance.

But it was not true that the law contained "full Constitutional safeguards," and it was extremely doubtful whether the earlier Attorneys General would have publicly supported any measure that lacked them. Moreover, it was unlikely that any of them would have backed the use of wiretapping and bugging against just about anyone in the country, as permitted by the current law. Robert Kennedy was away from the Senate, campaigning for the Presidency, when the wiretapping section of the Crime Bill came up for a vote, but he announced that had he been present he would have voted to strike that section entirely. His reason, like the reason given by other opponents of the measure, was that it was anything but carefully considered and carefully drawn. For instance, it permitted the President, on his own initiative and without any safeguards whatever, to order secret surveillance of any person or group that in his opinion posed a threat to "the structure or existence of the government"—a phrase that could be interpreted to include war protesters, civil-rights demonstrators, participants in a national labor dispute, and members of right-wing and left-wing movements.

The law also permitted the Attorney General, United States Attorneys, Assistant United States Attorneys, state attorneys general, and local district attorneys to tap or bug anyone who had committed, was committing, or was about to commit a crime punishable by a year or more in jail, as long as a judge in their jurisdiction approved the request. And the law further permitted all the foregoing public officials to tap or bug for forty-eight hours without a judge's permission if they decided that an "emergency" existed; the definition of the word was left up to them. The principal authors of the legislation—Senator John L. McClellan, an arch-conservative Democrat from Arkansas, and Senator Roman L. Hruska, an arch-conservative Republican from Nebraska—contended that it would provide an invaluable weapon in the war against crime, particularly organized crime. Most of their support came from policemen and prosecutors, who are invariably eager to have any new method to help them perform their duties.

The opponents of the law—mainly leaders of bar associations, law professors, civil-libertarians, and members of Congress who feared that the new law constituted a long step toward a police state—contended that the crimes people were most concerned about were street crimes, and that muggers, rapists, and holdup men were unlikely to discuss their intentions beforehand or their accomplishments afterward over the telephone. As for use of the law against organized criminals, it was pointed out that the first time it proved effective gangsters would devise other means of communicating with each other. That would leave the police and prosecutors with a lot of equipment and no one to listen in on—except perhaps their political enemies, likely subjects for blackmail, or anyone whose activities promised an earful. Finally, the opposition said, although the federal government might be expected to employ such devices with some restraint, there was no assurance that state and local authorities would be at all circumspect; in fact, an unscrupulous district attorney and an unscrupulous judge could certainly harass, and possibly even control, an entire town or city through secret surveillance.

In the State of the Union Message of 1967, President Johnson told a joint session of Congress, "We should protect what Justice

Brandeis called the 'right most valued by civilized men'—the right to privacy. We should outlaw all wiretapping—public and private —wherever and whenever it occurs, except when the security of this nation itself is at stake, and only then with the strictest governmental safeguards." Attorney General Clark accepted even that use reluctantly. "Nothing so mocks privacy as the wiretap and electronic surveillance," he testified before a congressional committee that was considering the passage of such a measure. "They are incompatible with a free society."

If Clark was the only Attorney General to oppose wiretapping except in matters of national security, he was also the only one in the last thirty years or so to take strict precautions to see that it was not abused in the name of preserving the Union. Attorney General Kennedy, for example, accepted F.B.I. requests for permission to use taps and bugs in national-security cases without question. "The assistant director of the bureau would come in and hand Bob a slip of paper asking for such permission, and usually he'd sign it without even looking at the name of the person to be tapped or bugged," one of Kennedy's associates in the Justice Department said not long ago. "Half the time, we didn't even have a record of it on file, so we had no idea of who was under surveillance for what." Clark, on the other hand, insisted that the F.B.I. provide him with a description of each person to be tapped or bugged, a detailed explanation of the reasons for suspicion, and information about what the bureau expected to find out. He was the only Attorney General within a generation who turned down the bureau when he found its explanations too flimsy or the safeguards against involving innocent people too loose.

Clark was deeply suspicious about both the usefulness of this kind of snooping and the motives of the people who wanted to use it. "It's rather ironic that the very men who insist upon our using wiretapping have refused to give us the manpower that we've requested for two years—seventy-five specialists to supplement our

38

Strike Forces in the organized-crime field," he said. "If we had those seventy-five specialists, we could have three to four more Strike Forces going constantly over the United States. And they could secure more indictments and more successful prosecutions than by devoting the same manpower to tap or bug. It takes two to six men to man a single wiretap or bug." For this reason, Clark believed that such surveillance was wastefully inefficient as a law-enforcement device, and that none of its advocates had ever made the kind of case for its use that would "meet the heavy burden of proof our values require" before such widespread intrusions of privacy were allowed. Asked if he also felt that the supporters of a law like this had a taste for sneakiness, he replied, "I do indeed."

Above all, he was most concerned about the creation of what he called "a tradition of surreptitiousness by law enforcement." In discussing the possibility or, he feared, the likelihood of this coming about, he explained, "If we create today traditions of spying on people, the time may not be far distant when a person can hardly speak his mind to any other person without being afraid that the police or someone else will hear what he says and therefore know what he thinks. Because of the size of our numbers and the denseness of our urban society, it will be difficult enough in the future for us to secure some little sense of privacy and individual integrity. We can trap ourselves, we can become the captives of our technology, and we can change the meaning of man as an individual."

Many observers believe that by far the greatest contribution the Department of Justice can make in the endless struggle to control crime in this country is through the assistance and advice it provides to local law-enforcement agencies, which must deal with about ninety-five per cent of all the crime that is committed. One of the ironies of Clark's career as Attorney General was that although his reputation as a crime-fighter was very low with the man in the street, it was very high with the man in police headquarters. For example, Quinn Tamm, head of the International Association of Chiefs of Police, said that Clark had "done more to help local law enforcement than any other Attorney General." Many local law-enforcement officials agreed. Donald D. Pomerleau, the police commissioner of Baltimore, stated that Clark had provided more "enlightened leadership" and greater "sensitivity to the problems of law enforcement" than any of his predecessors. Bernard L. Garmire, the chief of police in Tucson, said that Clark had contributed more to "improving the calibre of police officers than any other Attorney General in history." One reason for his standing with heads of police departments was that he got to know more than a hundred of them around the country on a first-name basis, and in the process he also got to know their problems at first hand. When he went out on the road to make a speech or attend a meeting, he usually stopped by to see the local police chief.

Herbert Jenkins, the chief of police in Atlanta, has recalled being astonished to get a telephone call from Washington one day late in 1967 informing him that Attorney General Clark was to be in Atlanta in a couple of days and would like to meet with him. "I'd been chief here for twenty years, and in that time every Attorney General had been here at one time or another, but none of them had ever talked to me," he said later. "Ramsey came over to the police department and spent several hours asking my opinion of this and that. He talked to my staff, to men on the beat, to people working in the slums. It had a big effect on us. And by listening to us he got us to listen to him."

When men like Jenkins listened, they discovered that Clark was keenly aware of their problems, and, of course, they were gratified when he told them, as he often did, that the policeman was "the man in the middle" and that because of his place in a society torn by social upheaval he was "the most important man in America today." And they were obviously pleased by his constant appeals for higher salaries and greater prestige for all law-enforcement personnel. To attract and keep the best men available, Clark recommended that the average salary currently paid—in cities of half a million population or more, it ran from sixty-six hundred dollars for rookie patrolmen to a top of seventy-six hundred dollars, whatever the length of service—should be increased to a degree that no one else had ever dared suggest. He proposed that patrolmen in similar-sized cities start out at ten thousand dollars a year and go up to a top of fifteen thousand dollars. Noncommissioned officers, he went on, should be paid from fifteen thousand to twenty thousand dollars, officers and division heads from twenty thousand to thirty thousand dollars, and chiefs and administrative directors from thirty thousand to fifty thousand dollars.

Although the pay scale undoubtedly seemed wildly inflated even to many of the policemen who heard him propose it, Clark argued that the money would be well spent on men who were properly qualified for their jobs. "We must recognize how important professionalization of police is," he told a meeting of police chiefs late in 1968, and went on to define professionalization as meaning college-trained patrolmen, college-trained officers who had proved their proficiency on the job, and specialists with advanced degrees in criminology, police science, public administration, law, medicine, psychology, and sociology. "Americans pay less than twelve dollars and fifty cents [per capita a year], on the average, for all police services," he told his audience. "Surely we are willing, even anxious, to pay more."

A few months earlier, the federal government had shown that it was prepared to pay more for improved services when Congress passed a bill setting up a Law Enforcement Assistance Administration, which was empowered to help local police departments, courts, and correctional systems upgrade themselves. The bill, which grew out of a project devised by Attorney General Katzenbach and implemented by Attorney General Clark, provided that the L.E.A.A., under the supervision of the Department of Justice, could spend a hundred million dollars in fiscal 1969 and three hundred million dollars a year in fiscal 1970, 1971, and 1972 in grants to states that set up approved programs for recruiting, training, and paying policemen; for modernizing their equipment and reorganizing their departments; for developing advanced rehabilitation techniques and other means of easing the return of convicts to society; for bringing their court systems up to date; for setting up crime-prevention programs in schools, colleges, and welfare agencies; for making loans to policemen who wanted to start or complete college studies; and for conducting research in all areas of law enforcement.

While the L.E.A.A.'s approach to the problem of crime in the United States was generally considered the most enlightened and most promising one ever developed, some participants in the struggle to enact it were deeply concerned about a couple of changes that were made in the Administration's original proposal as it passed through Congress. One was that the fifty million dollars originally requested by the White House for the first year was doubled, with most of the addition being earmarked not for upgrading law-enforcement agencies but for increasing their ability to control riots and organized crime. This led critics to suspect that money vitally needed for modernizing the country's antiquated law-enforcement machinery would instead be used to buy tear gas, mace, armaments, and wiretapping equipment.

Even worse, in the opinion of these critics, was a successful move led by Republican members of Congress, with the active support of former Vice-President Nixon, who was then campaigning in the primary contests, to require that all federal grants be given directly to states that developed generally approved programs, rather than, as the original measure stipulated, to localities with specifically approved programs. This amendment—known as the block-grant amendment—created a precedent that threatened to ultimately deny the federal government the right to say how its money was to be spent. Further, since state legislatures were still controlled by rural interests, despite the Supreme Court's redistricting orders, a large part of the government's money, it was charged, would be likely to end up not in the crime-ridden cities it had been intended for but in relatively placid towns and villages, and not for the purposes originally set down but for whatever local authorities felt would most enhance their law-enforcement practices. Many small-town police officers, it was suggested, might be somewhat less interested in going to college to study criminology or in boning up on the latest technological developments in police science than in getting pay raises, purchasing new prowl cars and fancy uniforms, and laying in supplies of the latest weaponry.

In Clark's view, the last eventuality was the most dangerous if it occurred before the police were professionalized. "The law could be a disaster," he said, and went on to explain, "The way it's written, even funds that aren't specifically set aside for riot control could end up being spent to stockpile arms for use during riots or demonstrations. It's another potential, and an enormous one, for repression. If the police have all that elaborate armament and are as untrained and undisciplined as many of our policemen are today, they may be inclined to use it in riot situations. After all, that's what they will be given it for. And if they do, this country will be in the gravest danger. There will be a bloodbath, and that can only lead to repression and more bloodshed and more repression." Clark's fear of this outcome was far deeper than he ever expressed publicly. "The worst way to preserve peace is by cracking down, but that's exactly what a lot of people want done," he has said in private. "Take the situation down at South Carolina State College, in Orangeburg. In February, 1968, students there demonstrated against a segregated bowling alley. They were just kids, and there was no need for the use of maximum force. In fact, there probably wasn't any need for force at all.

Before we could move in and take action against the bowling alley for violating the civil-rights laws, the cops—a bunch of big, burly state troopers who far outweighed and outnumbered the youngsters —waded in and began shooting. When it was all over, three kids were dead and nearly thirty more were wounded. The black people down there are so embittered that it will be years before they get over it, if they ever do. Next time, they'll probably come armed."

Asked whether he thought events of this nature could produce a revolution if there were enough of them, the Attorney General thought for a minute, then answered, "I never used to believe that this country could become so divided. But I do now."

Of all the forms of crime that are on the increase in the United States, one of the most alarming is the illegal use of narcotics. There are around sixty-three thousand known addicts in the country (half of them in New York City) and possibly an equal number who are unknown. Whatever their number, they contribute a disproportionate amount to the crime rate. In fact, some experts attribute three-fourths of all the serious crimes committed in New York and Washington to addicts—a figure that, many believe, may also apply to other large cities. The illegal use of narcotics in this country fell off gradually from 1900, when the number of addicts was estimated to be two hundred and fifty thousand in a total population of only seventy-six million, until 1960, but then it rose sharply. Between 1960 and 1968, arrests for all crimes rose by a little under eleven per cent, but arrests for violations of the drug-and-narcotic laws rose by nearly a hundred and sixty-five per cent.

The increase was not, as many people have imagined, confined to the dispirited inhabitant of the black slum. While narcotics violations were limited almost entirely to that class ten years ago, drug use has more and more afflicted middle-class suburban residents, until today the ratio is half and half between blacks and whites. Most of today's addicts are young. The rise among the young in all categories of crime between 1960 and 1968 was sixty-four per cent, but their arrests for possessing and selling narcotics went up by a staggering seven hundred and seventy-four per cent. Among all age groups, close to ninety per cent of those arrested for violating the laws on addictive drugs had criminal records, and seventeen per cent of them were armed, presumably to enable them to commit other crimes to support their habit.

It is an exceedingly expensive one. A heroin addict—the principal user involved—needs between fifty and sixty dollars a day to keep himself supplied. Since an addict is rarely able to hold down an ordinary job, let alone a job paying that kind of money, he must steal money or else merchandise that can easily be converted into money. As a rule, stolen goods bring about ten per cent of their value in cash, so, theoretically, the country's sixty-three thousand known addicts must steal three and a half million dollars a day in cash or thirty-five million dollars a day in merchandise, or a combination of the two, in order to survive. In trying to raise funds, the addict most often relies on muggings, holdups, or burglaries, and in the course of committing them he not infrequently assaults or murders his victims. Since crimes of this kind—the kind that frightens the ordinary citizen most—constitute only twelve per cent of all crimes reported in the country, and since many, perhaps most, of them are the work of addicts, it is clear that control of the illegal use of narcotics and the rehabilitation of those addicted to them would greatly reduce the crime rate on this level and also immeasurably alleviate the public anxiety.

Although the narcotics addict, like any other offender, must finally be dealt with by changing the conditions that drive him to such a desperate course, right now the problem is so acute that it can be met only by getting him off the street. In the past, that was often difficult to do because the federal authority to take that step was legally fragmented. Until 1968, the federal government divided responsibility in this field between the Bureau of Narcotics, a part of the Treasury Department, and the Bureau of Drug Abuse Control, a part of Health, Education, and Welfare. For a long time, it was believed that most users of LSD were otherwise lawabiding youngsters out for a hallucinatory thrill, but it was finally learned that some forty per cent of them had also been committing other crimes. And it was found by federal agents from the Bureau of Drug Abuse Control, which had jurisdiction over LSD, that nine out of ten of its possessors also possessed marijuana, but *that* drug came under the jurisdiction of the Bureau of Narcotics. Absurd as this conflict was, and critical as the need for effective government action to control drug abuse had become, no one did much about it until Clark recommended that the two agencies be combined in a single Bureau of Narcotics and Dangerous Drugs, with a staff expanded by fifty per cent, and that the new agency be set up not in Treasury or H.E.W. but in the Department of Justice, where it obviously belonged.

Few changes in government are easier than creating a new agency, and few changes in government are harder than disbanding an old one. Although the staffs and the programs of the two bureaus were expected to be largely retained under Clark's proposal, it met with the kind of fierce opposition that comes from entrenched bureaucrats who know the rules and dearly love them as they are. Nor are members of Congress, who cling to *their* rules with some devotion, much more open to change. In this case, though, the need for amalgamation was so overwhelmingly clear that even a Congress as deliberately sluggish as the Ninetieth was forced to accept it. "It was one of the most important changes ever made in the Department," Vinson said after the new bureau was set up. "It will have an immense impact. But, of course, hardly anyone knew it was all Ramsey's doing, so somebody else will get all the credit for its success."

"There are few better measures of the concern a society has for its individual members and its own well-being than the way it handles criminals," Attorney General Clark told a conference of the American Correctional Association in the summer of 1967. "No element is less deserving, easier to forget, and more difficult to work with. The history of penology is one of the saddest chapters in the story of man. Here, self-inflicted, is an incredible amount of human misery." Misery, he added, was the lot not only of the prisoners themselves but of the victims of the crimes that had sent them to prison, the victims of the crimes they would commit when they got out, and finally society as a whole. "Intelligence and self-interest tell us today that we must work diligently and effectively with those who commit crime," Clark went on. "We must rehabilitate as many as have the capacity for rehabilitation. The question is not whether to be tough or tolerant. The question is what is effective."

He pointed out that the tough, eye-for-an-eye solution might work if people who committed crimes were sent to prison and kept there for good. But since ninety-five per cent of them were returned sooner or later to society, that method was bound to be tougher on it than on them. And the tougher a prison system was the tougher would be the convicts who emerged from it, many of whom went there as first offenders—confused youngsters without criminal natures, or those with no more than a mild grudge against society. The first were almost certain to fall in with hardened criminals, the teachers in these giant crime schools, and to come out educated and confirmed in the ways of the criminal life. And the second were almost certain to emerge with an implacable hatred toward the society that had sent them there. As Clark put it, "Many prisoners, finally overcome by man's inhumanity to man, put aside forever all compassion, to rely ever after on cunning."

Whether the threat of imprisonment is a deterrent to crime has long been debated, but there can be no debate about whether the fact of imprisonment serves that purpose, for it clearly does the opposite. Three-fourths of all prisoners convicted of committing felonies were previously convicted of committing misdemeanors, usually in their youth. Half of them will go on to commit other felonies when they leave prison, and, in fact, will be responsible for four out of five serious crimes that are reported. These statistics have led Clark to conclude, "Corrections is a key, a very major part of our total opportunity to reduce crime. If we cut the rate of recidivism in half—and science tells us we can—a major part of our crime will be eliminated." Not much of it had been eliminated up to that time, he added, because until Congress passed the act setting up the Law Enforcement Assistance Administration there had been "no major national investment in corrections research." The little that had been carried out, however, had demonstrated that recidivism was clearly one element in the crime rate that could be controlled, particularly among the young.

Each year, two million people pass through the nation's two hundred and fifty major prisons and reformatories (only twenty-eight of which are federal establishments), a third of a million of them being in residence at any given time. Although only a twentieth of the total number of prisoners remain prisoners for life or die behind bars, until recently almost nothing was done to prepare the rest of them for their return to the outside world. Before the L.E.A.A. was established, the United States spent one and a tenth billion dollars on all its prisons—or about one-tenth of one per cent of the gross national product. Moreover, of that billion plus, ninety-five per cent went to pay for custody and only five per cent for reforming —or, as some call it, "coddling"—criminals.

Shortly after Clark became Acting Attorney General in 1966, he reported that thirty state prisons for adults had no vocational training whatever; that only five states had halfway houses (small centers that aim, and have been highly successful, at serving as decompression chambers for prisoners who are reëntering society); that twelve states had no probation services for adults who committed misdemeanors (usually the first kind of crime anyone commits), seven states had only the barest form of probation services, and the rest were almost universally understaffed by unqualified workers. Nearly half of all state probation and parole officers took care of a hundred cases at a time, or twice the recommended maximum.

As for the nation's thirty-one hundred local jails, through which an unrecorded number of people pass each year, they were, and are, far worse. "These jails have extremely limited, if any, diagnostic and treatment programs," Myrl Alexander, director of the Federal Bureau of Prisons, said not long ago. "Personnel are untrained, and most jails serve only as human warehouses and crime factories—places where impressionable younger offenders may learn the ways of crime. And no significant improvements in local jails have taken place in nearly a century." Still, if jails have no work or study programs, no recreation, no separation of prisoners by age or criminal history, at least their inmates do not ordinarily stay in them for long. Prisons, on the other hand, constitute home for ciminals for many months or years, and even the boy or man who enters one of them with some measure of hope and determination and courage usually is forced by conditions to give up. Once he has, he is inclined to forget what the outside world is like. And when he returns to it, he is almost always utterly unprepared psychologically, socially, and financially to cope with freedom. "Traditionally, inmates are still returned to society on the day of release with little more than a suit of clothes, a bus ticket, and a few dollars," Alexander pointed out. "The majority have no families to whom they can turn for assistance and no job or job prospect." Indeed, it is surprising that only half of them soon commit other crimes.

Society's self-destructive way of treating those who have offended it remained the rule until Robert Kennedy took office as Attorney General. "Within thirty days, there was a crescendo of interest in this bureau that we'd never seen before," Alexander said while serving under Clark. "Before two months were out, we had got four halfway houses that we'd been begging for fruitlessly for years. Kennedy got us a hundred thousand dollars for each of those and another hundred thousand for research on the best way to run them. Research was, and still is, one of our primary needs, because we know shamefully little about offenders individually, what group they should be put in with for maximum results, and what are the best techniques for each group. In fact, we know very little that is useful about whole specialized groups of offenders."

When Katzenbach took over the Department, it turned out that he was as concerned about rehabilitation as Kennedy, especially study-and-work programs during imprisonment. Katzenbach had been a prisoner of war for two and a half years in Germany, and he had studied so assiduously during that period that when the war ended and he returned to Princeton, where he had spent two years before entering the service, he was able to pass his final exams almost at once.

"Then Ramsey took over, and things really got moving," Alexander went on. "He can't think of crime without thinking of corrections, especially youth and young-adult corrections. He wants to move the system out of its medieval ways and get rid of all the crippling old myths, the shibboleths, the public's indifference, and the urge toward puritanical revenge. Because of his approach, some of the old attitudes are dying out. In fact, it's downright amazing how things have changed in less than a decade. Many of us on the lower levels—the professionals, that is—have wanted to make these changes

38486

for many years, but the impetus had to come from the top. It finally did."

The over-all change in emphasis from punishment to rehabilitation has taken a number of forms in the most advanced federal institutions. One of the most important departures—at least judged by its effect in cutting down the rate at which ex-convicts become convicts again—is that from hopeless drudgery on a rock-pile or ditch-digging squad to specialized schooling and job training suited to current labor-market needs. Belief in the new approach has become so strong among penal officials in federal prisons that all inmates except those who are physically disabled are required to put in a full day at either a work or a work-study project. In the past, about the best vocational training a prison inmate could hope for was learning to make mailbags or license plates. Since the only manufacturers of mailbags and license plates happened to be prisons, the experience did not go a long way toward preparing anyone for a job outside. Today, however, prisoners are taught such skills as linotype and printing-press operations, electronic-cable assembling, aircraft welding, and computer programming. They are also taught everything from how to read and write to advanced college subjects. Once they are released after this intensive training, they can have reasonable expectations of getting jobs that pay from five hundred to seven hundred dollars a month, compared to perhaps half that much as unskilled laborers, which was the most they could hope to earn, honestly, before.

Under the Federal Rehabilitation Act of 1965, which was drafted by the Department of Justice, prison officials were given far wider latitude than ever before in devising new methods for preparing inmates to reënter the outside world. Most notably, prison officials were given the power to commit or transfer adult prisoners to "residential community treatment centers," or halfway houses; to grant prisoners unescorted leave for up to thirty days for such purposes as visiting seriously ill or dying relatives, attending funerals, or going

51

to talk with prospective employers and to look for somewhere to live when they were finally released; and to allow inmates to spend their days working or studying in neighboring communities. A few months after the act was signed, on September 10, 1965, several hundred federal prisoners had regular jobs outside the walls and others were attending colleges and universities. Under this system, about five thousand federal prisoners have earned better than four million dollars while incarcerated, which has taken hundreds of their dependents off relief rolls. Some industries in areas where there are severe manpower shortages have set up training programs in nearby prisons, so that inmates will get a head start on their work-release participation and will be fully qualified when the time comes for parole. To help locate industries with manpower needs, Clark set up a pilot project in Atlanta, in 1967, to collect and collate information about job opportunities in that area; then prison training could be coördinated with business needs.

All in all, the training program has been so successful that Alexander expects some seventy per cent of the federal-prison population to be trained outside government institutions by 1979. The in-prison training and work programs have also been highly successful and highly rewarding, both for the prisoners, who are allowed to send their earnings home or to put them aside for later use, and for the government, which sells the products they make. Last year, Federal Prison Industries, Inc., a government corporation that runs forty-eight prison manufacturing plants, producing everything from office furniture to electronic assemblies for the space program, had gross sales of fifty-five million dollars and was able to turn over a five-million-dollar profit to the Treasury. The federal model has been imitated fairly widely by the states, twenty-seven of which now have similar programs.

Of all the crime committed in this country, the largest proportion committed by a single age group is committed by fifteen-year-olds, and the greatest need of all is for rehabilitating these and other young offenders. "Since 1960, adult crime has either maintained a level or declined slightly," Clark told a meeting of the nation's governors at the White House early in 1968. "Not so juvenile crime. . . . It has risen far more rapidly than the population growth—up fifty-eight per cent in seven years. Prevention of delinquency among juveniles in the long run is the most important thing we can do. This is where all of our growth in crime is." In 1968, more than half of those in federal prisons were under the age of thirty, and more than a third were under the age of twenty-five. This brought the average age of federal prisoners down to twenty-eight, the lowest in history. At the same time, the kinds of crime they were locked up for were becoming more and more serious; for instance, twice as many people were convicted in federal courts of bank robbery in 1968 as in any other peak year. And, of course, the earlier a person embarks on a life of crime the more crime he will commit during that life.

At the White House conference, Clark told his audience, "Perhaps the most important statistic in law enforcement is this: Eighty per cent, roughly, of all convictions for serious crimes are of people who were convicted, usually as a kid, for a misdemeanor. We spotted them then. We knew their potential. They contribute most of the crime. Why haven't we tried to do more about it?"

The most promising attempt so far to do more about it began on December 9, 1968, when Attorney General Clark officially dedicated the Robert F. Kennedy Youth Center, in Morgantown, West Virginia. The facility, which is set in a deep natural amphitheatre and looks like the campus of a small, fairly well-endowed college, is planned to house three hundred and fifty youngsters, ranging in age from sixteen to nineteen. The inmates are a cross-section of youthful prisoners in other federal institutions, so that the success or failure of the center can be measured by comparing its rate of recidivism with that of federal youth institutions elsewhere in the country. Like other youthful prison inmates, those in the center show the same general intelligence distribution as non-deliquent youngsters across the country but are about five years behind them in educational background and much further behind in work skills. The educational program runs from basic reading and writing through high-school studies, and additional courses are provided at West Virginia University, nearby, for those who can handle the work.

At the same time that the boys are brought up to or beyond the level of seniors in high school, they are given basic job training in four general fields—technical services, graphic arts, electricity-electronics, and aerospace—and then get intensive training in areas that they show special aptitude for. While the boys are being schooled in vocational and academic skills, trained counsellors concentrate on guiding them away from their old gang habits to more socially acceptable ways of gaining some measure of status. And as they do, they are rewarded with better quarters, more personal freedom, and even a form of earnings. In short, the center constitutes a small society that is designed to give youngsters the chance they ignored or were denied in the big society outside.

"If we know anything, we know that corrections can rehabilitate," Clark said at the dedication of the center. "We know the younger the offender the better his and society's chance. Let us begin with the young." It was a beginning full of promise, for earlier, less elaborate experiments along this line, principally several conducted by the California Youth Authority, had shown that criminal relapses among youngsters could be cut in half. But the beginning also promised to be costly, in view of the expense of the plant itself, its upkeep, and the unusually high ratio of trained staff to inmates. Of course, in the long run the outlay would be infinitesimal compared to the cost of keeping hardened criminals behind bars on and off for most of their lives. Then, too, there was the cost in money and suffering that their crimes would result in if they were repeatedly sent back to society in no better shape than prisoners have been in the past.

If the experiment at the Kennedy Center proves successful, the federal government will undoubtedly duplicate it elsewhere. But that will take years, and in the end will affect only a relative handful of the country's criminals. Senator Edward M. Kennedy, who was present at the dedication ceremony, brought up this point when he said of the center, "Its lessons are meant to be learned and applied in every state and community. It succeeds as a model only if it is copied. It fails if it remains unique."

During the 1968 Presidential primaries and the Presidential campaign, Nixon, building upon earlier attacks against "the Warren Court" from the extreme right wing, repeatedly charged that the Supreme Court was guilty of "seriously hamstringing the peace forces." The Court has no means of defending itself against such charges, since if it is to be effective it has to stand above all partisanship. Once again Clark felt that someone in a high position had to speak out against what he regarded as demagoguery, and once again he chose the occasion presented by the meeting of the Women's National Press Club to do it. "When Mr. Nixon attacks the Supreme Court, he may appeal to the fleeting prejudices of a majority, but he assaults our greatest champion of those who suffer most," Clark said. "He undermines our confidence in our system. He attacks the one branch of government that has moved unfalteringly toward equal justice under law."

Since becoming Deputy Attorney General, Clark had been deeply involved in a campaign to help all courts move closer toward the ideal of equal justice. One result was the opportunity for state and local governments to upgrade their courts through grants provided by the Law Enforcement Assistance Administration. Another was a radical improvement in the operations of the District of Columbia

Court of General Sessions, which handles almost all felony arraignments and all misdemeanor cases in the District. Unlike most federal courts, which display little of the frantic hubbub common to state and local criminal courts, General Sessions, which is under federal jurisdiction, was as depressing a place as the worst big-city criminal court in the land. Although it was directed by judges appointed by the President and served by United States Attorneys as prosecutors, its docket was so crowded that delays of a year or more were not uncommon, and the building itself had been so neglected that it struck nearly anyone who entered it with the chill of despair. Because of the rather grubby nature of its work, the court had long been a stepchild in the federal family. Finally, the Johnson Administration, prompted by the Department of Justice, instituted sweeping reforms, including the addition of more judges, more United States and Assistant United States Attorneys, more court aides, more probation officers, and a complete refurbishing of the building itself.

The improvements had a striking effect, not just on the defendants who passed through the court but on the states that used the new approach as a model. Their greatest need was for reducing court delays, for, as all law-enforcement experts agree, whatever deterrent effect punishment may have is utterly lost if a long time passes between the commission of a crime and the punishment for it. Clark hoped that another effect of the change would be to demonstrate to policemen, prosecutors, judges, and corrections officers how dependent on each other they were. "If the police effectively apprehend persons charged with crime but prosecution is lax, little good is done," he told a meeting of the Criminal Law Section of the American Bar Association. "If prosecution is firm and effective but courts cause long delays, little good is done. If police, prosecutors, and courts are all models of efficiency but correctional efforts fail to rehabilitate, the treadmill has only speeded up."

In private, Clark has expressed regret that the two groups most strongly opposed to modern rehabilitation methods are the two groups that stand to benefit most from them in the long run—policemen and prosecutors. Although shortsighted, their opposition is not difficult to understand. "If a policeman risks his life to arrest somebody and then the guy is let off on probation or after serving a brief sentence, the cop is bound to get sore at whoever let him out," Clark explained. "And the same applies to prosecutors, who sometimes have to try the same defendant over and over." (According to another high official in the Department of Justice, the law-enforcement official who has been the most determined opponent of probation or parole, at least for certain defendants, is J. Edgar Hoover. "Anyone who was sent to prison for doing something against the F.B.I. or who was personally arrested by Hoover himself, which used to happen quite often, has no chance of getting out before he's served his full sentence," this man said. "It doesn't matter if he's the most model prisoner that was ever in the place. Hoover puts pressure on parole boards in these cases, and they always go along with him. Of course, that means the reform of criminals is set back, because if the inmate himself sees that exemplary behavior gets him nowhere, other inmates see it, too.")

As Attorney General, Clark worked to transform the Department's age-old approach of "the flinty-eyed prosecutor" into one that more closely resembled what he called a ministry of justice, in which the objective would be not the stern application of the law to some but the fair application of it to all. And in such a ministry, he held, fairness would mean fairness to defendants across the board, on the part of policemen, prosecutors, judges, and prison officials. Throughout the history of the United States, the rights guaranteed by the Constitution have been unalienable only to those who were wealthy or astute enough to hire counsel to assert them. The rest—the great majority of criminal defendants—have been mostly the poor, the ignorant, the unwary. In a sickening number of cases—five thousand lynchings of Negroes in the half century preceding the Second World War, for example—"justice" has been the summary will of the mob. And in a far greater number of cases those who had no rights because they didn't know they were supposed to have them were summarily dispatched to jail or prison without a chance to defend themselves, let alone a chance to have someone else defend them.

In New York City the standard practice among criminal lawyers —as often as not, legal hacks who hang around courtrooms hoping to pick up a fee or two—is to attach themselves to potential clients at the time of their arraignment. Most often, the clients are Negroes, who are almost always hopelessly bewildered by court procedures. The lawyer's most common approach under these circumstances is to persuade, or more often instruct, the defendant that his only hope of avoiding a stiff sentence is to plead guilty to a charge one rung down the ladder from the one brought against him—assault, say, instead of armed robbery—and then to offer the plea to the district attorney. Unless the crime was particularly hideous or the defendant is particularly notorious, the district attorney will usually accept the offer. Except for sentencing, that completes the case.

In the end, everyone but the defendant is happy—the arresting officer because he won't have to spend hours or days attending a trial, the prosecutor because he has obtained another conviction for the record without preparing and arguing a case, the judge because it doesn't add to the congestion of his docket, and the lawyer because he has earned a sizable fee (usually paid by strapped but grateful relatives of the defendant) for a few minutes' work. In the process, which is known in New York courts as "a shave and a haircut," no one bothers to ask whether the defendant is guilty or innocent. It is doubtful that there is a policeman, a prosecutor, a defense lawyer, or a judge in the country who has not participated in the process. It takes place thousands of times a day throughout the country, and it is the oldest and clearest example of disrespect for the law in the name of order.

Something Has Gone Terribly Wrong in America

The idea of a ministry of justice is believed to have originated with Jeremy Bentham, who incorporated it in his proposal for a Constitutional Code. In the United States, the subject was first broached by Roscoe Pound, dean of the Harvard Law School, in 1917. Nearly half a century passed before the concept of elementary fair play toward ignorant and poor defendants in criminal cases was broadened and laid down as a firm rule—this time by the Supreme Court. In a series of decisions beginning in the late nineteen-fifties—the Mallory, Escobedo, Gideon, Wade, and Miranda decisions particularly—the Supreme Court laid down new rules to compel police, prosecutors, and lower courts to give poor and ignorant defendants the same protection against violations of their Constitutional rights that well-to-do defendants with enough sense to hire lawyers had possessed all along. Efforts to implement the Court's decisions within the Department of Justice were not pressed with any vigor until Robert Kennedy took office, in 1961. His interest in the subject seems to have grown out of another interest—poverty, especially as it affected crime. Law-enforcement officials had long been aware that most crime was committed by the poor upon the poor, but as the crime rate began to rise precipitously during the fifties, the middle and upper classes began to be increasingly affected by and afraid of it. That meant, of course, that it was on the way to becoming a political issue.

To find out what effect poverty had on crime, Attorney General Kennedy set up a Committee on Poverty and the Administration of Federal Criminal Justice, which came to be known as the Allen Committee, after its chairman, Francis A. Allen, a professor of law at the University of Chicago. Early in 1963, the committee submitted its report, which demonstrated that the effects of poverty on crime were far greater than anyone had suspected, and which recommended, among other things, that the government revise its bail system, since it effectively violated the Constitution by keeping people in jail for long periods before trial if they were too poor to post bond;

that paid counsel be provided for the needy in all criminal cases; and that an Office of Criminal Justice be established within the Department of Justice to see that all actions of the federal government in criminal matters were conducted fairly.

On March 8, 1963, President Kennedy sent Congress a bill incorporating the Allen Committee's recommendation that paid counsel be provided for needy defendants in federal criminal proceedings—fortuitous timing, it turned out, because ten days later the Supreme Court handed down its decision in Gideon v. Wainwright, which stipulated that all criminal defendants in state courts had to be given the help of counsel if they asked for it and were unable to pay the price. These events prompted Congress to pass the Criminal Justice Act of 1964, which accomplished a large part of what the Allen Committee had recommended. Robert Kennedy's final act as Attorney General was to announce—on August 10, 1964, in a speech before the Criminal Law Section of the American Bar Association—the formation of an Office of Criminal Justice under the Deputy Attorney General.

"We intend that this office will deal with the whole spectrum of the criminal process, from arrest to rehabilitation," he said. "We intend that it will deal with social problems that affect the criminal process, such as narcotics, or juvenile delinquency, or the right of privacy. We want it to be a voice inside the Department and a forum outside the Department. Perhaps, above all, it is our hope that this Office of Criminal Justice will be only the first step in dealing with what I believe is one of the most aggravating problems of criminal law: the wide—and widening—gulf between law-enforcement officials on the one side and other legal figures concerned with protecting the rights of the individual on the other."

When Katzenbach took over as Attorney General, Clark became his deputy, and when the time came to present the budget request for the new office before Congressman Rooney, Clark was chosen to make the case for it. "Rooney thought it was a lot of foolishness,"

Clark said later. "We asked for a hundred thousand dollars, but were lucky to get fifty-five thousand." Because Rooney continued to think that the approach was foolishness, the Office of Criminal Justice has never had enough money or staff to do the job it was set up for. Even so, the office's accomplishments have been out of all proportion to its size. One of its first assignments was to prepare a syllabus of subjects it might look into. This was later used by the President's Commission on Law Enforcement and Administration of Justice, more commonly known as the Crime Commission. By the time the commission was announced, on July 26, 1965, the Office of Criminal Justice had prepared an extensive agenda. The pertinence of this document prompted the commission to choose as its director the head of the office that had compiled it, James Vorenberg, who had formerly been a professor at the Harvard Law School.

In setting out to study the nation's system of criminal justice, almost the first thing the commission discovered was that there was no system. "They found that there was such a widespread and deep fragmentation of authority among the various agencies responsible for the administration of justice that no systemic approach was possible," Daniel J. Freed, who was director of the Office of Criminal Justice under Attorney General Clark, said shortly before leaving that post. "For instance, a judge looks at the administration of justice one way. A corrections officer looks at it in a different way. And a policeman looks at it in a still different way. There is no authority—except, perhaps, the implicit moral authority of the Attorney General and the Chief Justice of the Supreme Court—to give them a cohesive overview. That's what we try to do. Although we have no operational authority whatever, our job is to find ways of bringing about coördination in the federal system and in the District of Columbia by helping the agencies that have such power to use it effectively."

Among the most successful projects worked on by the Office of Criminal Justice were the Law Enforcement Assistance Act of 1965, a seven-million-dollar pilot project that led to the creation of the three-hundred-million-dollar-a-year Law Enforcement Assistance Administration in 1968; the so-called "fair-trial, free-press guidelines," which amount to ground rules that allow the press to give the public a fair idea of what is happening to defendants in criminal actions but also protect such defendants against prejudice resulting from undue publicity; the expansion and modernization of the District of Columbia Court of General Sessions; and the Bail Reform Act of 1966, which codified a number of important reforms in the method of trading money for freedom.

To demonstrate that justice under law must at last be made equal in practice as well as in theory, Clark once cited the French cleric Félicité de Lamennais, who lived through Napoleon's time and the Revolution of 1848 and who observed that every stable government in history had depended on the resignation of the poor to being poor. "The poor in this country are no longer willing to accept poverty," Clark added. "Nor are they willing to accept the injustice that has always accompanied it. Events no longer give us a choice about having or not having true criminal justice. Without it, we won't survive."

The nineteen-sixties have been a decade of protest—against poverty, against the denial of civil and human rights, against military service and the Vietnam war, and against politics-as-usual. Much of the protest has been directed at the federal government and has involved the use and abuse of its property. When this has happened, federal authorities have had to decide what the government's response should be, and these decisions have been up to the Attorney General. One of the most difficult of the decisions was whether a permit should be given for the participants in the Poor People's Campaign to enter Washington in May, 1968, and take up residence there in Resurrection City. President Johnson, mindful of the scandal that followed General Douglas MacArthur's violent routing of the Bonus Marchers from their tents and shacks on Anacostia Flats in 1932, and perhaps fearful that federal troops would have to be called in again to disperse the poor—this time the black poor —preferred to have the affair prohibited altogether.

However, Clark was convinced that the protest not only was valid but was guaranteed by the Constitutional rights of assembly and free speech. He was also convinced that if the protesters were not given a legal and orderly means of expressing their grievances they would resort to illegal and disorderly means, which would bring on what the President feared most. Accordingly, the Attorney General and other Department of Justice officials met time and again with the leaders of the march to work out arrangements that would be satisfactory to both sides. After several weeks of negotiations (including the weeks during which the marchers slowly made their way from Alabama to the capital), agreement was finally reached on a route and time for the arrival, a place for Resurrection City, conditions for its construction and operation, and a fixed period for its occupation. Dr. King had been scheduled to lead the march, which he hoped would generate support for an open-housing law.

Before the marchers reached Washington, Dr. King was assassinated, riots swept through more than a hundred cities across the country, including a particularly violent one in Washington, and Congress passed the Civil Rights Act of 1968, which included the open-housing provision Dr. King had asked for. Although the pressing specific reason for the march had been removed, Dr. King's successor as head of the campaign, Dr. Ralph Abernathy, apparently felt that it was too late to call it off, and proceeded as planned. By the time the marchers reached the capital, the temper of its residents, both black and white, was near the breaking point, and it took daily and sometimes hourly negotiations between the Department of Justice and the leaders of the march to keep the situation under control.

"Dr. King's means, as always, had been purely non-violent, but after his death some really violent-tempered militants moved into the march and into Resurrection City," one of Clark's aides said afterward. "It was clear that they hoped to provoke a confrontation that would create a violent, and preferably televised, response by federal authorities. All the elements of disaster were present, but Ramsey averted it by patiently talking with Abernathy, who didn't want violence any more than he did, and finding ways to meet those parts of the militants' demands which were legitimate. That way, he slowly siphoned off the rage, and kept the peace." Nevertheless, Clark was widely criticized from both sides—by Negroes because he had been too firm and by whites because he had been too soft.

Much the same reaction attended his conduct in enforcing the Selective Service laws. If circumstances permitted, Clark kept cases that seemed to constitute violations of the law within the Selective Service machinery as long as he could, chiefly because he felt that many of those who refused to register for the draft or who burned their cards and resisted induction were sincere young people who could be better dealt with through bureaucratic channels—at least at the beginning, when there was still time to persuade them to change their course—than through arrest, trial, and imprisonment. At the same time, he did not hesitate to resort to the latter means when the former failed.

Although Clark was as vigorous in this respect as any other Attorney General, and prosecuted over fifteen hundred draft cases in federal courts during 1968 alone, once again he was persistently attacked by people on the right for doing nothing. And he was attacked with equal vehemence by people on the left when he did something—most of all when he prosecuted Dr. Benjamin Spock and four others for allegedly "counselling, aiding, and abetting" young men to evade the draft. "We got a terrific amount of flak after that indictment," Vinson, who, as head of the Criminal Division, was responsible for prosecuting the case, said afterward. "The question facing us was: Do we go after speech or do we go after conduct? There was far more pressure on us to haul into court some of the hairy, foulmouthed kids who so aroused the public during the march on the Pentagon than there was to prosecute someone like Dr. Spock, who had proceeded on his course with great dignity. But Ramsey knew that the legal problem was conduct, not speech. And since Dr. Spock had violated the law in our view by his conduct—intentionally, as he made very clear—the only proper course was to prosecute him. A political-minded Attorney General, on the other hand, might well have left him alone and dragged the offensive kind of draft protester into court. That's one way government repression could start."

Many who support Clark on other grounds still attack him for the way he chose to prosecute the five men—on conspiracy charges rather than on charges that they had committed specific acts in violation of specific laws. For his own part, Clark said recently, "I have always had grave doubts about conspiracy charges in a legal sense, and I have doubts about the Spock case. But, at the time, the essence of all the events leading up to the march on the Pentagon indicated a common course of action in which these individuals were primary participants. One could believe that Spock was morally right —as I may have, in fact—and still believe that the laws had to be enforced. As the nation's chief law-enforcement officer, I had the duty to prosecute Spock and the others when, in my judgment, the facts showed a violation of the law. If you don't enforce the law, it becomes shapeless." Pausing for a moment, he went on, "Conspiracy charges are fairly common legal devices—to a degree, because they're easier for the prosecution. Under the press of daily business in the Department, I never had time to sit down and thoroughly sort out what I thought about conspiracy, legally speaking. I was remiss in that, I'm afraid. If I were Attorney General now, I would be inclined to prohibit the use of conspiracy charges altogether." In any event, Clark let the judge in the case know that the Department would recommend that no jail sentence be imposed after Spock and the other defendants were found guilty. The judge retorted that he didn't want a formal recommendation, and gave them two years. As with all the other cases that Clark filed as Attorney General, he did not discuss any aspect of this one beforehand with the President.

Another way government repression could start, Clark believed, was by forbidding the exercise of legitimate dissent on the ground that it might produce violence. Once again, when the march on the Pentagon was announced in October, 1967, the President was opposed, and so, it appeared, were most members of Congress and a large majority of the public. But once again Clark was convinced that the project was entirely Constitutional and that it would be better to find some legal way for it to occur peacefully than to stifle it. "We had endless talks with the leaders of the march beforehand," he recalled later. "We not only found a legal way for them to carry out their aims—including their aim of getting arrested by forcibly trespassing on government property—but we also learned what they were planning every step of the way. That made it possible for us to plan our response calmly and carefully, which is extremely important, since in a crisis one is likely to act too rashly when the unexpected occurs. Rashness can only mean trouble, and in a time like this one, trouble can be the spark that sets off an explosion."

On October 5, 1966, John Doar, then head of the Civil Rights Division, testified before a House subcommittee in opposition to a bill providing that anyone who crossed a state line with intent "to incite a riot, or to organize, promote, encourage, or carry on a riot, or to commit any act of violence in furtherance of a riot, or to aid and abet any person in inciting a riot or committing any act of violence in furtherance of a riot . . . shall be fined not more than $10,000 or imprisoned not more than five years, or both." Doar opposed the measure on several grounds. To begin with, he testified, it seemed to be a clear violation of the First Amendment guarantees of the rights of free speech, peaceful assembly, and travel. Second, riot control was a job for local police, since local riots constituted local crimes, and local crimes were the Constitutional responsibility of local authorities. And, third, it would be exceedingly unfortunate if the public was misled into believing that any such law could prevent riots.

Above all, the part of the bill that most concerned Doar and Clark, whom he spoke for, was the part that defined a riot as "a public disturbance involving acts of violence by assemblages of three or more persons." As he pointed out, this provision made large, peaceful demonstrations virtually impossible, since most of them were organized and participated in by out-of-staters, who would be liable to punishment if three or more people on hand created a disturbance —including such people as local right-wingers, who could attack law-abiding out-of-state demonstrators and thereby make their targets, but not themselves, subject to federal imprisonment and fines, or, for that matter, such people as the police, who could accomplish the same purpose by creating a riot, as they have in the past. In any event, the bill kicked around in Congress for a year and a half, and then, following the riots after Dr. King's death, Congress passed it as a rider to the Civil Rights Act of 1968.

In the course of the week or so that the riots lasted during the spring of 1968, Clark remained on duty around the clock at the Justice Department—either in his office on the fifth floor, in the command center down the hall, or in a small room above his office where there was a cot, a desk, a television set, a telephone, and an Exercycle. Getting by on a couple of hours' sleep a day, he spent most of his time receiving and evaluating reports from around the country. The national authority over civil disorder has traditionally been asserted, with extreme reluctance, only when local authorities concede that they are utterly unable to maintain control, and it was the Attorney General's delicate task to determine when that point had been reached. When the point was reached, it was his responsibility to recommend to the President, who had to approve the decision, that federal troops be moved into the troubled area at once.

One of the most severely afflicted cities that spring was Chicago, where many stores and homes were pillaged and burned down. Accordingly, Clark was not at all surprised to get a telephone call from Chicago urging that federal troops be dispatched there immediately, but he was very much surprised that the call came not from the mayor or the governor, one or the other of whom was required by law to make the request, but from the United States Attorney for the Northern District of Illinois, Thomas Foran. According to the Attorney General's aides, Clark was the calmest man in the Department throughout the crisis, but this was one time he allowed himself to display impatience. He said that since Foran was in no position to know what was happening elsewhere in the country, he was in no position to make a judgment about whether the President could spare federal troops just then; that such a request had to come from the mayor or the governor; and that before it could be granted, evidence had to be supplied that local forces were inadequate.

"What's the matter with the Chicago Police Department?" Clark demanded. Foran offered no answer to that, or to the other points, so the conversation was terminated. Clark was more than impatient when he later learned that Foran had called him from Mayor Richard J. Daley's office, with Daley at his side. Although a United States Attorney is theoretically responsible to the Attorney General, he is in practice more likely to respond to the person who recommended him for his job—usually the most powerful politician from his party in the state. In this case, Mayor Daley was that politician, and he was apparently trying to use a federal officer to provide federal intervention so that he would not have to admit publicly that he was unable to maintain control in his own city. After the riots were over, Clark let Foran know how he felt about what had happened, but, as later events were to demonstrate, Foran's loyalty to Daley was unaffected.

Something Has Gone Terribly Wrong in America

When the anti-war demonstrators threatened to descend on Chicago during the Democratic National Convention that August, Daley again turned to the federal government for help—this time directly to the President, to whom he appealed for a strong federal presence in the form of Army troops. The President convened an advisory group consisting of top White House, Pentagon, and other senior officials to consider the matter. All but one of those on hand voted to approve Daley's appeal. The one holdout was the Attorney General, who believed that the response was far too large for the threat, which, he suspected, had been magnified out of all proportion by Daley. Once the President decided to dispatch troops to Chicago, the matter was largely out of Clark's hands. But he sent Deputy Attorney General Christopher to Chicago with the mission of assessing the need for the actual use of the troops and of convincing Daley that the best way to assure a peaceful Convention was by offering the demonstrators a peaceful outlet for dissent. Daley was infuriated by the move. He reluctantly agreed to see Christopher a couple of times during the two weeks he was there, but adamantly refused to so much as talk with the demonstration leaders. Instead, he angrily attacked Christopher, Clark, and the entire Department of Justice for encouraging "outside agitators," who, he declared, were out to ruin the Convention and the city, too.

Chicago hippies and Yippies who had originally planned to participate in the anti-war demonstrations now began to change their minds. Having observed Daley's grim inflexibility at first hand, and having heard his expressions of determination that there would be no repetition of the spring riots (which Daley attributed to Clark's success in persuading the Chicago police chief not to "shoot to kill arsonists and shoot to maim looters," as Daley wanted), the local crowd of young dissenters circulated a warning through their underground press that out-of-towners should take him seriously. "The cops will riot," came the message from Chicago. "The word has gone down—'Brutality be damned!'" But the New York contingent, which was to supply most of the demonstrators, continued to take the whole matter lightly. A team of reporters from the London *Sunday Times* later reported:

> Nothing daunted, the New York Yippies continued to pile on the politics of the put-on—much of it seemingly calculated to offend Daley's sexual puritanism. The list of Yippie projects, by no means exhaustive, included ten thousand nude bodies floating in protest in Lake Michigan; the mobilization of Yippie "hookers" to seduce delegates and slip LSD into their drinks; a squad of 230 "hyper-potent" hippie males assigned to the task of seducing the wives and daughters of delegates; releasing greased pigs in the Loop area; a mass stall-in of beat-up automobiles on the expressways; the insertion of LSD into the city's water supply; Yippies dressed in black pajamas to dispense handfuls of rice to the citizenry; and the infiltration of the right-wing with crewcut Yippies who, at an opportune psychological moment, would exclaim, "You know, these Yippies have something to say."

Daley took all this quite seriously, and so, it seems, did representatives of the F.B.I., the Secret Service, and the Chicago Police Department. Daley placed an around-the-clock guard on the city's water supply; he also ordered the city's twelve thousand policemen to go on twelve-hour shifts, and persuaded the governor to send in six thousand National Guardsmen and the President to supply six thousand Regular Army troops, equipped with rifles, flamethrowers, and bazookas. Reliable estimates put the number of demonstrators in Chicago at the beginning of the Convention at no more than two thousand. And when they were later joined by others, from Chicago and nearby areas, it is believed they numbered at the most around ten thousand. Of these, all but two or three hundred were peacefully inclined, and their principal weapons were vituperation and obscenity. Officials in the Department of Justice who had had wide experience in such matters were convinced that Chicago could easily have accommodated a hundred thousand demonstrators without serious consequences if arrangements had been handled with circumspection.

Reports brought back from Chicago by a contingent of observers that Clark had sent there to watch events before and during the Convention convinced the same officials that the police had indeed rioted, as was charged in a subsequent report by Daniel Walker, head of a study team for the National Commission on the Causes and Prevention of Violence. Of course, Mayor Daley denied all the charges, and polls showed that some two-thirds of the public applauded the behavior of the Chicago police. That finding astonished even some of the most cynical appraisers of the public mind, because it meant that, for the first time in the nation's history, a large majority of its citizens supported the right of the police to beat hundreds of unarmed and unresisting men, women, and children into insensibility.

"Dick Daley opened another gate to tyranny in this country," one high official in the Department of Justice said later. "If it is left open by a failure to punish—clearly and thoroughly—those who committed the acts of terror and intimidation, then any mayor or governor in the country can take the law into his own hands and get away with it."

After the Chicago police riot, Attorney General Clark found himself under intense and growing pressure to act. The demands were not that he call the police or the mayor who loosed them to an accounting but that he prosecute the demonstrators under the 1968 anti-riot law. Much of the pressure came from members of Congress who had assured their constituents that the law would prevent riots and were now expected to explain what had gone wrong. Some of the pressure came from Daley, who hoped to absolve himself by persuading the government to condemn others. But most of the pressure came from the President, who in some measure had been driven from office by demonstrators like the ones in Chicago. After Clark's legal staff assured him that no grounds existed for federal prosecution of the demonstrators, he refused all demands for it.

Instead, he resorted to a Reconstruction statute, enacted in 1866, that made it a federal offense for any policeman to deprive any citizen of his civil rights by inflicting summary punishment on him without due process of law, and instructed United States Attorney Foran to initiate proceedings under it against nine policemen—the ones who appeared to have inflicted the most brutal summary punishment. To see that his orders were carried out, Clark sent a couple of Department aides to Chicago to keep an eye on things. Foran duly proceeded as ordered, and submitted the evidence to the Federal District Court for the Northern District of Illinois for consideration by a grand jury. As it happened, the judge who convened the grand jury was the chief judge of the court, William J. Campbell, who is said to be very close to Mayor Daley. Although grand juries, especially federal grand juries, are supposed to be wholly free of outside influence as they deliberate, they are actually quite susceptible to the influence of the presiding judge, if he cares to exert it.

According to inside reports, Judge Campbell cared to very much. He ordered that a daily transcript of the jury's proceedings—with nothing left off the record—be prepared and delivered to his chambers each day, and he frequently summoned the jurors before him to deliver instructions on what they should consider and in what light they should consider it. (When the Walker Report was released, Judge Campbell angrily attacked its timing as an attempt to influence *his* grand jury, as he put it, and added that the grand jury might want to investigate the matter for possible contempt-of-court action.)

In the capital, a few liberals in Congress urged Clark to press the case to a conclusion before the election—or, at least, before the inauguration of a new President, who might appoint a new Attorney General with different ideas about justice. Since both the judge and the prosecutor were in a position to guide the grand jury,

Clark was largely helpless, and the case was still pending when he left office. Shortly before he did, he was asked if he had changed his mind about not prosecuting the demonstrators. "No," he answered firmly. "And if the new Administration does prosecute them, that will be a clear signal that a crackdown is on the way."

Of all the duties that have been given to the Department of Justice, perhaps the most politically explosive is that of redressing the wrongs that have been the common lot of Negroes in this country, particularly in the South, by protecting and asserting their civil rights. That task is up to the Civil Rights Division, which was established by the Civil Rights Act of 1957. At the outset, the division's authority was limited to enforcing the little-used Reconstruction statutes already on the books. The Civil Rights Act of 1960 broadened that authority, by making obstruction of school integration a federal crime and by setting up a system of federal referees to settle voter-registration disputes. Then came the Civil Rights Act of 1964, which empowered the Attorney General to initiate suits against discrimination and segregation in public facilities, public schools and colleges, and places of employment; allowed him to intervene in private suits seeking relief from the denial of equal protection of the law because of race, color, religion, or national origin; and provided for the termination of federal funding for any state or local program under which such discrimination was practiced. The federal-referee system set up by the 1960 act for voter-registration disputes proved inadequate, and this led to the Voting Rights Act of 1965, which prohibited the use of literacy tests and other such devices as criteria for registration or voting; it also provided that the Attorney General could appoint federal voting examiners to register voters in counties where existing practices deprived Negroes of a chance to vote, that he could appoint election observers to make sure that voting procedures were conducted fairly, and that he could take civil and criminal actions against any person or any organization that violated the law. Finally, the Jury Selection and Service Act of 1968 prohibited racial discrimination in picking federal juries, and the Civil Rights Act of 1968 prohibited discrimination in most housing in the United States.

During Clark's last year in office, the Civil Rights Division was expected to carry out these immense responsibilities with a hundred and six lawyers and a hundred and eleven clerks, working on a budget of two and a half million dollars—or enough manpower and money to do a respectable job in one of the larger states. After Congress passed the open-housing act, Clark asked Congress for enough money to hire fifty-five additional employees to handle the huge work load that was expected to descend on the division when the law went into effect, on January 1, 1969. Congressman Rooney turned him down.

When the century-long denial of civil rights to Negroes results in civil riots, as it has more and more in recent years, it is up to the division to find out whether there were violations of the civil-rights laws during the riots and whether the public, the police, and the courts observed the legal proprieties in the aftermath, when the urge for revenge was strong. All this is done with the hope that in the long run the success of the division's efforts will help to make desperate outbursts a thing of the past, but the immediate job of heading them off before they start has more and more become the responsibility of a fairly new part of the Department of Justice—the Community Relations Service. This was set up by the Civil Rights Act of 1964 "to provide assistance to communities and persons therein in resolving disputes, disagreements, or difficulties relating to discriminatory practices based on race, color, or national origin . . . whenever, in its judgment, peaceful relations among the citizens of the community are threatened."

Something Has Gone Terribly Wrong in America

The kind of "community" in which such assistance is most urgently needed was described by a resident of the Watts section of Los Angeles after the riots there in 1965. "We suffer most of the crime, vice, disease, ignorance, poverty, hopelessness, and misery of the whole city," he said. "Every advantage and opportunity, like all leadership and power, is absentee. Our landlords don't live here. Store managers and clerks and others who work here drive back and forth from their homes. Even politicians and preachers are absentee. They don't live in our part of town. When the sun goes down, there ain't nobody here but us and the police."

Although the conservative forces in this country created and maintained conditions in places like Watts, the liberal forces, by promising too much and delivering too little, altered those conditions just enough to make revolt against them inevitable. It has long been standard liberal dogma to argue that the only way to control crime, including the crime of rioting, is to change the circumstances of poverty, ignorance, and lack of opportunity that produce it. But people who are involved most directly argue that while this has to be the long-range goal of the nation, the problem of crime, particularly the crime of rioting, can't wait. Clark has often made this point, and on one occasion when he did, in a speech to the Women's Forum on National Security, early in 1968, he went on to describe briefly what life for a youngster in a slum was like. "In a nation where only three and a half per cent are unemployed . . . one-fourth of the Negro boys and one-third of the Negro girls cannot find jobs, and for many who do there is low pay and little chance to advance," he said. "The poor, young Negro lives in physical and psychological loneliness. He is cut off from his chance. Fulfillment, the flower of freedom, is denied him. A small disadvantaged and segregated minority in a mighty and prosperous nation, he is frustrated and angry." Since that frustration and anger, multiplied several million times, was threatening to burst out at any moment, Clark said, he was convinced, especially by what he had learned from the experience of the Community Relations Service, that the only way to stop this from happening was by immediate action that produced immediate results.

Almost the first thing that the staff of the C.R.S. learned was that practically no one outside the country's slums had any idea of what went on inside them. Nor, they found, had anyone even begun to devise realistic ways of dealing with the barbed tangle of problems that beset them. Roger W. Wilkins, a young Negro lawyer who had been with the service since its inception and was its director for three years, recently described how, after a flurry of riots in 1964, he and his staff had gone into various black slums around the country. "We talked to mayors and found that generally they just didn't know anybody in the slums except the ceremonial leaders—the black ministers, black businessmen, black politicians," he said. "White leaders had almost no contact at all with the *real* leaders, the indigenous militant leaders. We found that these men who were totally unknown to the white powers were a considerable power in their own right. It was clear to us that if anyone could get things done, they were the men. So we tried to bridge the gap between white mayors and these black leaders, and to find the real issues, the real problems, the real friction, and then look for real solutions."

At the start, the C.R.S. concentrated on small towns in the South where the issues seemed manageable, and it also concentrated as much on the white side of the tracks as on the black side. But when Wilkins took over, in late 1965, he shifted the focus to large cities, in both the South and the North, where the most explosive problems were, and he also gave the program a strong black emphasis. "I built up a cadre of black men, whom I hired away from various poverty programs, social agencies, police departments, and the Civil Rights Division," he explained. "They're the heart of this organization. These guys are tough—really tough. They're not easy to handle, and, believe me, they're nobody to tangle with. Anyway, they go into the slums and get to know the people who count. It doesn't take long to find out what's going on once you're sensitized to this sort of thing. When they've learned what the main problems are, they try to lay down lines of communication between the real slum leaders and the white power structure. If necessary, the man in the field can call on us for any additional help, such as turning on aid for a specific program from one of the federal agencies, if that's in order. But the important thing is not for the man in the field or the people here to solve the problems. His job, and our job, is to help the people in the black community find a way to solve them on their own."

The C.R.S. operated in about a hundred and twenty-five cities during 1968, and Wilkins spoke of one Midwestern city (anonymous because of a "confidentiality clause" in the law that set up the C.R.S.) as offering a particularly good example of the sort of work that was done. The C.R.S. representative who was sent to the city found that it was almost hopelessly divided. The slum section was split up into groups, following various leaders who had various, and often conflicting, aims. And the mayor and other white leaders persisted in dealing with ceremonial black leaders, and refused even to talk with the black militants who ran things.

The C.R.S. man first met with the mayor and finally persuaded him to get together with the militants to see if anything at all could be agreed upon, and then he met with the militants and persuaded them to join together in a single group to pursue the aims they had in common. After that, he looked into the operations of a contract-compliance committee, which had been set up by the city to assure equal-employment opportunities in all city work contracts; he found that it functioned primarily to continue segregation and the lack of opportunity. Through the mayor, who was beginning to realize that if he didn't take action soon he would end up with a rebellion on his hands, the C.R.S. operator managed to reorganize the committee to make it serve the purpose it had been set up for; then it was expanded to undertake a program of recruiting workers from slum

schools, with the participation of militant leaders as well as traditional civil-rights groups, and of urging private employers, with or
without city contracts, to hire more Negroes. Next, he turned to a
citywide committee made up of businessmen, industrialists, and
civil-rights workers who had been getting together only when a crisis
was at hand, and persuaded them to hire a full-time professional
director and to set up offices in the slum to conduct job interviews
in. (That effort proved so successful that the committee became a
continuing operation and soon branched out to see what it could do
to improve slum education, housing, and relations with the police.)

During most of the C.R.S. man's stay in the city, the atmosphere
was comparatively calm, until the arrest of a black man by a white
policeman under disputed circumstances set off a week-long riot.
Ordinarily, the Community Relations Service feels that it cannot
accomplish much in riot situations, since most people are too carried away to listen to pleas for constructive action. In this case, however, the C.R.S. representative had established enough contacts and
created enough confidence in himself on all sides that he was finally
able to get the militants and the city leaders together. He convinced
the former that they had to include moderate Negroes in any group
of spokesmen if they wanted city officials to take it seriously, and
before long a coalition of militant and moderate adults, along with
a sprinkling of teenagers, was formed. He also convinced them that
they had to present their grievances specifically and clearly. In the
end, the coalition drew up a twelve-point outline of what they
wanted, and when it was given to the mayor and the city council
eight of the points were accepted immediately and most of the others
were approved shortly afterward. That was enough to calm tempers,
and the riot subsided.

"The coalition now has a broad enough base to be truly representative, and it has had enough success to prove that it's needed,"
Wilkins said not long ago. "The feeling today is that this city has
made a start toward working out its problems peacefully."

As Wilkins sees it, successes of this nature are vital if constant outbreaks of violence, and perhaps even a civil war, are to be averted. "It could come—far more quickly and easily than most people realize," he said. "The racial problem today can be described in two words—'white fear.' If that fear becomes much stronger, the only possible outcome is white repression of blacks on a broad scale. To show how it could start, and end, take what might happen if another civil-rights leader like Dr. King were assassinated. Say that afterward twenty black militants got together and decided to take revenge. Say that they divided up into groups of four in five different cities, and that each of them vowed to kill one policeman at the same hour on a given night. Say that ten of them succeeded, five of them wounded their targets, and five of them missed. The conspiracy would be announced the next morning on the 'Today' show. By the time Walter Cronkite came on that evening, this would be a different country."

In evaluating such a development while he was still the Attorney General, Clark said he believed that the country the United States would then most resemble was the Republic of South Africa. What was ultimately needed to avoid that outcome, he also believed, was time and the determination to use it to make visible improvements on every block in every slum in the country. "Whether we have the time needed will depend more on the policeman than on anyone else," he told the Women's Forum a couple of weeks after state troopers fired into a group of students at South Carolina State College. "This is why he is the most important American in 1968. He works in a highly flammable environment. A spark can cause an explosion. . . . If he overacts, he can cause a riot. If he underacts, he can permit a riot. He is a man on a tightrope. . . . Police-community relations is the most important law-enforcement problem of today and the years ahead. Every officer must be a community-relations expert. He must serve the public, and the public must respect, support, and compensate him for the vital role he plays.

Open communications with the entire community must be developed. He must reach the unreachables. He must know the man whose name nobody knows. . . . In the final analysis, police-community relations measures the difference between an authoritarian government executing its will by force and fear and a free society protecting the lives, the property, and the liberty of its citizens through public service."

It seemed like a hopelessly tall order, but Clark and those who worked with him were convinced that it could and had to be filled. In various speeches, Clark often observed that the worst kind of lawlessness was police lawlessness, because it left no one to enforce the laws. According to Deputy Attorney General Christopher, Clark's attempts to remold police departments and police thinking, thereby making them capable of handling civil disorder and keeping federal forces out of it, was possibly the most important program he undertook while in office. "The question always is whether you move in with force or get rid of the grounds for the disorder," Christopher said. "Whenever Ramsey saw a boiling kettle, he didn't turn up the gas under it by sending in federal troops but instead he tried to let off steam in various ways. Usually, he sent in some men to look things over—maybe me, maybe Wilkins, maybe both of us. For instance, I've been on the scene of just about every major riot since Watts. We've found that there's a quiet way to settle things more often than one might imagine. We ordered the integration of a beer parlor near a Negro campus down South and stopped trouble that was on its way to being explosive." When disorder couldn't be averted and local police seemed in danger of being overwhelmed, he went on, there was invariably a clamor for use of the greatest possible force—federal force in the form of Army troops. "The pressure for this has been unbelievable," Christopher said. "It has been so strong and so unrelenting that the President and the Attorney General have had to resist it as a pure act of will. They knew that if they gave in, our Constitutional system would soon end."

Something Has Gone Terribly Wrong in America

Clark was asked privately, while he was still Attorney General, about this situation, and he said, "Actually, the police have by far the best opportunity to stop riots before they get out of hand, because the police are on the scene and can move at once. The Army, by contrast, always insists on not doing anything until it is attacked. It insists on having overwhelming force before responding to an attack. And it insists on reconnoitring the field thoroughly to determine what its response should be. These factors mean that it would always be too late, because usually being half an hour late in a riot is being too late. And if it was too late, it would undoubtedly act with maximum force to make up for it. In the end, there would only be more bloodshed."

Despite these drawbacks, he continued, most of "the dynamics of the time" called for federal intervention during riots. "Local police chiefs want the Army because their men hate and fear riot duty," he explained. "Mayors want the Army because it relieves them of direct responsibility. Governors want the Army because it takes the political responsibility out of their hands. Negroes want the Army because soldiers are far less antagonistic and far less likely to be itchy-fingered than Guardsmen or local police. And the Army wants the Army because it gives them something to do. Right now, they're over there in the Pentagon, in a special division they recently set up with an appropriation of twelve million dollars, playing at training troops for riot duty. What we could do with that money in the Community Relations Service!"

Of the pressure on President Johnson to use federal troops in local disorders, Clark said, "It has been incredibly strong, not just on the part of the groups I've mentioned but on the part of his advisers. Very few people, especially those closest to him, oppose the pre-positioning of troops in and around our cities. They say it's the only solution. But I'm dead set against it, and so is President Johnson. What we must do instead is expand, train, and pay better salaries to the police forces around the country. Otherwise, those who are putting on the pressure will win, and half a million men will be brought back from Vietnam and trained in riot control—that is, to be a federal police force. That's what we've never had, and what we've always said we didn't want. It has the potential for the worst kind of disaster, because there's no telling which way a monolithic military-police organization might go. President Johnson has stood up to the pressure all along, but a new President might not be able or willing to."

The Attorney General expressed this view a few months after riots had engulfed more than a hundred cities and the fear of an uprising was especially strong. When he was asked what might happen if troops were garrisoned in and around the nation's largest cities and a President refused to use them in a particularly bloody riot out of fear that their participation would only make it bloodier, Clark put a hand over his eyes for a moment. Finally, he nodded, as if facing something reluctantly, and lowered his hand. "It is quite possible that the commanding generals would get together and take over," he said. "Of course, like putting the troops there in the first place, it would all be done in the name of saving the country."

II

The Transition

Shortly before six o'clock on the evening of November 6, 1968, Attorney General Clark convened the staff meeting that he ordinarily
held every Wednesday night with a dozen or so of his top aides to go
over the events of the past week and to discuss plans for the following one. On this occasion, the agenda was quite different, for a few
hours earlier the election returns had become sufficiently complete
to confirm that Nixon had won the Presidency. The meeting was
held in the Attorney General's formal office—a room some seventy
by thirty feet, with a twenty-foot domed ceiling—which was
equipped with W.P.A.-style allegorical murals, a capacious stone
fireplace, rich panelling, an enormous red-and-blue Oriental rug,
several red leather couches and easy chairs, and, along one side, a
large conference table with a dozen straight-backed leather arm-
chairs; having found this baronial chamber less than cozy, Clark
preferred a small corner room off one end of it as his working

quarters, and reserved the main office for meetings and ceremonial events.

As his aides came in—the Deputy Attorney General, most of the nine Assistant Attorneys General, and the heads of several offices, bureaus, and services—it was clear that they were weary from having stayed up until early morning waiting for the election results to become clear, and that most of them were deeply discouraged by the outcome. A few of the men on hand were either Republicans or what is known in government parlance as "career executives"— that is, non-political specialists in their fields—and had reasonable expectations of being kept on by the new Administration. But the others were Democrats who had been brought into the Department of Justice by Presidents Kennedy and Johnson and were certain to leave as soon as the new President took over. To most of them, though, the possible loss of position and work they had become devoted to was far less important than the threat posed by a Nixon Administration to the mission of justice.

Clark and his senior aides were confident that their methods, hammered out of long experience and hard, slogging work, were the soundest way—to combat crime, to create equal rights for all citizens, and to modernize the machinery of justice—and they were convinced that the results of their work in the last few years were beginning to show up. All of them were deeply concerned that Nixon and the man he chose to be Attorney General might dismantle the structure they had carefully designed and laboriously built.

The meeting was sombre—"the most sombre one I ever attended," a participant said later. The Attorney General spoke for about ten minutes on the obligations that the men present would have during the transfer of executive power, and in the course of his talk he touched on the specific responsibilities of all division, bureau, office, and service heads in the Department to keep their operations running smoothly. In passing, he mentioned that several of the career men present would probably be kept on by the incoming Administration. (He did not mention that the director of the F.B.I. would also undoubtedly be retained, since Hoover, though officially a subordinate of his, always behaved as if he were an equal, or at times superior, official wholly independent of the Department's control, and never attended such staff meetings.)

Then Clark observed that the over-all change in personnel in the Department would in all likelihood be fairly small if, as he expected, most first and second assistants to the Assistant Attorneys General were also kept on, since most of them were nonpartisan career men. When Attorney General Kennedy took over the Department in 1961, he went on, only one assistant was replaced. As for those who would be asked to leave, or at least not asked to stay, Clark made a special appeal to them to carry on their business as they would if they were continuing in office, urged them not to be dismayed or cheerless, and concluded, "Above all, we must remember how fortunate we are to have been here to serve this mission."

Several of those listening to him had entered the room not just dismayed and cheerless but embittered. One of them was Roger Wilkins, the young Negro head of the Department's Community Relations Service, who had decided some months before to leave C.R.S., whatever the outcome of the election, for a similar job with the Ford Foundation, which was willing to spend considerably more for the same kind of effort in the slums than the two million dollars annually allotted the Department of Justice by Congress. Wilkins was deeply fearful of what lay ahead for the country under a Nixon Administration.

"I was down in Fredericksburg, Virginia, attending a C.R.S. meeting when the election returns came in," he said later. "I was so discouraged that I said, 'If that's the kind of government this country wants, to hell with it!' Anyway, I figured I'd better get back up to Washington for the staff meeting that night. I did, and I've never been more impressed by anything in my life than I was by what Ramsey said to us. He made the most graceful, generous, open, and positive speech about how our task was to serve justice by making sure that the new people had the greatest possible opportunity to learn what the real problems facing the Department were and what we had been doing to solve them, and by creating the least possible conflict in getting the new Administration off to a smooth start. He compared the transition to a relay race and told us that our job from that point on was to hand over the baton in such a way that no one slowed down or lost a step. When I came into that room, my mood was terrible, but Ramsey changed it. He pointed out to me that the Community Relations Service was especially vulnerable because it was regarded with suspicion by Congress, and that the only way to preserve its vital function at this critical time was by the fullest and most wholehearted coöperation with the new people. He made me see that it wasn't Wilkins or the Democratic Party that was at stake, it was the country."

While Clark's appeals were unremarkably characteristic of the man, they were also precisely in line with the wishes of President Johnson, who was determined to set a firm precedent for the orderly transfer of executive power. Historians will undoubtedly say that this attempt was a success. Aside from a few angry disputes over basic policy, the most crucial of which occurred in the Department of Justice, the transfer of power in the executive branch was unprecedentedly smooth. In fact, it was probably the greatest love feast that the government has engaged in during a transition since Woodrow Wilson succeeded himself.

Congeniality has been far from the rule in past transitions. Despite the rapidly growing size and complexity of the federal government over the years, there were no rules whatever governing transitions between one President and another until 1964, when

Congress passed the Presidential Transition Act; and that measure did little more than urge everyone in the outgoing Administration to help everyone in the incoming Administration get settled, and provided four hundred and fifty thousand dollars to each side to facilitate the process. That still left the basic arrangements up to the outgoing President, and, as Henry F. Graff, professor of history at Columbia University, has observed, his only guides are "his sense of duty, his knowledge of history, and his notion of the fitness of things."

Some Presidents have lacked or have dispensed with all three. Both John Adams and John Quincy Adams, for example, refused even to attend their successors' inaugurations; in fact, the former went so far as to move out of the White House in the dead of night so that he wouldn't have to face Jefferson. Andrew Johnson also refused to attend the swearing-in of his successor, General Grant, and as an excuse for his absence held the most ineffectual Cabinet meeting in history during the inaugural ceremony. When Herbert Hoover departed from office, he left behind the last small government, which, as he admitted in a confidential letter to Senator David A. Reed, a conservative Republican from Pennsylvania, he had done his best to preserve by trying to persuade President-elect Franklin Roosevelt to commit himself to policies that would have destroyed nine-tenths of the New Deal before it got started; of course, Roosevelt realized what Hoover was doing and refused.

As it turned out, Roosevelt had more opportunity to make arrangements for his actual assumption of the Presidency than any of his successors, since he was the last President-elect to have a hundred-and-twenty-day interregnum between his election and his inauguration—a period that was cut in half by the Twentieth Amendment, passed in 1933, which moved the inaugural date from March 4th back to January 20th. If this change reduced an incoming President's capacity to create a new Administration, it also reduced the dangers inherent in having two governments—one responsible but weak and the other not responsible but strong—and yet no government.

Just before the transition of 1960-61, Professor Graff pointed out what more and more men in the higher reaches of government were becoming increasingly concerned about—"not only that the times are perilous but also that the Presidency is a place of power for which men contend with passion, and that at significant junctures in the past it has been yielded up only in a mood of fierce anger." And Graff added, "Today, an interregnum marked by partisanship without bridle could be a national nightmare and disgrace."

A dozen years earlier, Harry Truman, who was fully aware of the possibilities for disaster in the country's unsystematic approach to the transfer of Presidential power, became the first Chief Executive to attempt to avert it by arranging an orderly transition that would become a precedent for future changeovers. Despite the bitterness of Thomas E. Dewey's campaign against him and his own swashbuckling fight to retain the Presidency, Truman managed to stand aside from the battle long enough to issue detailed orders to all members of his Cabinet instructing them to draw up memoranda on the operations of their departments for their successors under Dewey. Four years later, before Truman announced that he would not run again, he issued the same kind of orders. By then, Senator Joseph R. McCarthy had demonstrated how close one unscrupulous politician could come to producing a national nightmare and disgrace. Deeply concerned about what might happen during a transition period in which the political atmosphere was poisoned by the Republican use of McCarthy's charges that the Democratic leadership was guilty of willful treason, Truman was more determined than ever to clear the air by putting the transition process above politics and, as the saying went, to help the incoming Administration "land on its feet and running." Above all, he hoped to establish a precedent that would survive any subsequent national lunacy like McCarthyism and become as much an established custom as, say, the President's right to conduct foreign affairs or issue legislative proposals to Congress—matters that Professor Richard E. Neustadt has described as "Presidential common law."

The Republicans would have no part of it. After twenty years of being out of power, which inevitably created a measure of irresponsibility, and after participating in one of the most mendacious campaigns in American history, which compelled those who presided over it to believe their own oratory as the only way of preserving their self-respect, the Republicans were bound to regard the Democratic Administration as the repository of all domestic iniquity. Truman, of course, was the arch-fiend, and when he wrote to General Eisenhower shortly before the election and suggested that the two men meet privately to discuss the transfer of the White House to the Republicans in the event that they won, Eisenhower curtly replied by letter that "our communications should be only those which are known to all the American people." When Truman got the letter, he scrawled a "Dear Ike" note in longhand saying, "I'm extremely sorry that you have allowed a bunch of screwballs to come between us."

According to Charles S. Murphy, who was Special Counsel to President Truman at the time, the clash had been caused mainly by Eisenhower's failure to defend his old commander and patron General George C. Marshall when McCarthy called him a traitor. "President Truman believed that General Marshall was the greatest living American—perhaps even the greatest American, living or dead," Murphy explained recently. "Truman was enraged by Eisenhower's disloyalty to the man who had made him. And, as usual, Truman was not hesitant about letting his feelings be known. Of course, that enraged Eisenhower, probably more than it would have under different circumstances, because in this case he was clearly in the wrong and must have known it. Despite Truman's anger—I never saw him angrier, before or after—he insisted on doing everything he could to provide for an orderly turnover of the Presidency.

If it had been up to me, I wouldn't have provided a damned thing."

After the election, President Truman invited President-elect Eisenhower to meet with him and to designate representatives to deal with the various departments and agencies. This time, Eisenhower could hardly refuse, since the election was over and the business of changing Administrations had to commence if the country was not to be paralyzed. The meeting took place soon afterward. General Eisenhower conducted himself with propriety but in an icily formal manner, and from Truman's point of view the affair was an utter failure, for he was unable to convince the President-elect that no attempt was being made to Hoover the new Administration into accepting current policies but, rather, that the purpose of the meeting was to arrange for the least disruptive changeover. Eisenhower's intense hostility toward Truman and his inability to believe that a lifelong politician could put the country's well-being above politics made it impossible for him to consider the offer sincere.

Laurin L. Henry, who made a study of the 1952-53 transition for the Brookings Institution, found that General Eisenhower's refusal to accept President Truman's offer of full coöperation caused the new Administration to land on its knees and crawling:

> Many of the Eisenhower appointees had neither the time nor the inclination to engage in serious discussion with their predecessors of the subtleties of departmental administration or the whys and wherefores of existing policy. Some of them simply did not know enough about the business to enter such discussions without serious loss of face. Furthermore, schooled by Republican doctrine to distrust all works of Truman and the bureaucracy, they were fearful of being misled or "captured." In the absence of any signal from Eisenhower that they were expected to take advantage of such aids, the Republican appointees tended to give but token recognition to efforts to help them by people already in the executive branch, choosing to receive advice from more "reliable" sources in Congress, the business community, and Republican-allied interest groups. . . . Republican opposition to what was done in

the government during the twenty years of Democratic rule had become so generalized that many of Eisenhower's appointees approached their jobs with the assumption that most of the government's policies were wrong, most of its programs were badly administered, and most of its leading officials were incompetent or worse. Therefore, the notion of maximizing continuity and keeping on an even keel while plotting new courses meant little to them. They were not stepping into a going organization, they were receivers in bankruptcy.

As soon as the Republicans took over, they threw out an unprecedented number of officeholders, instituted humiliating security investigations of those who could not be fired, put anyone who had had a part in devising or implementing Democratic policy on the shelf, and treated the entire bureaucracy, which had the task of running the government on a day-to-day basis, with unremitting and demoralizing mistrust. In Henry's opinion, General Eisenhower's attitude crippled his Administration for close to a year, while other observers felt that it never fully recovered from the effects of its initial suspicion and contempt.

Apparently, President Eisenhower either did not share these opinions or he went on believing that what was bad for the Democratic Party was good for the country, for when the time came for him to hand over the government to the opposition he did exceedingly little to smooth the way. As late as a month before the election, he had taken no steps to prepare members of his government for the task of informing and assisting a new Administration. Finally, once the election was over, he formally offered President-elect Kennedy "full coöperation"—an offer that was made, in the opinion of some insiders, with the conviction that it would be no more welcome than Truman's had earlier.

However, Kennedy eagerly took the President up on it, and sent his people into the executive branch to learn their jobs as soon as they were appointed. Unlike their predecessors, they were grateful for any and all information and assistance, and as soon as they had absorbed it came back for more. Moreover, it was quickly made clear to the incumbents that there would be no housecleaning like the one carried out by the Republicans, and this assurance greatly boosted the morale of the bureaucracy and encouraged its members to help out the newcomers as much as they could. "Cordiality and courtesy are evident on both sides," the *Times* noted in an editorial at the time. "This constructive approach to a transition period that is difficult under the best of circumstances only emphasizes how serious could be the dangers in this interregnum if the men and the circumstances were different."

The two and a half months during which a President-elect prepares for his assumption of office are usually more crucial to his future and to the future of the people he is to govern than any comparable period during his time in the Presidency. It is in this interregnal hiatus that he must begin devising the policies that will determine the course of his Administration for four or eight years and, in some important respects, the course of the nation for decades. His goal, naturally, is to do what he believes is best for the country and, along the way, to demonstrate that his government is superior to anything the opposition can offer. Aside from the character, intelligence, and outlook of the President-elect himself, the most important elements in any transition are the character, intelligence, and outlook of the men he appoints to high posts in his Administration, for it is ultimately through them that he will view the problems confronting the country and through them that he must administer its government. The task of selecting these top aides is by nature an exceedingly complex and delicate one, and it is made even more complex and delicate by what is perhaps the most serious drawback in our traditional manner of transferring executive power—that is, a new President must choose the men best qualified to nurture and prune the innumerable twigs on the executive branch in ways that he deems most productive, but he cannot conceivably know if these men will ably carry out his policies, since he cannot know what those policies should be until the men have got settled in office and have learned what the real problems facing the government are. And the learning process is inevitably delayed by his appointees' initial preoccupation with the counterfeit problems that are the hyperbolic staples of all political campaigns.

Among the gravest problems facing President-elect Nixon and his aides was one that he had created in order to get elected. Having repeatedly blamed the rising rate of crime—including criminal protests against the war in Vietnam, the selective-service system, and racial injustice—on the incumbent Administration, and having laid the responsibility for dealing with these and other kinds of lawlessness at the door of the White House, it was bound to be one of the first things awaiting him as he prepared to take up residence there. And it was bound to be a far more serious problem than it had been before he played on, and thereby increased, the fears of millions of citizens that they were about to be assaulted or murdered, which could only increase their demands that he take immediate steps to protect them. Further, the right-wing guardians of the repressive mood in this country were certain to renew these demands as a way of keeping them uppermost in the public mind, in the hope that the new President would then be compelled to meet them by recasting and restricting the Supreme Court and by encouraging policemen around the country to crack down on all left-wing dissidents, lawbreaking and law-abiding alike. Citizens who feared that this would lead to further repression and ultimately to a form of domestic tyranny found their only comfort in the political truism that a Presidential candidate is not the same thing as a President. In another Brookings Institution report, entitled "Agenda for the Nation," which was published shortly after the election in 1968, Kermit Gordon, former Director of the Bureau of the Budget, commented on the difference:

> Between the election and the inauguration, the new President and his lieutenants must make the jolting transition from the slogans and simplifications of the election campaign to the intricate task of constructing workable policies and programs. In designing the rhetoric of the campaign, the goal was to win the hearts of the voters; in hammering out the policies of the new Administration, the goal is to solve problems. The problems are always vastly more complex, and the new Administration is always considerably less confident of its ability to solve them, than the rhetoric of the campaign can admit. The full complexity and intractability of the problems will be seen more clearly in the cold light of the post-election scrutiny.

What the new President's policies would be—especially his policies on the domestic crises that were driving the nation toward deep division and possibly civil war—were expected to remain unclear for several weeks or months. The earliest inkling of them was looked for in the kinds of men the President-elect chose for the top posts in his government. If there was increasing concern on the part of outsiders as the weeks wore on over Nixon's slowness in forming his government, there was increasing desperation on the part of insiders who found that they were faced with a severe shortage of willing and capable applicants. Apparently, Nixon had hoped for a coalition government—a coalition of Republicans, that is—to unite his party. But some of the Party leaders he was believed to want in his Administration found their disagreement with him on basic policy matters too great to be patched up even superficially, and rejected the feelers that his people put out to see if they were interested.

Democratic Administrations had largely drawn their top manpower from the academic and legal professions. Few of these men seemed to find Republican philosophy compatible with their own, and this led the recruiters in the Nixon camp to fall back on the only other sizable pool of skilled workers available to them—businessmen. As it turned out, not many of these were eager to leave rewarding occupations in a booming economy for anything less than a Cabinet post. And although there were only a dozen Cabinet posts, it took the President-elect five weeks to fill them to his satisfaction, which further delayed the transition, since none of the second- and third-level positions could be filled until the Cabinet was formed.

President Johnson had long since taken steps to make sure that the newcomers, whenever they arrived, would have all the help they could use. On September 11th, he asked the three major candidates for the Presidency to name representatives to deal with the White House through Charles Murphy, Truman's Special Counsel, whom President Johnson had chosen as "central coördinator" for the transition. Nixon named Franklin B. Lincoln, Jr., who had been an Assistant Secretary of Defense in the Eisenhower Administration and was a partner in the law firm of Nixon, Mudge, Rose, Guthrie, Alexander & Mitchell, as his representative, and Lincoln conferred several times with Murphy before the election. Early in September, Murphy sent memoranda to all Cabinet members describing the manner in which the President expected the "planning for an orderly transition of the Presidency" to be conducted. After requesting each Cabinet member to name a senior official who would be responsible for overseeing the transition process in his department, Murphy went on:

> You should begin planning now so that immediately after the election you will be prepared to assist individuals designated by the President-elect and Vice President-elect as their representatives in the period between election and inauguration. Each agency will have the major responsibility for briefing its own incoming management. As new

officials are designated and make contacts with outgoing officials, such time as may be necessary should be devoted to briefing them as they prepare to assume their responsibilities. The briefings, written and oral, should be concise and devoted to essential information which will have a high potential of usefulness to incoming officials and will serve their most immediate needs. Excessive length and detail of briefing materials should be avoided. Similarly, incoming officials should not be overwhelmed with unsolicited advice and recommendations. Lack of restraint in either of these respects will severely limit the utility of the transition briefings.

Attached to each memorandum was an outline for material to be covered in two volumes—or, as they came to be called, "briefing documents." The first was to cover "agency missions and statutory authorities, basic organization and functions, budgetary and financial information, key personnel, significant interagency relationships, significant intergovernmental relationships, legislative processes and problems, and policy and program issues [and] priorities;" the second was to cover "personal arrangements (nature and tenure of appointment, conflict of interest, compensation and benefits, supporting services), personnel policies and administration, internal communications, and program operations and administration." Murphy asked for the names of the officials designated to handle the preparation of the briefing documents in their respective departments by September 17th, for a progress report on transition planning in each department by September 30th, and for copies of the briefing documents by October 30th.

In the mid-nineteen-fifties, the Hoover Commission had made a study of how the executive branch might be better organized, and among its conclusions was the recommendation that each department make one post at the assistant-secretary level non-political, so that the man occupying it—a career executive—would be kept on by an incoming administration and thereby preserve some measure of continuity. In the Department of Justice, this was the Assistant Attorney General for Administration, Leo M. Pellerzi, a career executive with twenty years of government service, who had been general counsel to the Civil Service Commission until Clark brought him into the Department a year before. Clark passed Murphy's memorandum on to Pellerzi, who immediately went to work to carry out the President's orders.

At the Republican National Convention in Miami, the previous August, Nixon told what he believed was a secret session of Southern delegates (until the Miami *Herald* printed a verbatim transcript made from a tape recording of the meeting) that he was going to run the Department of Justice himself. "I am going to take charge of this, because I am a lawyer," he said. If his post-election scrutiny included reading the two thousand pages of briefing documents prepared by the Department for the edification of the new Attorney General, he may have been tempted to change his mind. While the influence of the man who runs that Department is enormous, so are his responsibilities, and even a quick perusal of that batch of transition papers would have revealed that the problems he would face were complex and intractable indeed.

Among those listed, for example, were controlling the multifarious activities of an estimated five thousand members of La Cosa Nostra, only two thousand of whom had even been identified; handling "the exploding volume of selective service cases," which had nearly tripled in four years, and which constituted "one of the major problems facing the Department;" investigating and prosecuting some thirty thousand yearly violations of eight hundred sections of the United States Criminal Code, including everything from bank robbery to misuse of federal funds in local poverty programs; revising laws to cut down the distribution of narcotics (arrests for the possession and use of "dangerous" drugs had risen by a hundred and sixty-seven per cent between 1960 and 1968, compared to an increase of less than eleven per cent for all other crimes), and getting ready for at least a hundred new "mind-altering psychotropic drugs" that are expected to be developed within the next few years; replacing ancient, fortresslike prisons, which breed rather than prevent criminality, with small, modern institutions able to offer those who have taken to crime a second chance that is often a good deal better than the first one they had; backing the Community Relations Service in its efforts to siphon off the fury seething in the nation's slums; enforcing a battery of complex civil-rights laws with a twentieth of the manpower needed; devising new legislation to assure equality and justice for more citizens; and persuading Congress to pay not just lip service but the bill for all the work that had to be done, and done soon.

In the President-elect's first post-election statement to the press, he said that "the great objective of this Administration at the outset" would be "to bring the American people together." There were those in the Johnson Administration who felt that Nixon's campaign had gone a long way toward driving the American people apart, but President Johnson and the leading members of his Administration were determined to provide all the coöperation and assistance they could, so that Nixon would have plenty of time to study the problems that had divided the people before he committed himself to policies that would make that division wider and deeper. Accordingly, it was with much more than an eye to the political amenities that President Johnson sent the President-elect a telegram the day after the election saying that he would do everything in his power "to make your burdens lighter on that day when you assume the responsibilities of the President." Nixon accepted the offer with alacrity and dispatched Lincoln that same day to the White House, where he met with Murphy and other Presidential aides for several hours to get the actual transition process started at once.

One of the first steps in that process was to make preparations for obtaining security clearances for Presidential nominees, who had to be confirmed by the Senate, and for White House staff members.

Although this is not required by law, it has grown into a custom in recent years, because it is the best way to protect a President from embarrassment later on if something awkward is revealed about a man's personal habits or background. The day after Lincoln's visit to the White House, he and Murphy met at the Department of Justice with Attorney General Clark to discuss the matter of such clearances, and Clark offered to instruct the F.B.I. to set up a special team to investigate new appointees, thereby cutting the normal clearance period of three or four months down to three or four weeks.

Shortly after the meeting, Clark said, "Lincoln suggested that I handle the clearances, but I told him that he and Mr. Nixon should have direct contact with the F.B.I. and should not bring me into it unless a nominee wanted access to classified material before the inauguration, in which case my duty would be to make a judgment about his trustworthiness on the basis of the F.B.I. report. I said that I would write Hoover and ask him to give priority to these clearances. I said that they should be run only on key White House personnel and Presidential nominees subject to Senate confirmation. I said that no more than three persons, and preferably only one, other than Mr. Nixon should be authorized to request such clearances. Also, not more than Mr. Nixon and one other person should be allowed to read them, because they contain gossip and a lot of embarrassing stuff and shouldn't go the rounds. In fact, I don't think that the person who *is* cleared should ever look at his own report. He'd be amazed at the slander and at what even people he thought were friends had said about him. Anyway, I told Lincoln that I didn't want to see the reports and thought only Mr. Nixon should."

Not long afterward, Hugh Sidey used his weekly column, "The Presidency," in *Life* to present quite a different account. "The usual rumors which follow in the wake of FBI security checks of candidates for jobs have not materialized," he wrote. "Nixon, who spent years of campaigning across the nation, knows many of his men well and does not plan to order checks until the last minute. He argued with incumbent Attorney General Ramsey Clark over having the reports go through Clark's office and won. They now come directly from J. Edgar Hoover, an old Nixon friend."

Although this story made Clark look like a snoop and a gossip, he said nothing about the affair publicly. In private, he remarked, "I've never spoken to Mr. Nixon in my life or had any communication with him. This was obviously planted in *Life* by someone on his staff. It is not a good omen at all."

In recalling the meeting, Murphy affirmed that there was no truth to Sidey's version of the conversation. "The letter that Ramsey later wrote to Hoover about how the clearances were to be handled contained a tiny ambiguity, and when Lincoln received his copy of it he called me to ask what it meant," Murphy said. "I told him that it meant exactly what we had decided on at the meeting. Lincoln and I had agreed from the start that our job was to de-escalate any lack of harmony, but I guess somebody on the other side was determined to get one last, unfair swipe in at Ramsey."

Early in the transition period, the President-elect's campaign manager and closest adviser, John N. Mitchell, who was being increasingly mentioned as the likeliest choice for Attorney General, stated that General Eisenhower's greatest mistake when he assumed the Presidency was his failure to dig deep enough in scooping out Democratic officeholders. Since Eisenhower dug deep enough to damage the work of his own government, some people in the Department of Justice feared that Mitchell's approach could make the Department incapable of action.

"If they end up with a lot of inexperienced people, that will mean crisis management," Clark explained. "We file two or three hundred cases a day, and many of them can't wait. Also, the pressures in a Department like this are so great that some men become drawn by the dramatic, firefighting aspects of the job and get to live for crises. They never see the beautiful architecture that is quietly burning away. And, of course, firefighters don't build houses. Above all, the Department needs people who can give themselves the time to use their ability and their judgment. Otherwise, they can have no consistent policy and thus no chance of keeping up with the terrific case load. If that happens, they end up like corks bobbing wildly on a sea of litigation."

Like other high officials in the Johnson Administration, Clark was perturbed by the extreme delay on the part of the President-elect in naming his Cabinet and getting its members acquainted with their new jobs as soon as possible so that they would have some idea of what to expect when they took over. "They're woefully, woefully behind," he said a month after the election. "If they don't come in here and take hold soon, they'll never catch up." Despite this danger, Nixon continued to proceed with the kind of caution that had typified his two-year campaign for the Presidency. While the reports that he was having difficulty in getting the men he wanted to join his government were true, it was also true that he preferred the perils of delay to the perils of haste. Shortly before the election, he had told a group of reporters that the transition period was crucial to a new President's success, "because if he makes poor decisions with regard to the selection of his Cabinet, with regard to his budget, and with regard [to policy] . . . it's going to be very hard to correct them."

By this time, it must have become clear to the President-elect that his choice of Spiro T. Agnew to succeed him if he died in office had been a poor decision indeed. Mitchell, who had recommended Agnew, was said to believe that the new Vice President would be a great help in the South. Others close to the campaign were not so sure. "Before Agnew's term is over," one of them said, "I'm sure we'll all be glad that he is not a quadruped." In all likelihood, the President-elect had not forgotten that General Eisenhower's awe of successful businessmen, and his inability to grasp the difference between running a large corporation and running the government, had led him to appoint some of the most arrogant misfits ever to serve in high posts in Washington—men like Charles Wilson, Secretary of Defense, who also missed the distinction between public and private interests, and George Humphrey, Secretary of Treasury, who had such faith in his own abilities and such contempt for the abilities of the civil servants who had to run his Department that he paralyzed the work of the place for months after he took over. In the end, President Eisenhower was never able to overcome the public belief that his Administration was run by and for big business.

The choice of a man to carry out the public mandate to control organized and unorganized crime, urban and campus rioting, and the threat of a black uprising must have seemed a far simpler matter to Nixon the candidate at Convention Hall in Miami than it did to Nixon the President-elect at the Hotel Pierre in New York. The day after the election, *Newsweek* reported, "According to one of Nixon's top planners, the President-elect's prescription for law and order is simple: 'We'll get a tough cop and tell him to go to work.'" (Speculation about who the "tough cop" would be centered for a time on former rackets-buster Thomas E. Dewey, who, it was said, twice was offered and twice turned down the Attorney Generalship. He later appeared to take himself out of the running for that or any other post in the federal government by stating, "We would get along just as well if we repealed the Fifth Amendment.")

While the choice of a tough cop would please many of those who had elected Nixon, it would further alienate those whom he had to mollify if he hoped to preserve peace at home, and perhaps the Union itself. "A hard-nosed crackdown by a hard-riding Attorney General, as if he were a newly appointed district attorney fighting a local crime wave, could, and undoubtedly would, invite a political reaction against the Nixon Administration of serious proportions," Richard Wilson observed in a column that he wrote for the Washington *Evening Star* late that November. "For it is the sad fact that much of our trouble today involves matters of race, economic and social status and values, concepts of morality, behavior, and personal belief which official repression might only serve to magnify. . . . A very clear distinction will have to be made in the Nixon Administration between measures curbing criminality and measures which, while curbing criminality, also repress social and economic aspirations and concepts of personal belief and behavior. It will not be easy."

Many of Nixon's opponents and some of his supporters believed that he had chosen Agnew in order to avoid having anyone around who was more personable or dynamic than he. In the view of one of the most embittered opponents of all, this limitation had compelled the President-elect to dig deep into the ranks of the undistinguished for his Cabinet. When he finally displayed its "extra-dimension" members on television, on December 11th, even people who were ready to give the new Nixon the benefit of their old doubts were dismayed. He had promised a youthful, idealistic Administration, and he delivered a collection of twelve men whose average age was over fifty and whose backgrounds revealed no sign of an ideologue. Each of them was skilled in his own specialty, but none of them seemed equipped to persuade the suffering, discordant, and impatient half-members of society not to tear it to pieces. Some viewers of the Cabinet's television debut—conducted in a manner that led to its being tagged "The Federal Ed Sullivan Show"—were also troubled by the clumsy promotional flavor of the affair, which suggested that the new Administration was going to be strongly influenced by the large number of advertising and public-relations men who were appointed to the White House staff.

The Cabinet member who was closest to the new President, of course, was Attorney General-designate Mitchell. About all that was known of him at the time was that he had a reputation for being unapproachably aloof and disdainful of weakness in others. "When you first meet Mitchell, he seems cold on the surface," a Wall Street acquaintance of his remarked not long ago. "But when you get to know him better, you realize that's only the tip of the iceberg." One man who had worked with Mitchell during the campaign considered this impression baseless. "He was always eminently decent to everyone around him," this man said. "Of course, he has a tendency to be blunt, but that's because he's made his way in life not through the use of public-relations techniques but through his brilliance in the field of municipal bonds. After all, he made two hundred thousand dollars a year on Wall Street, so why should he butter up people?" To others, the new Attorney General's background constituted his most serious drawback, for municipal-bond law is not known for its richness in human and social concerns. In Clark's opinion, the Attorney Generalship was primarily a moral job, and, along with many others, he wondered if a man who had devoted thirty years to accumulating money could suddenly turn around and devote himself selflessly to the public interest.

Roy Wilkins, head of the N.A.A.C.P., expressed regret that no Negroes had been appointed to the Cabinet, and added, "The one least likely to understand the Negro situation is John N. Mitchell, the new Attorney General. The administration of justice is an area where the Negro in past decades has taken a terrible beating. Mr. Mitchell, without question, is concerned with the law, but it is hard for the average white or black American to see how a Wall Street lawyer can appreciate the police and courtroom hocus-pocus which snuffs out the liberties and lives of many hapless citizens each year." Over in the Department's Civil Rights Division, a young lawyer who viewed the appointment with even deeper despair said, "I gather from those who know anything about Mitchell that he could stay here for four years and never use the words 'Negro' and 'youth.'"

During a discussion of the potential alliance between white youth and Negroes of all ages, Clark remarked, "This is the mix we're worried about. The students gave up the civil-rights battle for the most part to take on the government as the war in Vietnam got bigger and bigger and affected them more and more directly. But when it ends, there's every reason for them to join forces with the Negroes again." Continuing, he pointed out that the United States now had seven million college students, at least an equal number of young people between the ages of eighteen and twenty-one who were not attending college, and some twenty million Negroes. If even a small percentage of these groups got together and made common cause, they would constitute an immense force; ten per cent of the total, for instance, would be close to the number of men in the military services. They would also constitute a grave peril to the nation if they ended up either with undemocratic goals or with democratic goals that were forcibly repressed. "Youngsters spend their formative years breaking away from their parents' direction," Clark said. "If the police suddenly order them to turn around and go in the opposite direction—that is, back in their parents' direction —why, the kids will just flow over them. They would be extremely difficult to handle, unless the authorities were willing to use maximum force and shoot enough of them to cow the rest."

Many successful managers of Presidential campaigns in the past have been rewarded by being made Postmaster General. The campaign manager usually makes the deals that help put his man in office, and since the Postmaster General is the chief patronage-dispenser in the government, giving him this office is a convenient way to pay him off and at the same time give him a way to pay off some of the people he made deals with. Nixon's decision to name his campaign manager to the post of Attorney General was bound to produce complaints that the Department was a political arm of the White House—in a way that it hadn't been since Truman named his campaign manager, J. Howard McGrath, to head it in 1949. And the complaints were intensified because of Mitchell's campaign role in devising the so-called Southern strategy, which had reportedly included commitments to men like Senator Strom Thurmond, of South Carolina, to the effect that enforcement of existing civil-rights laws and pressure on Congress to enact new ones would be less than vigorous.

"The big question now is whether Mitchell will act on the substance or the politics of an issue," Clark said. "The man who has this job shouldn't be closely tied to the President." Mitchell was very close to the new President—a relationship that he repeatedly reminded others of after the election. On the other hand, no Attorney General in history had been closer to a President than Robert Kennedy, who had been his brother's campaign manager. When this was brought up, Clark nodded and said, "Yes, but Bob was fully aware of how essential it is to keep this job out of politics. When he took over the Department, he held a meeting with all his top aides, and the first thing he said to us was 'No politics—period. You don't attend political functions, you don't speak on political matters, you don't get involved in any way.'"

For his own part, Clark went on, he had never consulted President Johnson before filing a case, whatever its political implications might have been for the White House. "One of the main parts of this job is to find legal ways for the President to do what he wants to do," he continued. "All Presidents soon discover that if they can do something that's politically important to them through executive orders or legal maneuvers, they can sidestep legislation and avoid issues, and usually the public won't even notice what's being done. But the whole legal system can become shapeless if the Attorney

General allows the law to be used that way. I've tried to keep the sense of legal discipline intact here, but the pressures against you are tremendous, and, God knows, you pay a heavy price for resisting them. Now, if an Attorney General is over at the White House for lunch three days a week, it's not likely that he'll hold out for long. And if he takes this office solely to help the President politically, he probably won't even realize that he should hold out."

Clark's insistence on maintaining the Department's independence constantly amazed his subordinates and constantly irked the President. "Under former Attorneys General, the Public Information Office sent weekly memoranda to the White House informing the President about the Department's plans for the coming week," Cliff Sessions, who was Clark's press officer, said not long ago. "Since this had always been done, I went on doing it when Ramsey took over. But he heard about it and told me to stop. He said that it was none of the White House's business." (Under Mitchell, the custom has been revived.)

Mitchell insisted throughout the campaign that he would never take a post in the new Administration if his candidate won. He meant it, and held out as long as he could. It was small wonder that he would have resisted, above all, becoming Attorney General, since the Republicans' campaign strategy of misrepresenting what the man in that post or the man who succeeded him could do about crime made it virtually impossible for him to perform the duties of that office effectively. In short, he was being asked to sit down on the chair that he had scattered tacks on. Even after he took the job, he went on saying that he hadn't wanted it and that he intended to stay in it for no more than two years. "This is the last thing in the world I wanted to do," he said shortly after accepting the appointment. "I've got all the things I ever wanted. I'm a fat and prosperous Wall Street lawyer, which is just what I always wanted to be."

When this remark reached Clark, he shook his head dejectedly and asked, "How in the world can anyone do the job here with that kind of attitude? Bob Kennedy and the rest of us came here like a real shirt-sleeved crew. We sat down and asked what had to be done, how to do it, and then how to improve on doing it. When we came up for confirmation in the Senate, we were asked if we meant to stay on just long enough to get big reputations and then move on to cushy jobs in prominent law firms. That wasn't my attitude. I told them I hoped to stay on as long as I could do something to help."

After Mitchell was appointed, the press described his political views as ranging from conservative to deeply conservative. For instance, the *Times* said that he appeared to be "far on the conservative side," and *Human Events,* the newsletter of the extreme right wing, said that he was "known to have a 'J. Edgar Hooverish' view on law enforcement" and that he had come "highly recommended for his new position by several conservative sources, including Sen. Strom Thurmond." Everyone knew where Thurmond stood, and if any doubt about Hoover's views remained he laid them to rest by telling reporters on his way out of a meeting with the President-elect that "justice is merely incidental to order."

However, Mitchell himself had yet to be heard from. When he was, it was by way of an interview given to the *Evening Star,* which reported that he had said, "I've somehow got to dispel the notion that I'm a tough cop and an arch-conservative." In another interview—between Mitchell and a man he had asked to come work for him—the man explained that he wanted the job but that he also wanted to make it clear he shared most of Clark's views on how crime should be dealt with. "So do I," Mitchell replied.

The morning after the President-elect's mass introduction of his incoming Cabinet over television on December 11th, Clark telephoned Mitchell to offer his congratulations. Mitchell was too busy to come to the phone, but he returned the call a couple of hours later. Clark congratulated him on his appointment and offered whatever help he could give. Mitchell thanked him and said that he would need all the assistance he could get, whereupon Clark invited him to his staff lunch that day. Mitchell declined, explaining that he was engaged in White House briefings. Clark then invited him to his staff lunch the next day, but again Mitchell declined, saying that he would get in touch with him the following week.

As it happened, though, the two men met the day after this conversation—at a cocktail party for the outgoing and incoming Cabinets that was given at the State Department. The two men talked together for an hour or so, and the next morning Clark confessed that he had been deeply depressed by the encounter—most of all by the realization that Mitchell's background and temperament would indeed make it as unlikely as everyone had said that the new Attorney General would ever be able to understand the bitter discontent of Negroes and the young. "If he can't reach out and make contact with them, it looks hopeless," Clark said. Of course, he went on, it was possible that Mitchell would arrive by a different route at the same conclusions that practical necessity had compelled Attorneys General Kennedy, Katzenbach, and Clark himself to reach. But that raised the question of whether Mitchell would be temperamentally able to maintain even minimal rapport with the groups that such conclusions would compel him to deal with. "I also got the impression that he's a first-rate administrator and will use his time well," Clark added. "That will help."

In the course of their talk, Mitchell took advantage of the setting —the Diplomatic Suite—to see if he could negotiate a truce between the President-elect and the outgoing Attorney General. In spite of the bitter campaign attacks on Clark, Mitchell said, Nixon actually held him and his work in high esteem. Explaining that the attacks had merely been "a simplistic way to personalize the crime issue," Mitchell went on to say that both Nixon and he felt an apology to Clark might be in order, and suggested that Clark might open the door to this by publicly stating that he knew the charges made against him and his record had not been meant personally. Clark heard him out and then said mildly, "I guess that judgment should be left up to third parties."

If the President-elect found it difficult to get the right men for his Cabinet, he must have found it next to impossible to get the right men for the jobs immediately below that level. It was one thing to find a dozen successful businessmen and politicians who either wanted to cap their careers with the prestige that goes with a Cabinet post or to use it as a step toward other public office. It was quite another to find several hundred men who were willing to give up or postpone promising careers to take on the unglamorous, frustrating, day-and-night work that is the lot of the average Under-Secretary or Assistant Secretary—or, as these positions are designated in the Department of Justice, Deputy Attorney General and Assistant Attorney General. At the same time, sub-Cabinet positions demand high qualities of character and competence, because the men who hold these jobs must try to put the policies devised by the President and his Cabinet into effect on a day-to-day basis.

Once again there was an extended delay in filling these posts—so protracted, in fact, that the new President failed to fill more than a third of the top three hundred spots in his Administration by the time of his inauguration. Democrats charged that either he couldn't make up his mind about what men he wanted because he couldn't make up his mind about what policies he wanted carried out or the men he wanted had decided that their chief interest in the government was in being left alone by it. Republicans retorted that his cautious approach was part of the Presidential style he hoped to set—stability, moderation, continuity, and deliberation—as a means of soothing a troubled nation that was worn out by the flamboyant exertions of his predecessor. Actually, a more reasonable explanation was that neither Nixon nor his staff had spent much time during the campaign looking for men to fill these posts. In fact, it wasn't until two weeks after the election that he set up a small group to collect names of prospective appointees.

Although there may have been a shortage of qualified applicants, there certainly was no shortage of applicants. In a publicity stunt that left the new Administration wobbling on a high wire without a net below, the President-elect's office sent out form letters to everyone listed in *Who's Who* asking for recommendations about likely prospects for office in the forthcoming government. Since the requests produced thousands of nominations and only about three hundred offices of significance were open—almost all of which would inevitably go to friends and associates of high-ranking Republicans—the predictable result was thousands of disappointed and angry people who had worked and voted for Nixon and who might be expected not to go out of their way to help him again. Another result was that recommendations submitted by important Party leaders got buried in the piles of unwanted recommendations, which further delayed the selection process. (Three months after the inauguration, the recruiting staff was still frantically looking for letters from members of Congress, governors, and large campaign contributors who were infuriated by the Administration's failure even to thank them for their suggestions.)

By the time the Cabinet was announced, the number of promising nominees for sub-Cabinet posts had been narrowed down to around two thousand. These were divided among the twelve departments, and each Cabinet officer was given a thick black binder containing descriptions of the posts to be filled and a list of the most suitable candidates, with their biographies and letters of recommendation. It was reported that President-elect Nixon had instructed his Cabinet to pick the men they wanted either from the notebooks provided or from among their own associates but that he retained veto power over their choices and they over his recommendations.

The report was not entirely accurate. As it happened, Mitchell was in charge of the final screening process for all departments, which gave him a veto over any prospective nominee, unless, of course, the President or another member of the Cabinet insisted on hiring him. In the case of the men considered for the top jobs in the Department of Justice, a preliminary screening was conducted by the man who had been chosen (although the choice had not been announced) to serve as Deputy Attorney General. This was Richard G. Kleindienst, a forty-six-year-old Harvard-educated lawyer from Arizona, who had been national director of field operations for Barry Goldwater in 1964, a candidate for governor of Arizona that same year, field director for the Nixon campaign in 1968, and counsel to the Republican National Committee. Kleindienst was said to be somewhat to the right of Goldwater, but his own self-appraisal was that he was a conservative in economic matters and a liberal in human matters. (No one has ever been able to explain how this outlook—which General Eisenhower seems to have invented to describe his political philosophy—is possible, since liberalism in human affairs usually seems to require a liberal outlay of money.) In any event, Kleindienst also had a veto power of sorts over prospective appointments as long as he could explain to Mitchell's satisfaction why he had knocked someone off the list.

Mitchell had scarcely been named Attorney General before it was rumored that he would stay in the Department only until he had learned enough Constitutional law to qualify for a spot on the Supreme Court. The rumor somewhat cheered those who awaited his arrival in the Department with apprehension—until a new rumor sprang up to the effect that if he went to the Court Kleindienst would take his place as Attorney General. Several members of the Department predicted that this event would produce mass resignations on the part of the legal staff. In their view, it was bad enough that Kleindienst had been made Deputy Attorney General, since that post carried more power than most other sub-Cabinet posts in the government. The Deputy Attorney General not only runs the Department on a day-by-day basis and is in charge of the place when the Attorney General is not on the premises—as, in the nature of the job, he often is not—but also screens all prospective United States Attorneys and federal judges, which again gives him veto power, and directs liaison with Congress, which gives him an opportunity to try to revise legislation to his liking as it makes its tortuous, and largely secret, way through Congress.

After it was reported but before it was confirmed that Kleindienst had been picked for the second spot in the Department of Justice, Tom Wicker took the unusual step of appealing, through his column in the *Times,* to the President-elect to reconsider this decision. Asserting that the Cabinet and sub-Cabinet selections so far seemed "a grievous fumble, a missed opportunity to give the blacks and the poor a symbolic assurance that the new President is interested in them," Wicker went on to point out that the selection of two men who were clearly without experience in, and apparently without sensitivity to, the complex and perilous circumstances surrounding the contention over civil rights "might well jeopardize any remaining confidence, among the blacks, in the Nixon Administration."

As it turned out, Kleindienst was inexperienced in more than civil rights. At the start of a two-hour visit he paid Clark for a briefing on the Department, he suggested that he be dealt with on the assumption that he didn't know anything. "I found nothing to challange that assumption," Clark remarked afterward. Kleindienst had not even looked at an organizational chart of the Department and was stunned when he learned that it had thirty-five thousand employees; he knew neither the name of the man he was succeeding, let alone his duties, nor the name of the man in charge of the Criminal Division, which, with Kleindienst's enthusiastic support, had been such an issue in the campaign; he asked for summaries of all pending cases, and persisted in the request even after he was told that there were sixty thousand of them, that no one in the Department could conceivably be familiar with more than a tiny fraction of them, that some were literally older than he was, and that by the time summaries were completed—in half a dozen years, at best—they would be hopelessly out of date. He also wanted biographies, including political affiliations, of all employees in the Department; these were refused on the grounds that the product would end up half as big as *Who's Who* and would be as useless as that volume when it came to determining whether a man was a competent, loyal public servant, and that it was against both policy and common sense to force people to give up their right to a secret ballot. All in all, it appeared that the Nixon Administration was going in for on-the-job training in a big way.

One of the most important and difficult parts of the Attorney General's job, Clark once said, was "keeping a sense of balance in law-enforcement attitudes toward the very great tensions and anxieties that exist in the country today—tensions of the central city, of racism, of extremist activity, of youth unrest—and maintaining a fair and effective enforcement of the law that is neither repressive nor permissive." Although the choice of Mitchell and Kleindienst led Clark to suspect that the Nixon Administration would return the Department to its old role of acting like "a flinty-eyed prosecutor," he was still determined to do everything he could to help the new men by showing them what he and others in the Department had learned over the years about the problems facing it and how they had tried to solve them. "Probably the most difficult part of the transition is conveying our experience," he said. "Some newly arrived Cabinet officers want *no* help at all. Others want some help but are usually suspicious of what they get. And still others want all the help they can get and do their best to consider it objectively."

To preserve the integrity of the transition, President Johnson let the senior members of his Administration know that he wanted nothing done that might appear to be an attempt to commit the Nixon Administration to current policies. Clark wholeheartedly agreed with this dictum, and to make certain that the experience he hoped to convey was taken in the best spirit he did not put it down on paper, as his subordinates did in their briefing documents, but delivered it to his successor orally. Otherwise, he explained, it might have looked as if he were trying to create a written record that he could publicly refer to later in the event that the new Administration undertook programs that the old Administration had recommended; if Mitchell got that impression, Clark added, he might be inclined to reject all advice without even considering it. Clark also instructed his top aides to draw up suggestions for new programs and new procedures to make the Department more effective and easier to run. When an acquaintance remarked that probably no one else in political life had ever taken such a step to assure the success of someone who had blamed him for a good part of society's ills, Clark shrugged. He was not interested in the success or failure of the man who was taking his place, he explained, but was concerned only about the success or failure of the mission of justice.

The ideas that Attorney General Clark and his staff passed on to Attorney General-designate Mitchell and his staff were many and various. According to a memorandum submitted by Solicitor General Erwin N. Griswold, "The greatest defect in the administration of justice today is the delay in making trials available" to defendants. To remedy this, he recommended that the federal government set an example for state and local governments by sharply increasing the number of federal judges, federal prosecutors, and federal courtroom and detention facilities. He also wanted to see United States Attorneys and Marshals—there are ninety-three of each throughout the fifty states and territories—removed from the patronage system and put under the direct control of the Attorney General. And, finally, he proposed that the ministry-of-justice approach that Clark had been working toward be expanded and made an integral part of all government action in criminal cases.

To an unfortunate degree, the government is a set of interlocking anachronisms, and one of the most outdated of them all is the system of giving a new President the right to name all new United States Attorneys. Since they conduct most of the government's legal business in the field, one would expect them to be responsible to the government's chief legal officer, the Attorney General. Actually, though, each considers himself far more responsible to the man who persuaded the President to appoint him—normally, his state's leading political figure in the party that has won the White House. Once installed in office, a United States Attorney has little contact with the Attorney General but constant contact with the senator, representative, or political boss who got him his job. Of course, it is unlikely that these patrons support all of the government's aims, which makes any consistent legal policy impossible on a national scale. It also tends to make it unlikely that the government will succeed in any attempt to investigate or prosecute illegal conduct on the part of any friend, supporter, or associate of the politician who put the United States Attorney in office.

"The system reduces justice to a political pawn," Clark said in commenting on this archaic tradition. Another flaw, he went on, is that each time a Presidential election comes up, all United States Attorneys (and all of the nearly eight hundred Assistant United States Attorneys) begin to slack off work as they scout around for other jobs in case their party loses and the market is suddenly glutted with former United States Attorneys. "Justice should not have peaks and troughs like that," Clark observed toward the end of his term in office. "These men should be chosen for their professional skill, not their political friends. As things work now, the Department's constancy, its purpose, its mission are shattered every four or eight years. When we came into office in 1961, we found six United States Attorneys' offices in different parts of the country where no one even showed up on Inauguration Day or thereafter."

Assistant Attorney General Vinson, head of the Criminal Division under Clark, felt that the most critical problem facing his operation was "the development and retention of experienced personnel." Pointing out that many of the Assistant United States Attorneys around the country were in great demand by large law firms, Vinson expressed the belief that a large number of them took good job offers not because they wanted to leave but because they had so little security where they were. "Their departure with the outgoing Administration may be especially crippling" in view of the rising crime rate, he added, and urged the incoming Attorney General to devise ways through which many of these men might be persuaded to stay on before the exodus began. Vinson also called for expanded programs to train young attorneys for the Department, for a recruiting campaign to get experienced trial lawyers to join his division, for an improved system of collecting and collating information on organized crime, for more consumer-protection laws to safeguard the unwary, for a network of regional offices to handle the rapidly increasing number of fraud cases (particularly frauds against Negroes and the poor), and for more funds to expand the organized-crime section.

Stephen J. Pollak, head of the Civil Rights Division, saw his office's main flaw to be the relative ease in persuading capable lawyers to work there but the abiding difficulty in keeping them for more than a year or two in the face of the eighteen-hour days, seven-day work weeks, and three-month periods away from their families that were their common lot. Although the simplest solution would have been to hire more lawyers and spread the work out among them, Congressman Rooney would never have approved anything that sensible, so Pollak could only suggest that "a special recommendation be made to the new Attorney General to the effect that he and his new people should immediately embark on a program to encourage Civil Rights Division lawyers to stay on."

Alexander, director of the Bureau of Prisons, asked, first of all, for higher personnel standards and more people to meet them. For example, he pointed out, there were only nineteen psychiatrists and nineteen psychologists for the entire population of twenty thousand inmates in the federal prison system. Second, he urged large-scale development of model institutions—relatively small adult and youth facilities in and near large metropolitan centers—to provide a broad range of rehabilitation programs. In order to spread the most beneficial effects of such experiments to state and local prisoners, he suggested that local correctional agencies be allowed to use these centers for non-federal prisoners on a cost-sharing basis. Ultimately, Alexander continued, once the new centers were competently manned and successfully operated, they should be turned over to local control. Then, to study and treat special groups of offenders about whom almost nothing was known—mentally ill, violent, and mentally defective prisoners—he called for regional centers with highly trained personnel. Finally, he recommended that more funds be provided for new facilities to house small numbers of "adult repeaters," as a means of developing new rehabilitative techniques for "this heretofore unresponsive group."

Alexander's suggestions seemed to Clark among the most important that he passed on, because, as he often said, "repetition is the one factor in crime we can control." During the Presidential campaign, Nixon had recommended his own solution—putting twice as many people behind bars—but Clark pointed out that since most of the country's jails and prisons were little more then crime schools, this resort would only assure that twice as many hardened criminals emerged from them.

By the time the last work week of Clark's term of office came to an end—on January 17th, three days before the inauguration—he and Mitchell had conferred together for half a dozen hours. In the course of these meetings, Clark gradually revised his original impression of his successor. "I've been very impressed by him," Clark said at the end of this period. "In our talks, I've found him intelligent, wise, cautious, and highly professional. He seems sensitive to the problems surrounding civil rights, although he's inexperienced and somewhat narrow there. But he's wise enough to realize that he doesn't have the answers and that he has to learn, and learn quickly."

Before leaving office, Clark urged Mitchell to make full use of the funds provided for under the Law Enforcement Assistance Act to help—or, in effect, compel—local and state governments to improve their police departments, courts, and correctional systems, and to push for new legislation to help the new Bureau of Narcotics and Dangerous Drugs function more effectively. He also urged Mitchell to press for electoral reform and passage of stricter new laws to deal with corrupt practices by government officials, and said, "These would be good for the country, good for the Department, and good for your party."

Shortly after the Republican National Convention, Nixon's aides and a group of outside advisers met at Mission Bay, California, and set up thirty committees to study the major problems that then confronted the country or were expected to confront it within the next few years. Some of the initial conclusions were used during the campaign to impress the public with the imagination and resourcefulness of the candidate, until one of them—a statement to the effect that a modest increase in unemployment would be tolerable if it produced a sizable decrease in inflation—created such adverse publicity that, Mitchell said later, "we turned the task forces off and diverted our energies instead to the campaign." Once the campaign was over, the task forces were turned back on, and their findings began to pour into Nixon headquarters at the Hotel Pierre, along with the thousands of pages of briefing documents submitted by the Johnson Administration. It was like changing the kitchen staff in the middle of preparations for an elaborate seven-course meal that had to be served at once; no one on the new shift was sure what recipes had been used, what ingredients should be added, or whether the whole meal should be thrown out and a new one begun.

One basic change in the Justice Department that was contemplated by the incoming Administration was to make the Organized Crime and Racketeering Section of the Criminal Division a full division on its own. "This would be a very bad move, but they want to make it," Clark said at the time. "Although organized crime is hot stuff right now—a fashionable scourge—actually it makes up only a small percentage of the total crime afflicting this country. Making a change of this sort would create a hopeless conflict of responsibility and authority. Because of all the current publicity about organized crime, a new division devoted to it would get most of the crime-control funds appropriated by Congress, and a lot of lawyers would be enticed away from the Criminal Division, which has most of the real work to do. Of course, such a change would be popular with the public and on the Hill, but it would be purely political. I strongly advised against it."

The new Administration was considering another plan, which Clark also opposed, to appoint a Negro to head the Civil Rights Division and a white man to head the Community Relations Service, instead of, as in the existing setup, the other way around. In theory, it sounded good to have a Negro in charge of the Civil Rights Division. In practice, however, the change would have meant that the head of the division would be far less able to deal with white segregationists in the South, who might refuse to sit down at the same table with him or anyone representing him. And a white man in charge of the Community Relations Service could have destroyed it overnight. Seventy per cent of the people working in the C.R.S.

were Negroes, and the heart of the operation was made up of black militants who worked in the slums. "They would simply refuse to take suggestions, let alone orders, from a white man, however sincere he might be, because they would never believe that he knew the problems and shared their convictions," Clark explained. "But it would look good to have a white man in there fighting for his black brother."

Although these changes seemed politically productive, they were never made, apparently because their potentially disastrous social consequences finally became clear to Mitchell. That they were seriously contemplated, though, supported a contention made at the time by Deputy Attorney General Christopher—that the ambling pace with which the new Administration was approaching the problems it was about to inherit, coupled with a wholly unrealistic attitude toward them because of the top management's utter lack of experience, was bound to produce miscalculations. A miscalculation of this dimension also supported the contention made by Clark and others that nothing more gravely imperilled justice in America than an Attorney General whose instincts were essentially political.

After Mitchell took over the Department, he remarked that what had surprised him most during the transition and his first weeks in office was the spirit and dedication of the Department's employees. In large measure, this spirit and dedication had grown out of the conviction that Clark and his two immediate predecessors had inculcated in the key members of the Department—that no work in the entire government was more vital to the well-being and, indeed, the survival of the country than theirs. Along the way, most of these officials had also become convinced that their goals—full equality and true justice—could best be attained through the methods then in use.

"The new crowd probably isn't committed to civil-rights enforcement any more than they are committed to any other ideology," one career officer in the Department remarked during the transition.

"But they are practical men, and they will discover—let's hope soon —that the only practical way to keep this country in one piece is the way it's being done now. After all, the policies we follow didn't spring out of our foreheads full-blown. They are the result of trial and error, slogging hard work, long experience, and the lessons of history. They aren't really *our* policies, they're the policies of necessity."

Shortly afterward, Robert H. Finch, the newly appointed Secretary of Health, Education, and Welfare, publicly revealed that one crucial policy involving the Department of Justice didn't seem a matter of necessity to him. After meeting with the President-elect's task force on education, Finch told reporters that he was going to take "a long look at the guidelines" that had been laid down in the Civil Rights Act of 1964 to finally carry out the Supreme Court's school-desegregation decision of 1954. The guidelines—repeatedly criticized by the Republican candidate during the campaign, with the unmistakable implication that if elected he would take immediate steps to change them—required Southern school districts to show annual percentage increases in the number of Negro students attending formerly all-white schools if the districts wanted to continue getting federal education grants. Since few schools in low-income states like those involved could hope to stay open without federal money, the guidelines had been the most effective means devised so far for enforcing the Court's order. Accordingly, any plan to relax them struck many observers as an obvious payoff to Senator Thurmond for his help in putting Nixon in the White House.

When Finch was asked whether he intended to withhold federal funds to achieve desegregation, he answered, "There are other ways —such as community pressure—to achieve results." There being very little community pressure in the South for desegregation outside Negro communities, the remark prompted Clark to issue a statement warning about the upheaval that would follow any relaxation of the guidelines. In 1963, the proportion of Negro children in schools that had once been exclusively attended by white children was one per cent, he said, while under the guidelines it had risen by the end of 1968 to twenty per cent. If the forces of law were turned against Negroes, he added, they would quickly lose the little remaining respect they had for the law and would give up all hope of attaining full citizenship by peaceful means.

A few days after the election, President and Mrs. Johnson were waiting on the south portico of the White House as a limousine drew up and President-elect and Mrs. Nixon got out. Mr. Johnson was surprised to see Mitchell emerge behind them, and concluded at once that he was going to be the second most important man in Washington. Of course, Nixon's reliance on his former law partner was by no means exclusive, but it was great enough to force Mitchell to sacrifice the time he might otherwise have spent in learning about his forthcoming responsibilities in order to assume the burden of overseeing the entire transition. The main result was that three weeks before the inauguration not a single representative of the new Administration was at work in the Department of Justice. This promised great trouble in the future for the new management, but it created some trouble right then for the incumbents. Men who knew they would be replaced had long since made arrangements for other jobs and were eager both to get settled in their new work and to keep their promises to Clark that they would stay as long as they were needed to brief their successors.

"I guess we're the transition's stepchild," one of Clark's aides said on the last day of 1968. "We've set aside some offices, but no one has shown up to use them. The rumor is that someone will be coming in the day after New Year's, but we don't really know. It's a crazy way to start a new government."

JUSTICE

The rumor was correct. On January 2nd, the first member of the new Administration to appear for full-time duty arrived at the Justice Department. A twenty-eight-year-old lawyer by the name of Kevin P. Phillips, he had been administrative assistant to a conservative Republican congressman, Paul Fino, of the Bronx, for three and a half years before going to work in the Nixon campaign as an assistant to Mitchell. On December 23rd, Phillips made a telephone call from New York to Pellerzi, the Assistant Attorney General for Administration who was handling the nuts and bolts of the transition, and explained that Mitchell wanted him to move into the Department and start preparing the necessary groundwork for the new Administration's takeover.

Pellerzi assigned Phillips the suite of offices that had been set aside and, at his request, transferred to his staff a young lawyer from the Land and Natural Resources Division who had worked for Nixon during his 1962 gubernatorial campaign in California, and sent a secretary-typist from the administrative pool to assist them; at the same time, Phillips got in touch with a young lawyer who had been chairman of Law Students for Nixon and asked him to be on hand at the Department on January 2nd. Shortly after noon that day, the four of them got down to work. The first job the Phillips group tackled was reading the briefing documents the outgoing Administration had prepared for the Department. Phillips, who was deeply mistrustful of anything the Democrats had put their hand to, soon decided that this material was too cumbersome to be of much use and turned instead to a number of documents he got from the Bureau of the Budget and one he got from the Justice Department's Office of Legal Counsel called "Duties and Responsibilities of the Attorney General," which, though it had been drawn up in 1959 and was somewhat out of date, had at least been prepared under a Republican Administration.

From this material, Phillips compiled a description of the Attorney General's job, and then he turned to the areas where the greatest troubles might be expected the soonest—civil rights, crime, and slum-dweller relations with the police. He and his staff wrote digests of all civil-rights laws and of key federal criminal laws, ending with the Omnibus Crime Control and Safe Streets Act of 1968—with emphasis on Title I, which set up the Law Enforcement Assistance Administration, and Title III, which gave federal and local officials the right to place wiretaps and bugs on anyone who had committed, was committing, or was about to commit a crime punishable by a year or more in prison. After that, Phillips's group put together data that had been submitted by the Department to the Bureau of the Budget in preparation for President Johnson's 1970 budget, which was due to be revised by President Nixon shortly after he took office.

Then the Phillips staff compiled descriptions of about a hundred pieces of legislation that the Department had proposed or intended to propose to Congress, along with a list of the likeliest clashes over issues when the Ninety-first Congress convened a few days later. Memoranda were also prepared on the Department's involvement in certain pressing urban problems and its responsibilities vis-à-vis the District of Columbia. Since most of the Department's business with Congress is conducted through the Senate and House Judiciary Committees, Phillips and his staff drew up biographies of their members, which included information about where each man stood on important issues and the relative influence of the chairmen and the ranking members of both parties, along with an assessment of the strength of the coalition between Southern Democrats and Northern Republicans, which was expected to be more influential than ever. Finally, Phillips prepared a paper describing the procedure to be followed in the confirmation hearing that Mitchell would have to attend before the Senate Judiciary Committee in a couple of weeks.

The Brookings Institution study of the 1952-53 transition had observed that what any President-elect needed most of all was "advisers who had been studying the issues in several key areas long enough to have recovered from the shock of discovering how complicated most issues are when they are approached with responsibility for action." Although Phillips was far from being a Presidential adviser, his role of deciding which facts were important and which were not, as well as the way in which he described both sides of certain issues, was bound to influence Mitchell, a very important adviser.

When Phillips was asked, after he had been on the job for a few days, what had surprised him most about the place he replied, "Nothing really surprised me, except perhaps the weakness of the administrative structure and the way the lines of command here are tangled and broken. I can't say that I've been overwhelmed, as I thought I'd be. Of course, I didn't know what many of the people here did, but the operation ceased to awe me when I saw the disorganization. Much of the Department—that is, the technical side of it—runs itself. And the decisions made by the Attorney General don't seem overwhelming to me. In fact, the responsibilities of the job strike me far less than when I got here five days ago. The main problem is that there is no real command system, which leaves things too fragmented. It's an unresponsive mechanism. But Mr. Mitchell is a terrific administrator. And that's just what this place needs most."

In an article published in *Commentary* a few months earlier, Daniel P. Moynihan enumerated some of the mistakes made by liberals in the Kennedy and Johnson Administrations, and added, "High on any such list would be our disposition to be too much interested in ideas, especially if they are new, and too little interested in administration." Phillips was dismayed to find that he could agree with a Democrat on anything—even a Democrat like Moynihan, who had been chosen as a key White House staff member by the President-elect—but he conceded that in this case he emphatically did. "It's time for the tired, old, competent people to come in and make things work," he said. "We've had enough of the innovations of the wide-eyed idealists. They spent more money on finding out how long it took a termite to eat a building than they did on feeding people. They went into the slums and got the people's hopes up and then didn't deliver. That just made things worse. Some of these idealists have done far more damage to the country than the Morgans and the Insulls did. Most of them have been too interested in their own little bailiwicks, in preserving and expanding their power, and too little interested in the poor. They have misled the people in an attempt to keep their own gravy trains running. It's time we got these hypocrites out of town and began administering."

When Phillips was asked whether he had in mind merely a more orderly process of carrying out current policies, he shook his head vigorously and said that while he had nothing to do with devising policy, he nonetheless had some ideas of what would ultimately have to be done. "We're going to have to change things here basically from Clark's approach," he went on. "For example, I absolutely disagree with the theory that you can upgrade the poor by giving them things like better housing. That liberal idea is wholly without substance. The most important thing you can give the poor is a sense of community and history and their place in both. As matters stand now, most of the current government programs have hurt, not helped, the poor." Asked further if the poor could be given a sense of their place by way of education, Phillips again shook his head. "I don't believe in education for most people," he said. "Teach them how to use a lathe and let it go at that. Also, it's time we stopped being soft. We mustn't be afraid to get in there and crack a few heads."

Phillips had expected to find the Department of Justice "an all-knowing monolith," he said, but instead he found that "some of the Assistant Attorneys General, who really run things, are not very knowledgeable," although he did not explain how he had reached this conclusion when, by his own account, he had assiduously avoided all contact with them for fear of political contamination; as he put it, "Those are all political men." (Actually, only one of these men—Edwin L. Weisl, Jr., son of the New York political leader and head of the Civil Division—could have been considered a political figure, and because he was he had little influence on Clark and even less on policy.)

On his first day in the Department, Phillips was invited to join Clark and his senior aides at a staff lunch in the executive dining room, but he was reluctant to accept. "I felt that they were all political people—you know, Democrats—and, of course, I'm a Republican," Phillips explained later. As it happened, several of those at the lunch, which he finally attended, were non-political career officials, and at least one, Solicitor General Griswold, was a lifelong Republican. Everyone on hand knew that Nixon had placed an embargo on all policy discussions between his aides and outsiders for the time being, so the lunch conversation was mostly small talk. However, Phillips seemed tautly uncomfortable, and to put him at his ease Pollak, head of the Civil Rights Division, politely asked where he had gone to law school.

"Harvard," Phillips answered, and resumed eating.

Pursuing the subject, Pollak asked what class he had been in, and when Phillips told him Pollak asked if he knew a student in the same class who had later worked for the Department.

"I didn't have any contact with the other students," Phillips replied, and added, matter-of-factly, "I wasn't interested in the law. I went there only to further my career in politics."

The reaction of the others in the room—particularly Griswold, who had been Dean of the Harvard Law School before becoming Solicitor General—was one of barely controlled astonishment, but Phillips seemed unaware of it. "There were various personalities there," he later said of the lunch. "Of course, Clark came up through the ranks and is more chummy with his staff than an outsider would be. But Mr. Mitchell will be the only personality in that room when he takes over. The others will be his assistants." (When Mitchell was later asked whether he agreed with the theory that Phillips had developed in his recently published book, "The Emerging Republican Majority," he replied, "I don't really have a practice of sub-scribing to the theories of my aides. It generally works the other way.")

Phillips's charge that the top level of the Department of Justice was too politically oriented apparently was derived from the belief that only Democrats were politically oriented, for it would have been difficult to imagine three more intensely political men than Mitchell, Kleindienst, and Phillips. That is, it would have been difficult until the names of some of the men chosen to serve as Assistant Attorneys General were revealed. Although their appointments were not an-nounced until after Mitchell took office, four of them were present in the Department during the final week of the transition. Of the four, three had recently run for political office—Will Wilson, the new head of the Criminal Division, who had run unsuccessfully in Texas for both governor and senator as a Democrat, and then switched parties; Jerris Leonard, the new head of the Civil Rights Division, who had given up his seat as a Republican member of the Wisconsin legislature to run, unsuccessfully, against Senator Gaylord Nelson, a Democrat; and William D. Ruckelshaus, the new head of the Civil Division, who had been beaten that fall by Senator Birch Bayh, Democrat of Indiana. The fourth, Richard McClaren, the new head of the Antitrust Division, had not been involved in politics; he had been an anti-antitrust lawyer for business. In other words, six of the first seven men to come into the Department on the top level were essentially politicians.

To Clark this was the most unfortunate development so far. "Political men are usually ambitious men," he said after the appoint-ments were made. "One has to be especially careful of the ambitious men who come in here, exhilarated by their position and power, and get carried away."

And Christopher elaborated on this danger by saying, "Our whole philosophy has been that you have to depoliticalize this operation as much as possible. When the Attorney General was the President's campaign manager, the Deputy Attorney General was a campaign field director and gubernatorial candidate, and three Assistant Attorneys General recently ran for office, you are politicalizing things, no matter what kind of face you try to put on it. We've avoided people of this sort like the plague. Once they've run for office, even unsuccessfully, they're likely to want to run again. That is, they lost the gal last time but they're going to get her the next chance they have. That creates the danger that the way civil-rights, criminal, and anti-trust suits are handled will be less than pure. Once the Department becomes political, of course, the mission of justice must suffer."

The danger that men whose outlook is essentially political may use their positions to create new or stronger political constituencies and opportunities for themselves is not the only peril in such a course. Perhaps even more important is that once in office they may be disinclined to oppose political moves by a superior, however damaging to the cause of justice these might appear to be to them, because an open fight over an issue could damage or destroy any hope for a political future within the party. (In any event, a tally made six months after the inauguration revealed that seventy-three per cent of Nixon's appointees were Republicans; in the Department of Justice, the figure was nearly a hundred per cent.)

On the plus side of the ledger, Mitchell indicated to Clark that he was not going to make the clean sweep of officeholders left over from the outgoing Administration that many had anticipated. In fact, he went so far as to ask both Clark's executive assistant and his private secretary to stay on in the same capacities. "That indicates a high level of professionalism and confidence," Clark said. "These offices aren't easy to manage, and this shows that Mitchell realizes it. It also shows he's not worried that they'll listen in on his phone calls or tip me off about the latest hot memo from the White House." To Clark's further satisfaction, all of his own aides who were being replaced arranged to stay on until the end and to be available for consultation afterward.

Their behavior during the transition was typified by the way Roger Wilkins conducted himself after he recovered from his initial despair over the results of the election. "I've done my best to be absolutely correct," he said during the last days of the transition. "The only way I can hope to preserve the integrity of this agency is by dealing as openly, candidly, and honestly with the new people as I possibly can. The least we can do is give them the benefit of our doubts and all the help we can. Of course, some of them don't want any help of any kind from us. I can understand their attitude, and I don't blame them for not trusting us. They feel that this Administration has goofed up from beginning to end—war, riots, student discord, rising crime. In their view, we've failed miserably. We're a bunch of wide-eyed romanticists who don't know how to tie our own shoes. Their reaction is bound to be exaggerated because they've been out of office for eight years, and from the outside the problems always look simple. And the fact that they won a Presidential election seems to them to prove that they're right. Why should they come in here and take instructions from losers?" He paused for a moment, and added, "I wonder how omniscient they'll feel when *their* term ends."

In the final three days of his administration, Clark filed three major anti-trust cases against large corporations, which brought an avalanche of criticism down on him from conservative newspapers around the country. An editorial in the New Bedford, Massachusetts, *Standard Times* called him "the weakest, most inept member of the Johnson Administration" and charged that his "week of vindictiveness against his successor and the new President was an indictment of himself." The cases involved, first, the charge that General Motors, Ford, Chrysler, and American Motors had conspired together for nearly fifteen years to delay the development and use of pollution-control devices on automobiles; second, the charge that the Atlantic Richfield Oil Company and the Sinclair Oil Corporation were planning a merger that, according to the Antitrust Division, was illegal; and, third, the charge that I.B.M. had monopolized the three-billion-dollar-a-year computer market.

Clark conceded that to a degree these cases might inhibit his successor by compelling him to press them to a successful conclusion or leave himself open to the charge that he was soft on lawbreakers if they were big enough. "Still, we had no choice but to go ahead," Clark went on. "Big companies often lie in wait for a transition period, because they figure the Department's attention will flag then. Some of them want to negotiate with us for mergers during the transition, when everything is up in the air. Others want to make their move during and after the transition, when the flux is at its peak. And still others want to make their move after the inauguration, before the new people get settled in."

Atlantic Richfield and Sinclair, by announcing their intention to merge on January 17th, compelled the Department either to act while still in office or to let the companies proceed in a fashion that it believed to be illegal. As for the other cases, Clark said, "We spent two years investigating these matters, and if they were turned over for review to people who aren't even here yet and who aren't experienced, it would take two more years to go over the whole thing again. By then, it might be too late to remedy the damage we feel has already been done. In general, I think it's wrong either to hurry things or to leave the hot potatoes behind. For instance, I've got a reorganization plan for the Department that I think is good, but I wouldn't put it into effect because it's a policy matter and should be left up to the new people."

Before filing the three anti-trust suits, Clark informed Mitchell of his intentions and explained that major cases of this kind were certain to be difficult and controversial. "We can discuss them, but that might make it appear that you were endorsing our actions," Clark told him. "Although the decisions are mine, you will have to live with them, so you may want to know what I'm going to do and why." Finally, they agreed that Clark would call Mitchell before making any move of consequence and provide him with the details. In turn, Mitchell discussed with Clark the people he had in mind for top posts in the Department and the people he was going to ask to stay on—all with candor and amicability.

"The time we've had together has been very beneficial, I feel," Clark said a few days before leaving the Department. "I only regret that there wasn't time for all the new people to work together in the same way with the men they're replacing so they could get to know the personalities and the issues before taking over. You can be an awfully good lawyer and make an awful lot of mistakes this way."

The Senate Judiciary Committee met on the morning of January 14th in its panelled hearing room on the second floor of the New Senate Office Building to consider the nomination of the Attorney General-designate. A couple of days earlier, the Nixon camp had heard that some liberal Democrats on the committee who resented the Republicans' campaign attacks on Clark intended to rough up the man who had devised them. To prepare Mitchell for this, Phillips was ordered to provide more information on the Attorney General's duties, and early on the morning of the fourteenth Kleindienst took the material and went to brief Mitchell over breakfast at his temporary headquarters in the Hotel Jefferson, a quietly elegant establishment not far from the White House.

The rumor turned out to be unfounded, for it soon became clear that Mitchell would be confirmed without serious opposition. The hearing opened when the chairman of the committee, Senator James

O. Eastland, the Mississippi protector of Southern womanhood and cotton subsidies, stopped chomping on a panatela long enough to say, "I'm going to vote to confirm you without question." This was quickly followed by similar expressions of confidence from other conservative Southern Democrats, including Senators John L. Mc-Clellan, of Arkansas, Sam J. Ervin, Jr., of North Carolina, and Robert C. Byrd, of West Virginia.

The committee's leading conservative Southern Republican, Senator Thurmond, was absent from the deliberations, presumably to create a protocol obstacle for any of his colleagues who might have been tempted, had he been present, to ask the witness whether he had made a deal to get the support of the Southerners led by Thurmond, but would have been unwilling to violate Senate courtesy by bringing up that subject unless Thurmond was there to defend himself; Thurmond arrived at the end of the hearing, just in time to vote for Mitchell when the committee went into executive session. The Southerners' eager support of the nomination also appeared to support the contention that Nixon had indeed made commitments in the South, through Mitchell, to ease the enforcement of civil-rights laws and to oppose adding any more of them to the books.

Senator McClellan took advantage of the forum provided by the hearing to expand on one of his favorite themes: the Omnibus Crime Control and Safe Streets Act had been passed nearly unanimously by Congress the year before, and yet President Johnson and Attorney General Clark had flatly refused to enforce two of its main provisions—one permitting federal, state, and local law-enforcement officials to wiretap and bug suspected criminals, and the other legislatively overruling two Supreme Court decisions designed to protect the Constitutional rights of defendants in criminal cases. Just about every leading legal historian and Constitutional-law authority in the country had opposed both provisions of the law, on the grounds that they were un-Constitutional, ineffectual in the struggle against crime, and aimed not at criminals but at the liberal majority on the Court. Even many of the members of Congress who voted for the measure felt that McClellan had demagogically used the public's intense fear of crime to bully his colleagues into approving the law in the name of order. When McClellan asked Mitchell if he meant "to abide by the overwhelming voice of Congress," Mitchell hastily assured him that he did, whereupon McClellan said, "That is very gratifying to me."

The only question of substance asked by a Southerner came from Senator Ervin, who, in all likelihood, brought it up in a friendly manner to head off anyone who intended to bring it up in an antagonistic one. After remarking that most campaign managers in Presidential contests had been rewarded with the job of Postmaster General, he went on to say that to his way of thinking there was "something imcompatible with marrying the function of the chief political adviser and chief agitator with that of prosecutor of government crimes," and asked Mitchell whether he planned to act as chief legal officer of the country or chief political adviser to the President.

"Senator, I would hope that my activities in a political nature and of a political nature have ended with the campaign," Mitchell answered. "I might say that this was my first entry into a political campaign, and I trust it will be my last. From the termination of the campaign and henceforward, my duties and functions will be related to the Justice Department, and as the legal and not the political adviser of the President."

Nodding his approval, Ervin smiled and said, "Thank you, sir. I commend your answer."

Unaccountably, no one asked Mitchell about his highly political role in selecting and screening Cabinet members and their top aides.

In the course of the two-hour hearing, the only member of the committee to bear down on the witness was Senator Philip A. Hart, Democrat of Michigan, who had been one of only four senators to vote against the so-called Crime Bill:

SENATOR HART: The one statement that sticks in my mind in connection with [the Presidential] campaign most vividly was the President-elect's statement that we were going to get a new Attorney General. It had a lot of overtones to it. Now I believe Ramsey Clark has been a superb Attorney General. How will the conduct of the office under you differ?

MR. MITCHELL: Senator, I don't know as I can answer that in full. I believe that I can point out one difference which has been discussed here this morning, and that is perhaps the extent to which electronic surveillance may be used, particularly in the area of organized crime. I do not, of course, know all of the refinements of the workings of the Justice Department under the present Attorney General, and I think it would be presumptuous on my part to try and analyze the different activities of that Attorney General and to anticipate what my function and course of action might be in relationship to it.

SENATOR HART: Well, did the President-elect have any deeper analysis than you when he made his speeches?

MR. MITCHELL: I don't know as I can answer that question either, sir. I am sure that the points to which he talked related to specifics in this area of electronic surveillance. I believe that his basic approach to the discussion of the office of the Attorney General related to the pursuit of the prosecution of people engaged in organized crime. There was that additional area, as I recall his statements during the campaign.

SENATOR HART: I am sure you will check the record, and my reading of that record is that the pursuit of organized crime under Ramsey Clark has been more aggressive than at any other time in the history of this country. And if the only policy quarrel the President-elect had with Ramsey Clark's conduct was wiretapping, he was most imprecise in his speeches, as I listened to them. They were politically productive, but I think contributed nothing to the understanding of what really confronts this country.

A battery of television cameras had been set up in the corridor outside the hearing room, and when Mitchell emerged he was asked by a network interviewer the same question Hart had asked inside;

namely, how his stewardship of the Department of Justice would differ from Clark's. One principal difference, Mitchell answered, was that he would make use of electrical and electronic surveillance in cases affecting the nation's security. The implication was that Clark had refused to use such devices in these cases—or, in other words, that he had willfully jeopardized the security of the United States. He had not, of course—he simply refused to authorize whole-sale wiretapping and bugging *outside* the realm of national security —and if Mitchell had made that assertion inside the hearing room he would certainly have been corrected at once. But the interviewer apparently didn't know enough to correct the record, and that was the way it went out on the news around the country that night. A week later, *Time,* which had the time to get such matters straight, reported that Mitchell had promised in the hearing to "use electronic devices for 'national security and against organized crime,'" and added that Clark "had brusquely refused to use wiretapping."

Clark was far too accustomed to Republican misrepresentations by this time to let the latest one bother him. He was much more deeply upset by the new Administration's decision to employ wiretapping and bugging against any and all suspected criminals, because it constituted the first firm evidence that the President-elect and his Attorney General were going to continue playing politics by promis-ing the public that they would move aggressively against society's malefactors, whereas, in his opinion, they were doing little more than destroying every citizen's right to privacy. During the hearings, Mitchell promised the committee that in using secret surveillance the government would carefully protect the rights of the individual. There was no reason to disbelieve him. But the new Administration's acceptance of such surveillance would encourage state and local law-enforcement agents, who had exactly the same right under the new law that the federal government had, to use these devices, too. There was ample reason to fear that they would act far from circumspectly when they did, since local prosecutors and local judges are far less subject to public control than their federal counterparts.

The incoming Administration's unhesitating support of this perilous law immediately raised doubts about how the new President and his Attorney General would react to other crucial problems that were certain to come up within the next few months. Among them was whether the Law Enforcement Assistance Administration's appropriation of three hundred million dollars a year for the next three years would be spent in the crime-ridden cities that desperately needed the money or in small towns and villages where speeding and drunkenness were about the worst offenses, and whether the money that was spent would go for upgrading police departments, courts, and correctional systems, as the measure's sponsors had originally intended, or would go for wiretapping and bugging equipment, mace, tear gas, and anti-riot armaments, as the conservatives in Congress had amended the bill to allow. Clark and others in the Department who had watched helplessly as the right-wing Dr. Frankensteins in Congress assembled this monster feared that it would someday be used to fight Negroes and students rather than criminals.

Another fear was that the new President and Attorney General would carry out implicit pledges made during the campaign to weaken civil-rights efforts in the South by revising the school-desegregation guidelines, which had raised the proportion of black children attending formerly all-white schools from one per cent to twenty per cent, and that the new Administration might also sabotage the Voting Rights Act of 1965, which in four years had doubled the number of black voters in the Old Confederacy and had resulted in four hundred and seventy-nine Negroes being elected to public office. Clark was convinced that if there was retrenchment on these policies the little remaining faith Negroes had in the established system would vanish, and he publicly warned, "Nothing could be better calculated to irreconcilably divide the country than the failure to enforce the civil rights of all our citizens."

Kleindienst had reportedly promised to crack down on "draft dodgers," on "anarchistic kids," and on "militants" of all persuasions, and this threat led some high members of the Department to wonder if all dissent was to be stifled on the pretext that it amounted to subversion. In some quarters, student radicals were regarded as an even greater threat than the forces of organized crime, which was made alarmingly clear by a report that later appeared in the Chicago *Daily News:*

Undercover police investigations in Illinois are at an all-time high. In the Chicago area alone, more than 1,000 men from the FBI and various other federal, state, county and city agencies are working on supersecret assignment. "Our growing concern about subversives and militants, with their talk of armed revolution, has brought us a temporary shift in emphasis away from the organized crime problem," said Illinois State Police Supt. James T. McGuire. "I've never seen anything like the intensity of the current investigations in all my years in law enforcement," McGuire said.

The shift in emphasis was evidenced this week when dozens of undercover agents "monitored" the seventh annual convention here of the leftist Students for a Democratic Society. Deputy Chicago Police Supt. John Mulchrone, the department's resident expert in intelligence matters, said he had "upwards of 500 men doing undercover work." The new shift against subversives also was evidenced in an April speech by Mulchrone's top aide, Capt. Thomas J. Lyons, at a meeting of 600 police intelligence experts at Palm Springs, Cal. Lyons described the telephone interchange of information between police departments when a suspected subversive travels. . . . Undercover agents use a variety of investigative techniques. These include disguises, wiretapping, infiltration, and around-the-clock surveillance. Frequently they use "dummy" businesses operating from rented store-fronts, and assign policemen as drivers of trucks from nonexistent television repair companies or pizza parlors. Mulchrone said he often hires civilian men and women as informers and investigators. "We get people who've become disillusioned," [he said.]

Mayor Richard J. Daley was apparently prepared to prove that his panic during the Democratic Convention had been justified even if he had to invade the privacy of every citizen in Chicago and loose an uncontrollable witch hunt to do it. In the Department of Justice, a fear was growing that the federal grand jury then investigating what a report prepared for the National Commission on the Causes and Prevention of Violence called the "police riots" in Chicago might fail to produce indictments of even the policemen who had been most flagrantly brutal.

There was also some concern in the Department that if the police *were* indicted some of their victims would be, too. "Chicago author-ities have arrested and charged every leader of the demonstrations there," Vinson said shortly before leaving office. "There has been enormous pressure on the federal government to step in and prose-cute them, too. The basic question is: Should the federal government preëmpt what has always been a local responsibility?" Clark, of course, believed that it shouldn't. He also believed that if the federal government—in the person of Attorney General Mitchell—usurped this local responsibility the motivation would be purely political and the action would be a grievous blow to the public interest.

Another question about the new Administration's policies con-cerned the use it would make of the Office of Criminal Justice. De-spite that office's modest budget, Freed feared that Mitchell might consider even that outlay an idealistic waste of money and close the place down. Others feared that, if it wasn't closed down, its aim might be changed to such an extent that it would end up guarantee-ing less justice rather than more—particularly if it was used, as many people expected, to devise a system of "preventive detention," to keep criminal defendants locked up before they were tried. In Freed's view, preventive detention probably violated the Constitution, because it would amount to punishment before guilt was proved. "Still, there's a lot of political appeal in the idea," he went on. "Nearly everybody in Washington is scared to death that they're going to be mugged or worse, and, of course, such a law would keep a lot of hoodlums off the streets."

Over in the Community Relations Service, Wilkins was also worried about what would become of his operation when he left. "To do this job right, you have to deal with a lot of really tough, hostile people," he said. "The new Administration may not want to do that. They may decide to spend less time in the heart of the black communities, where the heart of the problem lies, and to deal instead with the middle-class blacks on the fringes, because they seem more constructive and are certainly more mannerly. Also, the new people may decide to face these problems only when strife is imminent or actual. We believe that's too late, that you have to solve the hottest problems before they ignite and set a host of other problems afire. We also believe that to accomplish this you have to constantly make large, visible changes, so that black people will see them being made and realize that things are getting better. But the new Administration may say, 'Hell, that's not our job. Our job is to run when the fire bell rings.' If that happens, one of these days several thousand fire bells will go off at once."

Clark shared this concern, but, above all, he was deeply afraid that President Nixon, under pressure from the military, the police, and most of the nation's governors and mayors, as well as many leading members of Congress, would give in to their pleas that he garrison troops around the country's major cities, so that they would be ready to move in at the first sign of disorder. Besides the danger that the military would thereby become a national police force of the kind that has always been resisted in this country, there was the equally great danger that a move of this kind would draw the final battle lines between the races.

Attorney General Clark's final responsibility before leaving office was to oversee the protection of the inauguration. "It's a nervous one to go out on," he said a few days before the ceremony. "There have been a lot of situations here that have been hard to judge, but they would have been a lot easier to live with if I'd been wrong." Inauguration Day presented two principal dangers, he went on, the first being a capricious psychotic and the second being an outburst like the one at the Chicago Convention. While extra precautions were to be taken against the former—such as stationing armed troops and police officers on all rooftops along the route of the inaugural parade and checking the identity of everyone who lived or worked in rooms with windows facing that route—little more could be done to stop an assassin who was willing to lose his own life in taking the President's. As for controlling a riot, Clark was confident that the Department and the other government agencies coöperating with it had that eventuality well in hand. His preparations followed the methods he had found successful in earlier confrontations between protesters and the government—chiefly, negotiations with the demonstrators to find out what their plans were and then further negotiations over suitable outlets for their dissent that would be both peaceful and legal.

The task of conducting these negotiations fell, as it often had in recent years, to Deputy Attorney General Christopher and his staff, who met repeatedly with demonstration leaders during the weeks before Inauguration Day. "There's a real technique to this kind of negotiating," Christopher said at the time. "We start from a strong bias that there are Constitutional rights to be exercised, and we're confident that we can provide a safe and legal way for these dissenters to express themselves. Consequently, we don't expect much trouble."

On the morning of January 16th, Christopher met for two hours with the chief of the Metropolitan Police Department, his deputy, the deputy mayor of the District of Columbia, the head of the Parks Service police, a representative from the Inaugural Committee, a man from the Secret Service, the local commander of the National Guard, a Marine Corps officer, and Kleindienst. Early in the meeting, Christopher brought up the subject of permits for the demonstrators as a preamble to the explanation he intended to make about the elaborate groundwork he had laid, the agreement reached with the leaders of the planned demonstrations, and his past experiences under similar circumstances.

Before he got to any of these matters, Kleindienst broke in and shouted, "No permits! Don't give *any* permits!"

Christopher began patiently explaining the preparations that had been made and the reasons for them. "He had been an observer in almost every major riot since Watts, and he knew what he was talking about," a participant in the meeting said later that day. "But Kleindienst wouldn't listen. He just kept pounding on the table and saying, 'No permits!' It was very much touch and go there for a while. Finally, the Republican from the Inaugural Committee managed to quiet Kleindienst down. But I'm afraid he didn't change his mind. He wanted to pre-position troops all over the city. That meant he could crack down at the slightest provocation. Of course, that would have been the best way to turn a small incident into a disaster like Chicago."

Since Clark and Christopher would officially relinquish office at the moment that Nixon was sworn in by the Chief Justice, the power of the Attorney General would then fall to the third-highest-ranking man in the Department, the Solicitor General, who had been asked to stay on. Until Mitchell was confirmed by the Senate and sworn in by the President the day after the inauguration, he was legally without power. In effect, this left the new President without the legal right to provide protection for the inaugural party even after he was in office. To remedy this situation, Clark took the precaution of appointing Mitchell and Kleindienst special assistants to the Attorney General, so that between the time that he departed and Mitchell was sworn in they would have the legal right to issue orders to members of the Department. Then, at ten minutes after eleven on the morning of January 20th, Clark rode down in his private elevator for the last time—fifty minutes before his term expired, because he had to get ready for the inaugural ceremony, which he felt he should attend to demonstrate, however modestly, the continuity of the government.

At the same time, Kleindienst was in the Department's "situation room" on the fifth floor, overseeing the protection of the inauguration. By means of a walkie-talkie, he kept in constant touch with those guarding the site of the inaugural ceremony, on the steps of the Capitol, and with those guarding the route that the President and his party would later follow to the reviewing stand in front of the White House. Throughout the ceremony and parade, Mitchell was followed around by a Navy commander who had a walkie-talkie tuned in to the same frequency as Kleindienst's. "I kept in touch with Mr. Mitchell minute by minute," Mr. Kleindienst said later. "The first trouble was the knots of kids at 12th and 14th Streets on Pennsylvania Avenue. They started throwing things at the President's car, so I ordered more troops into those areas and then let Mr. Mitchell know what I had done. We had security people ready to move in from three blocks away from the parade route. Clark hadn't wanted them that close, but I insisted. I think things went pretty well."

President Nixon did not think that things had gone at all well. In fact, he was said to have been bitterly offended by the demonstrations against him—which, indeed, were as ugly as they were futile—and to be determined not to allow anything that insulting to his office or to himself to occur again during his Presidency. One of Attorney General Mitchell's first official acts after being sworn in the following day was to announce that in the future he would deny permits to "activists" like those who had pelted the motorcade. Since a denial of the right to express dissent on the grounds that the applicant has previously broken a law or might simply be considered apt to break a law is forbidden under the First Amendment, it appeared that the new Attorney General either was unfamiliar with the Constitution or was prepared to ignore it.

III

Watch What We Do

"This morning, as for some days past, it seems exceedingly probable that this Administration will not be reëlected," President Lincoln wrote on August 23, 1864. "Then it will be my duty to so coöperate with the President-elect as to save the Union between the election and the inauguration; as he will have secured his election on such ground that he cannot possibly save it afterward." Everything that could go wrong for his Administration went wrong that summer. Confederate troops were encamped on the outskirts of Washington, the Republican Party was in bitter disarray, and Lincoln was widely being put down as a failure and a scoundrel by men in both parties. The Democratic National Convention was scheduled to open in Chicago on August 29th, and it was generally believed that who- ever was nominated was certain to be pledged to end the war on any terms he could get, and was equally certain to be elected in November. After the President finished writing the note, he folded and sealed it, and during a meeting with his Cabinet later that day he asked the members, some of whom were worse enemies of his than anyone in the opposition camp, to sign the back of the document without being told what it contained. Presumably, he wanted to have this evidence of his intentions in case he needed it later, and yet did not want to assure his defeat by letting it be known that he fully expected it. In the end, of course, the Union Army broke the Confederacy that fall, Lincoln was reëlected easily, and the note was never used.

Although the Union may have been in less peril at the time of the 1968 Presidential election, it was in graver domestic danger than it had been at any other time since the Civil War. And although President Johnson was not running for reëlection, he undoubtedly was troubled by some of the same fears that had beset Lincoln a century before. To a great extent, the causes underlying the danger to the Republic, like those that had brought on the Civil War, were racial. What seemed to concern the majority of voters most in 1968 —aside from the war in Vietnam, an issue that was largely removed from political debate during the campaign once peace talks began in Paris that spring—were the black riots that had engulfed a hundred cities across the nation and that, to many white people, were the most flagrant and frightening kind of criminal activity; the alarming increase in street crime, most of which was committed by Negroes; and the economic threat posed to millions of lower-class white men by millions of black men who were trying to extricate themselves from the bottom of the heap.

In the course of the Republicans' campaign to restore "law and order," Nixon repeatedly implied in the North that he would crack down on those who fomented disorder and those who committed crimes—by giving the police a freer hand, by locking up twice as many accused suspects, and by restricting the Supreme Court's efforts to give the poor and the unwary the same rights that the well-off and educated had asserted all along—and he repeatedly implied in the South that he would slow down the pace of integration. In sum, his campaign was largely aimed at cashing in on the white man's fear of the black man. But Nixon's victory at the polls presented him with much the same kind of dilemma that would have faced General George B. McClellan had he defeated Lincoln: How could the winner keep the pledges he had made to those who had elected him, and thereby maintain his power base, and at the same time do what was necessary to preserve the Union?

President Johnson had faced a dilemma of this sort when he went ahead with his plan to press for equal rights for all citizens, knowing full well that his policy would drive Southerners out of his party and thereby weaken, if not destroy, *his* power base. Following his election in 1964, he met with a group of Southern politicians at his ranch in Texas, and after listening to their arguments against his setting down firm guidelines to implement the Civil Rights Act of 1964 he finally said, "Nigger, nigger, nigger—that's all I hear. You might as well stop, because we're going ahead." Convinced that this course provided the only hope of saving the country—and his place in history—he went ahead, with unexpected and unprecedented vigor. That cut the heart out of the Democratic Party, and made Nixon's election possible.

Because of the ground that President Nixon had secured his election on, his "Southern strategy" of making the South the basis for his victory at the convention and his strategy, South *and* North, of appealing to the racist in white voters for his victory at the polls took on even more importance once he assumed office. Many watched with amusement as Nixon's chief lieutenant during the campaign and the transition, who had played a principal part in misleading the public into believing that any halfway competent Attorney General could easily solve the crime problem, took over that post. But others were less entertained by the ironies in Mitchell's appointment than they were apprehensive about his inexperience in national affairs, about his reputed hardline attitude toward any kind of public disorder, Constitutional or not, about his evident lack of contact and sympathy with the disenfranchised and the young, and, above all, about his role in carrying out the Southern strategy. Reporters persistently credited Mitchell with having devised this strategy, and he persistently denied it. Of course he hadn't devised that approach; Barry Goldwater had, in 1964. It hadn't worked then, because President Johnson was too popular and Goldwater was too impulsive, but there was no reason to believe that it wouldn't succeed for a cautious and experienced Republican candidate running against an impulsive and disorganized Democrat, who had been deprived of his party's historic base in the South and whose personal platform, in the middle of a terrible war abroad and riotous discord at home, was "the politics of joy."

Nixon was well aware that John F. Kennedy had not won the election in 1960 but that he, Nixon, had lost it, and he was determined this time not to try to win so much as to let his opponent lose. In any event, the larger question was not who had originated the Southern strategy but how it would be carried out after the election. Mitchell also persistently denied that he had made any deals with anyone, including such Southern leaders as Senator Thurmond, the Democrat-turned-Dixiecrat-turned-Republican from South Carolina. Indeed, Mitchell wouldn't have had to make any deal as such once it was known that Nixon had decided that the best way to win the nomination and the election was to get the South in his corner, for after he had accomplished his purpose he would have to go on pleasing the South to keep it there.

A few months after President Nixon's inauguration, he said that Attorney General Mitchell's views on the law were closer to his own than were the views of anyone else in his Administration. (The President also said that Mitchell was the man he had relied on most in forming his government and in conducting its business.) During the same press conference in which the new Attorney General promised to deny permits to "activists" who wanted to demonstrate, he also promised to provide more "vigorous law enforcement" than his predecessor. When a reporter asked what, exactly, he had in mind, Mitchell answered, "I would give you a specific instance that you might consider in relationship to the bail problem here in the District and other parts of the country, where many of the criminals that are apprehended are let out on bail and by the time they get back on the first case they are up on two or three more charges. I would point out, as to this bail situation, if it were straightened out and these defendants were not turned loose it would present a specific area in which there would be a decrease of crime."

At issue was a fundamental question about procedures for dealing with people arrested in the District of Columbia, whose growing crime rate Nixon had promised, time and again during the campaign, to deal with as soon as he took office. In the mid-sixties, a number of legal specialists in court procedures got together with a number of lawmakers in Congress who were concerned about the widespread abuse of bail practices to see what could be done to improve them in federal courts throughout the country. Under the existing system, a defendant who looked dangerous to a presiding judge was often assigned a high bail as a means of keeping him away from society. That meant, of course, that wealthy men or professional criminals with an organization behind them had little trouble getting out of jail, while the impoverished defendant stayed there—in other words, money was exchanged for freedom.

For the poor man who was arrested for a serious crime, this also meant that he would have to spend months in jail awaiting trial—in the District, for example, the average time between arrest and trial was ten months—that he would probably lose his job if he had one, that his family would probably have to go on relief, that he could not consult freely with his lawyer, and that he would be unable to search for witnesses who might testify on his behalf (a task that few court-appointed lawyers would bother to undertake). Moreover, he might be worse off in a local jail than if he had been convicted and sent to prison, since prisons provide vocational and recreational facilities that jails invariably lack.

Under the leadership of two conservative senators—Ervin, a Democrat, and Roman L. Hruska, a Republican from Nebraska, both of whom had done remarkably farsighted work in reforming the archaic eye-for-an-eye vengeance that had long been passed off as "rehabilitation" in the nation's prisons—Congress passed the Bail Reform Act of 1966. One of the effects of this statute was to prohibit the assignment of bail, either high or low, in all non-capital cases that came before federal courts unless a judge had demonstrable reason to believe that a defendant would not appear for trial.

The greatest impact of the new law was on the District of Columbia, where all criminal cases are under federal jurisdiction. Within a year or two of the law's passage, there was growing alarm in the community over the way some defendants who had been released pending trial were committing other crimes—"free crimes," as they were known on the streets, since most courts were too crowded to try defendants on any but the first offense, and if they weren't, defendants were usually sentenced to concurrent terms for two or more offenses. As everywhere else in the country, crime was on the rise in Washington, and since much of it there was publicly —although incorrectly—attributed to "bail criminals," a movement inevitably got under way in Congress to reform the Bail Reform Act. Just about everyone agreed that some kind of remedy was essential, but there was wide disagreement on what form it should take. Among the various proposals suggested, the two most popular were an old one, calling for an increase in federal-court personnel to cut down the delay between arrest and trial, and a new one, "preventive detention," which would permit federal judges to refuse bail to any defendant in a criminal case if his release threatened to endanger the community.

The first proposal would be expensive and Constitutional, since it would actually provide the "speedy" trial that the Sixth Amendment theoretically guarantees. The second would be cheaper and, in the opinion of its opponents, un-Constitutional, since it would amount to suspending due process by punishing an accused person before he was found guilty by a jury; moreover, as a device for preventing "free crimes," it put the punishment before the crime. "I have misgivings about imprisoning a man for crimes he has not yet committed and may never commit," Senator Ervin said of the preventive-detention approach. "Preventive detention in non-capital cases is repugnant to the traditions of a liberty-loving people."

Attorney General Mitchell's implicit support for the approach indicated that he found it no more repugnant than he had the un-Constitutional suspension of citizens' rights on the ground that they might be "activists." Anthony G. Amsterdam, a professor of law at the University of Pennsylvania, described both preventive detention and the suspension of citizens' rights on the ground that they might be "activists" as "not merely repressive but un-Constitutional." He added, "I accept the proposition that President Nixon and Mr. Mitchell may have a popular mandate to lead the nation through the wilderness of such sterile and self-defeating posturing for four years, until we learn that violence is not curbed by counter-violence. I object, however, to ignoring plain Constitutional mandates in the process. . . . They are among the most priceless safeguards of liberty won and cherished by this nation. When the Attorney General is heedless of them, he does more violence to the nation than the course of conduct which he urges could possibly hope to prevent."

During the transition, Clark suspected that Mitchell would come out for preventive detention because it would be relatively cheap and politically rewarding, particularly in urban centers where crime and the fear of crime were high and Nixon's vote-getting strength was low. For his own part, Clark was implacably opposed to the plan, both because it was un-Constitutional and because its impact would fall mostly on Negroes—a point, he feared, that would not be lost on the black community—which would further divide the races and bring open conflict between them closer. As Tom Wicker later wrote in his column in the *Times,* preventive detention was "sure to be perceived in the ghetto as one more way of making second-class citizens of black Americans—one more way of reacting punitively to the victims of conditions that breed and even encourage crime and violence, rather than of launching any real or effective attack upon those conditions."

What worried Clark and his top aides most during the transition was that their successors would "politicalize" the operations of the Department, which they saw as the gravest danger of all to the even-handed administration of justice. Clark had refused to consult with the President before filing any suits, whatever their political implications, and during his stewardship of the Department he consistently put down any attempts on the part of his subordinates to please the President or other party leaders by conducting official business in a manner that would be politically rewarding. But Mitchell appeared to be turning the Department of Justice into a political mechanism overnight, by placing political figures in the most crucial posts there and by advocating the use of wiretaps and preventive detention, both of which seemed to be aimed at the politics rather than the substance of the crime issue. In view of Mitchell's unfamiliarity with the governing process on a national scale, his well-known disdain for social theory, and his ignorance of the historical background of the contending forces in the country, there was no reason to believe that he was aware of the threat to the commonweal he was creating. And in view of his single-minded dedication to the President's political fortunes, there was no reason to believe that he would alter his course even if he became aware of it.

A week after Mitchell assured Senator Ervin in the confirmation hearings that from "the termination of the campaign and henceforward, my duties and functions will be related to the Justice Department, and as the legal and not the political adviser of the President," a reporter asked the new Attorney General at his first press conference, "Mr. Mitchell, because of your closeness to President Nixon during the campaign, it has been speculated that he will seek your advice during this Administration on matters even outside the legal sphere. Would you clarify a little bit on that in detail?"

"Yes, I will be available to do whatever the President asks me to," Mitchell answered.

By the Attorney General's own account, as described in an interview that he gave Milton Viorst, which was published in the *Times Magazine* a few months later, the President had asked him to do a good deal, including taking on such tasks outside the Department as working closely with the National Security Council, with the government's secret intelligence operation, and with the Urban Affairs Council. "I think you can come to your own conclusions about the range of advice I give the President," he said after describing these duties. "I guess I see him once a day or more, when I go over to the White House. And during the course of the day we usually talk on the phone several more times. In the evening, he frequently calls me at home; I have a direct line from the White House switchboard. I think he hears my views on most important questions, and I think he values my judgment." After the election, Mitchell went out of his way to let acquaintances know how close he was to the President-elect personally and how broad his advisory role was politically, but his making this public suggested more than insecurity or disregard for a senator's right to an honest answer in an open hearing. Indeed, it suggested that from the outset he had been, and meant to go on, playing politics.

As time wore on, events demonstrated that he was playing the game rather poorly. By and large, even the most intelligent men who spend their lives accumulating money rarely have the experience to operate skillfully in the incredibly complicated and subtle world of politics. In Mitchell's case, his determination to make the Department of Justice a political arm of the White House while failing to realize the importance of not making that determination obvious left him open to the charge that he was serving the President's political interest, not the public interest. And however much Mitchell denied the charge, as he repeatedly did—"There were no political considerations in the choice of any of these people," he said of his top appointees in the Department—the charge remained. It was difficult to see how Mitchell could have known that Kleindienst, whom he described as "made for the job," was qualified, since neither man had an inkling of what the position entailed when Kleindienst was chosen.

Leonard demonstrated that he had no emotional commitment to the civil-rights cause by retaining his membership in the all-white Order of the Eagles (which Mitchell was aware of when he chose him to head the Civil Rights Division), until the public outcry by civil-rights forces compelled him to resign from the Eagles shortly after taking office. Just before he did, the National Association for the Advancement of Colored People in Wisconsin, his home state, observed, "It's too late in the day to recognize that the issue of membership in the Eagles is a sensitive one with the black community. His resignation at this time would demonstrate that he is a politically aware person and not that he has a fundamental understanding or sympathy with the people he is supposed to represent."

And it was reported that Wilson, who got his job through Senator John Tower, the ultra-conservative Texas Republican, took a dim view of men who had been close to Clark, because he feared that they were likely to be contaminated by Clark's conviction that vigorous enforcement of the law had to be balanced by equally vigorous fairness toward defendants. "Clark's trouble was that he was philosophically concerned with the rights of the individual," Wilson said after he was installed in office. "Our concern is more an orderly society through law enforcement. Clark put too many restraints on the law-enforcement agencies. He was like a football coach warning his players not to violate the rules when he should have been telling them to go in there and win."

Wilson's first change in policy after taking office was to switch the emphasis of the Criminal Division from dealing with crime in general to dealing with crime in La Cosa Nostra. That was clearly a political move, for organized crime, though popularly believed to be the most pressing part of the crime problem in this country, is a relatively small part. However, many law-enforcement officials in the country have found that it is a profitable one to talk about. The public fear of this dark and greatly exaggerated menace transforms the most ordinary man who promises to deal with it into a public hero. And his promise pries money out of the poorest and most reluctant legislature.

Just before the inauguration, Wilson's predecessor, Fred M. Vinson, Jr., told him, "You may not believe this, but it would be easy to check out: When I took over this division, I hired only one man whose political affiliation I was aware of, and I was only aware of it by accident, not because I had looked into it. In fact, in all those cases with political overtones that I prosecuted here, I indicted many Democrats but only one Republican." Wilson was less impressed by the number of Democrats indicted than he was by the news that one Republican had been indicted, and after taking over the division he summoned the lawyer who had prosecuted that case and demanded to know which party he supported. Dumbfounded by this invasion of privacy, the man would only say, "Mr. Wilson, I don't care if they're Democrats or Republicans. If they've broken the law, I'll prosecute them." Since if he fired the man Wilson would have been placed in the position of being open to the charge that he didn't want Republicans prosecuted, he was forced to let the matter rest for the moment.

Some other holdovers from the previous Administration found different ways to hang on to their jobs. John Ingersoll, head of the Bureau of Narcotics and Dangerous Drugs, which Clark had set up the year before in a widely praised reorganization of the government's efforts to control narcotics but which had not yet had time to produce the results expected of it, called a press conference after the new Administration took over, and said that the fight against addiction had "failed miserably"; two weeks later, Mitchell announced that Ingersoll was being kept on. Subsequently, it emerged that Attorney General Mitchell meant to concentrate heavily on the misuse of narcotics in this country. Of course, that was a laudable goal, but he left some doubt about his motives and his regard for fair play when he said not long ago, "The former Administration failed utterly to do anything about narcotics." To be sure, it had failed to a degree, as any Administration faced with a task of this magnitude was bound to, but his remark suggested that he hoped to make political capital out of this issue by falling back on the same kind of misrepresentation that Nixon had used in his radio speech on crime during the campaign. Mitchell's charge also ignored several innovations undertaken by the previous Administration—two major laws enacted in two years to deal with drugs and to rehabilitate those who fell victim to them, and the consolidation of the government's struggle against the drug scourge into the new bureau that Ingersoll headed.

During Mitchell's first press conference, a reporter asked if all his new assistants were Republicans, and the Attorney General answered, "As far as I know, yes." Still, he insisted that there was nothing political behind his choices. Freed, who had come into the Department during the Eisenhower Administration, disagreed with his new boss's appraisal. "Everybody in the Department knows that politics is playing a far larger part here than it has at any other time in the past decade," Freed remarked shortly before he departed, a couple of months after Mitchell took office. "For one thing, being a Democrat here is a huge obstacle to one's advancement now."

The politicalization of the Department was inevitably bound to create problems for Mitchell himself, since few really able practicing lawyers are willing to subordinate their dedication to the law to someone else's political designs. As a result, topnotch lawyers were unwilling to come to work for the Department, and it was questionable whether the topnotch lawyers already there—in surprising numbers—would be able to sustain the kind of morale and enthusiasm that had led them to put in long hours at relatively low pay under Clark's stewardship. Ultimately, of course, the work of the Department was bound to suffer; in time, that was bound to reflect adversely on Mitchell, and, because of his close association with the President, on the entire Administration. In sum, the victors belonged to the spoils.

During the transition, it was often said in Washington that President-elect Nixon had chosen his Cabinet in the same manner that he had chosen his Vice President—to make certain no member of it would outshine him. It was also said that some of the men he had selected followed this principle in choosing *their* subordinates, which led to the expectation that the new Administration might be as lacklustre as any since Millard Fillmore's. Anyway, on this basis it might be argued that Attorney General Mitchell's choices were not so much political as they were personal. "There's always the danger that a Cabinet member will avoid first-rate men when he picks his staff," Clark said in the course of a private discussion on this topic during the transition period. "That's far likelier in government than it is in the commercial world, because here the spotlight is always on. The opposite approach was one of the Kennedys' greatest strengths. They weren't afraid of anyone, so they went after the best men they could find." A prominent Washington attorney later remarked that a couple of men who were considered for high posts in the Department under Mitchell and then were turned down "would have been glittering jewels in any Administration's crown," and the *Times* called the men who were finally selected an "unpromising cast."

If Attorney General Mitchell's selections suggested some sort of insecurity, that impression was strengthened by his apparent conviction that men can be measured by what they earn. After he reluctantly agreed to take the post of Attorney General, he continually let it be known that his decision meant he would have to leave a two-hundred-thousand-dollar-a-year law practice, which, as he put it, had included "some of the biggest clients in the country." And in explaining to Viorst how he had defended himself before a group of Party leaders who questioned his ability to run the Nixon campaign, he reported having said, "I've made more money in the practice of the law than Nixon, brought more clients into the firm, can hold my own in argument with him, and, as far as I'm concerned, I can deal with him as an equal."

Any transfer of the Presidency from one party to another inevitably creates tension and conflict. In the transfer of power from the Johnson Administration to the Nixon Administration, there was only one public clash, and that one, which did not occur until shortly after the inauguration, lent substance to Clark's fears about what would happen if the Department of Justice was turned into a political branch office of the White House. The origins of this clash went back to the previous fall, when President Johnson nominated a number of men to be federal judges. Most Presidential nominations to the federal bench are approved by the Senate more or less routinely, but the contention over the nomination of Justice Abe Fortas to be Chief Justice caused the Senate to delay consideration of five names President Johnson had presented for lesser judgeships. When the Ninetieth Congress adjourned, the nominations lapsed.

President Johnson could have given the five men recess appointments, which would have put them on the federal bench until the end of the forthcoming session of the Ninety-first Congress, and hoped that the Senate would confirm them sometime during the year. But Clark opposed recess appointments on principle. "When a judge has that lack of security," he once explained, "there are all sorts of subjective pressures on him—'If I do this or don't do that, will it work against my confirmation?'—and all sorts of direct pressures from people who say, 'If you don't do this or do do that, we'll get Senator So-and-So to block your confirmation.' And all a senator from a prospective judge's state has to do to block his confirmation is to notify the Judiciary Committee that he opposes it. I saw what happened to one judge who was given a recess appointment but wasn't confirmed. It ruined his life. His reputation, his career just vanished, and it caused his family terrible pain." For these reasons, Clark convinced President Johnson that recess appointments for judges were undesirable, and the President made none of them after 1965, when Clark became Deputy Attorney General, with responsibilities that included screening nominees for federal judgeships.

In the cases of two of the five nominees, sticking to his position was particularly difficult for Clark, since one of them, Harold Barefoot Sanders, Jr., who had been a close adviser to the President, was Clark's best friend. The other, Cecil F. Poole, United States Attorney for northern California, was possibly the best-qualified Negro lawyer in the country, and his appointment would have made him the first Negro judge on the federal bench west of the Mississippi. Among Poole's supporters were the American Bar Association's Committee on the Federal Judiciary, the San Francisco *Chronicle*, the

San Francisco *Examiner,* the Los Angeles *Times,* and the entire California Democratic delegation in the House of Representatives. Among his opponents were Senator George Murphy, Republican of California, who was reportedly considering a move to block him, and Senator Thurmond. "It's small wonder that young blacks figure that things are rigged against them," Representative Phillip Burton, Democrat of California, said of Murphy's reported threat. "Here's a Negro who has played the game according to the established rules and gets dinged for no apparent reason. I'll tell you, it makes it damned hard to face those kids."

Clark shared this view, but, he said, "I couldn't let my personal interest intrude, so I advised the President not to make recess appointments for *any* of the nominees. Instead, I urged him to send up all five names for confirmation—including Sanders and Poole. I figured that if we submitted them soon after the new Senate convened we'd have a slim chance of getting them through before the inauguration, on January 20th. And even after the inauguration the names would remain there unless withdrawn, and with a Democratic majority in the Senate it seemed quite possible that the Administration wouldn't fight over it. At least, it was worth a good try. If precedent was any guide, there was good reason to be fairly hopeful about our chances. In January of 1961, President Eisenhower sent four nominations for the federal bench to the Senate, and President Kennedy didn't withdraw any of them."

The President wanted Clark to clear the nominations with Senator Everett M. Dirksen first, in the belief that the Senator, as an old friend, would stand by him. But Clark objected, pointing out that Dirksen was undoubtedly under pressure to oppose the appointments at the start, and that if he did, this would destroy any chance the Administration might have. Instead, Clark recommended that the nominations be sent up cold, and he promised to see what he could do in the way of working on members of the Judiciary Committee, which had to clear them before they could go to the floor of the Senate for a vote. Since there was contention in the Senate at the time over several of President-elect Nixon's nominees—particularly Walter Hickel, who had been named Secretary of the Interior—there was an opportunity for the you-don't-block-our-nominees-and-we-won't-block-yours kind of political approach.

On January 9th, Clark was having lunch with the senior members of his staff in the Department's executive dining room when his secretary hurried in and handed him a folded piece of paper. Clark opened it and beamed. "The President is sending up the five names for confirmation," he announced. Some time earlier, Clark had arranged to inform Mitchell of any major moves he was about to make, so that the new Administration would not be unaware of important innovations just before it took over, and two days before the President's approval of his recommendation the Attorney General had told the Attorney General-designate about the matter. Since Mitchell was unfamiliar with the facts about the appointments, Clark described the five cases to him and went on to explain that ordinarily twenty-five to thirty-five vacancies occurred in federal courts every year, that there were already thirty-odd vacancies, and that a bill was pending to add sixty-seven judges to the federal bench—in short, that President Nixon would have a minimum of more than a hundred and thirty and a maximum of about two hundred and forty vacancies to fill in the federal courts during the four-year term to which he had been elected.

After the call from the White House, Clark got in touch with Mitchell and informed him that the five names had just been sent to the Senate. "I told him that we might not manage to get them through the Senate before the inauguration but that we were going to try," Clark recalled after leaving office. "He thanked me for letting him know and said he would advise the President-elect." Clark had to call Mitchell about something else an hour or so later, and Mitchell told him, "I just came from a meeting with Dick, and he says it is O.K. to proceed with the nominations of the judges." Since the

Deputy Attorney General is officially responsible for the clearance of nominees to the federal bench, Clark, who had never contemplated calling the President he served by his nickname, thought for a moment that the reference was to Richard Kleindienst, but then suddenly he realized that Mitchell was talking about Nixon. According to Clark, Mitchell went on to say, "Dick asked me to ask you to tell the President that he understands he may be in the same position himself someday, that he has no objection, and that he will not withdraw the nominations."

Clark said afterward, "It was clearly a gesture of good will toward the outgoing President, who had been extremely helpful and cordial toward Nixon during the transition." It was also probably an attempt to keep lines of communication open between the two men, in the event the new President wanted to call on the old President for assistance, as President Johnson on numerous occasions had called on former President Eisenhower. Still, Clark was uneasy about the speed with which the decision had been made, and assured Mitchell that there was no need for such haste. Mitchell replied that he had said as much to the President-elect but that he wanted to do this and he wanted President Johnson informed of his decision. Accordingly, Clark dropped his plans for trying to persuade the Senate to approve the nominations, and immediately delivered, verbatim, the President-elect's message to the White House.

Three days after the inauguration, President Nixon withdrew from nomination the five names that President Johnson had sent to the Senate. When news of this reached Clark, he was first stunned and then outraged. The move made it look not only as if he had failed to take the necessary steps to get the men confirmed while there was still time but as if he had misrepresented the situation to President Johnson. To make certain that the former President did not take this view, Clark telephoned him at his Texas ranch and described the circumstances of the case. Clark also decided to issue a press release outlining the episode, and that produced front-page stories in the papers the next day. When a reporter called Clark for further information, he was told, and reported, that the matter raised "a serious question" whether the new President "keeps his word." Later, the reporter asked Mitchell about his part in the affair, and was told that Clark's version went "far beyond the facts and the bounds of propriety." The only discussion that he had had on the subject with Clark, Mitchell said, was confined to his informing the outgoing Attorney General that the President-elect did not object to the appointments' being submitted. "It is apparently from this conversation that Mr. Clark erroneously concluded that President Nixon was committed not to withdraw the nominations," Mitchell added. Of course, since the President-elect had no power to oppose the appointments until he was President anyway, such a statement was meaningless.

On January 27th, President Nixon was asked, during his first press conference, about this issue, and he answered, "I did not have any understanding with the President directly, and no one, including Attorney General Mitchell, as far as I was concerned, had any discretion to agree to a deal that these nominations, having been made, would be approved by me." The statement amounted to a series of truths that added up to a lie. Indeed President-elect Nixon had not dealt directly with President Johnson; indeed Mitchell had not had the power to make such a deal; and indeed there was no guarantee that if he had made such a deal on his own President Nixon would be bound by it. But if President-elect Nixon made arrangements to approve, and thereby support, the nominations indirectly with President Johnson, through Mitchell and Clark, his press-conference remarks, while accurate, misrepresented what had happened. "His entire statement was an attempt to make it look as if I had tried to make a deal with Mitchell and had failed," Clark said afterward. "And that wasn't a candidate for office standing up there—that was the President of the United States."

Although the debate over who was lying got front-page coverage for several days, the real explanation of the matter was almost entirely ignored by the two dozen reporters who were present when it was offered, on January 29th, at the height of the contention. In the course of Kleindienst's confirmation hearings before the Senate Judiciary Committee, Senator Edward M. Kennedy asked the witness what he knew about the squabble over the judgeships. Kleindienst replied that he knew nothing more than Kennedy did, which produced smiles all around. Their conversation went on for a few minutes, and then Senator Dirksen broke in and said, "I want the record to show now that through channels I suggested to the President that he withdraw [the five names]. I do not know what commitments were made, and I did not care. They would not be binding on me. . . . So if anybody tries to make something of a breach of faith, there just is not any breach of faith, and it is a very simple picture." Apparently, if no one had broken a promise or lied to the Senator, no one had broken a promise or lied.

"Ramsey Clark has been extremely conscientious about his responsibilities in the transition," Attorney General Mitchell said shortly after he took office. "He did everything he could to make it as smooth as possible for us. He and his staff worked nights and weekends with us to facilitate the takeover. His personal conversations with me about the problems in the Department and what might be done to make matters work better here were also extremely helpful. He even prepared ideas for us to help the new Administration deal with these problems." Mitchell also said, in private, that he shared ninety-five per cent of Clark's ideas on the administration of justice but that the five-per-cent difference between them was extremely deep.

The principal difference, Mitchell explained when he spoke to Viorst, was that, unlike Clark, he believed the Department of Justice was "an institution for law enforcement, not social improvement."

The remark suggested that the new Attorney General was still playing politics—and campaign politics at that—for he was obviously saying that his predecessor had been less than vigorous in enforcing the law. As Mitchell, and everyone else who was familiar with the work of the Department under Clark's direction, knew, that charge was untrue. And, of course, a large part of federal law enforcement—reforming criminals, assuring equality for all citizens, and protecting everyone's Constitutional rights—does add up to "social improvement." The remark also suggested that the Preamble to the Constitution, with its promise to "promote the general welfare," was not uppermost in the Attorney General's mind.

At that stage in the new Administration, Attorney General Mitchell did and said little to indicate what other differences he had with the old Administration. But Kleindienst was less accustomed to keeping his own counsel, and at a lunch for Washington alumni of his alma mater, the Harvard Law School, he spoke more openly about some of the Administration's intentions. "Ramsey Clark is a nice guy, but he just wouldn't act," he told the assemblage. "As a result, the Ramsey Clark administration did a lot of theorizing about crime but it didn't take action. We're going to act, and act fast." Several of the lawyers at the lunch had worked in the Department under Clark, and were outraged by the statement. "I felt like jumping up and giving him a quick list of several dozen vital and lasting acts of Clark's," one of them said after the lunch. "But then I decided that anybody who was that injudicious and that ignorant of what had happened in his own shop would hang himself soon enough, so I sat tight." When Kleindienst went on, it was to say, "Take the inauguration as an example. We had a dispute about where the security troops should be stationed. I wanted them hidden in nearby alleys, offices, and basements, but Clark wouldn't listen. He said troops that close might appear repressive and cause a backlash. But after President Nixon was sworn in, *I* took over. I was up in the command center in the Justice Department, and when I heard there were militants on 12th and 14th Streets along the parade route I ordered out a few hundred more troops, and that cooled them off. You've got to crack down."

When negotiations on the November 15th peace march in the capital last year got under way, Kleindienst let it be known that because violence, from both the left and the right, was expected, the government might turn down the demonstrators' request for a permit and would airlift troops to the city from military bases around the country. The *Times* charged that "the Administration has been following a course calculated to increase the danger that the protest will turn into a violent confrontation" and added that "the Justice Department has been turned into a funnel for alarmist reports about militant penetration of the peace front—reports of the type that exacerbate tensions and thus serve as self-fulfilling prophecies."

A few days before the march took place, however, the mayor of the District, Walter E. Washington, met with the President and prevailed on him to order Kleindienst to compromise on the permit— presumably because the several hundred thousand people who were expected to participate in the protest would go ahead even without a permit, and thereby force the government into an armed confrontation of frightening magnitude. To make certain that federal authorities did not riot as Daley's police force had, former Attorney General Clark organized two hundred lawyers in the capital to serve as observers along the line of march and record violations committed by either side. "The country can't afford another Chicago," Clark said.

Almost all observers praised the demonstrators for their good spirit and orderliness on the march, but afterward Mitchell accused the organizers of the demonstration of fomenting the isolated incidents of violence that occurred, and added, "I do not believe—over all—the gatherings here can be characterized as peaceful." This suggested that the way was being prepared to refuse permits for future demonstrations. In view of Mitchell's reported assistance in preparing some of Vice-President Agnew's more undemocratic pronouncements, the Attorney General's statement lent ominous portent to Mr. Agnew's earlier proposals that "any civil disobedience must be prohibited by the authorities because there's no way to draw the line between what's responsible and what's irresponsible" and that in dealing with irresponsible elements the government can "afford to separate them from our society—with no more regret than we should feel over discarding rotten apples from a barrel."

In the course of an interview that appeared in the *Times* a couple of months after the Harvard Law School luncheon, Kleindienst returned to the subject of cracking down. "This Administration is prepared and willing and ready to act immediately," he said. "As soon as we're notified of danger, we'll have the National Guard in the armory and the Army on two-, four-, or six-hour alert. . . . We're going to enforce the law against draft-evaders, against radical students, against deserters, against civil disorders, against organized crime, and against street crime. We have several draft-evader cases in the process of being filed. If we find that any of these radical, revolutionary, anarchistic kids violate the law, we'll prosecute." Except for the intemperate language, the eagerness to use troops to quell disorders, and the promise about dealing with street crime, which is the Constitutional responsibility of local authorities, the statements about enforcing the law could have been made by Clark.

One of Kleindienst's aides, Donald E. Santarelli, a former Assistant United States Attorney in the District of Columbia who had been chosen by President Nixon personally to be Associate Deputy Attorney General, speculated around that time, somewhat more philosophically and calmly, on the Administration's attitude toward crime. "There will be a new enthusiasm and a tremendous new effort, with President Nixon at the helm, to do something about criminal justice," he said. "President Johnson's emphasis on combating crime seemed great because it brought things from zero to ten. But it wasn't systemic. The proposals were piecemeal and many were unsound.

Ours will be a whole look, a reorientation. There will be a massive new commitment to the effort in money and staff. The most important change here will be in the attitude and the atmosphere our new programs will create. People here now have hope."

Every Attorney General in recent years had done his best to get more money from Congress to fight crime, for it had become unavoidably clear to each of them that there was no great secret to dealing with crime; the answer was simple—more funds to upgrade police departments, expand and speed up the work of courts, and improve corrections systems so that they rehabilitated prisoners instead of making them into worse criminals. But every Attorney General in recent years had run up against the implacable opposition of Representative Rooney, chairman of the House subcommittee responsible for overseeing the Department's appropriations. Rooney scornfully dismissed just about every request for money to fund new programs or anything that smacked of experimentalism; he rudely attacked the facts and data supplied to the subcommittee and insultingly impugned the motives and judgment of most witnesses from the Department who appeared to testify on its behalf.

For example, Congress had set a ceiling of a hundred and six lawyers for the Department's Civil Rights Division when the Civil Rights Act of 1964 was passed. In the years since then, several major civil-rights laws have been enacted, including the Open Housing Act of 1968, which prohibited discrimination in most of the housing in the country. But Rooney adamantly refused to raise the ceiling on the number of lawyers allotted to the Civil Rights Division, although it was obvious that a hundred and six attorneys were enough, perhaps, to see that the laws were enforced in only one or two sizable states. Even Clark's request for more lawyers for his Strike Forces—despite their obvious success in forays against organized crimes—met with Rooney's brusque dismissal. However, when J. Edgar Hoover appeared before the subcommittee last spring to ask for an increase of four hundred and fifteen agents, two hundred and seventy-one clerks, and two hundred automobiles for the Federal Bureau of Investigation, at a cost of nearly nine million dollars (one of the few increases over President Johnson's budget that President Nixon allowed), Rooney left no doubt that Hoover would get what he asked for, as usual.

One high official in the Department under Clark was all for Hoover's getting whatever he wanted. "If he doesn't, he'll cut back on the bureau's work in the really important areas, like civil rights," he explained. "They don't like that kind of work in the bureau. They're statistics-crazy over there—you know, the periodic head count of all the wanted men captured—and investigation of civil-rights violations doesn't beef up the statistics much. They hated having to hunt for Dr. King's assassin. It meant putting five thousand agents on his trail, but in the end they would have only one more name on their roll of achievement."

About the only man in the Department, besides Hoover, who was able to deal successfully with Rooney was Wilkins, the director of the Community Relations Service. "It was an experimental approach, and of course Rooney thought the whole idea was preposterous," Wilkins recalled not long ago. "So I went before him and treated him with the utmost deference. He decided I was a good black Boy Scout, and treated me almost politely. In fact, he even gave us a little more money."

Some members of both the old and the new Administrations hoped that the campaign promises Mitchell had devised, and now was expected by the public to fulfill, would lead him to find ways of persuading Rooney to part with enough money so that the Department could produce clear results, which, they believed, would then persuade Rooney to part with still more money. However, though Rooney treated Mitchell with the respect due a member of the Cabinet, he treated his aides' explanations of why increased funds were essential with the same contempt he had shown their predecessors'. After the House hearings, one member of the Department suggested that President Nixon had chosen the wrong man to be Attorney General. "He should have picked Hoover," he said. "That way, Hoover would have got enough money out of Rooney to put ten men on the tail of every suspected subversive and still have enough left over to do something about the real crime problems facing the country."

Mitchell's solution for the rebuff he received in the House was to make a strong appeal for restoration of some of the funds cut there when he later appeared before the Senate subcommittee that had similar jurisdiction over appropriations for the Department of Justice. The principal restorations he asked for concerned the Criminal Division and the Bureau of Prisons. The latter request came as a surprise to many observers, until they learned that corrections was one important area in which Mitchell's conclusions matched Clark's. The task of rehabilitating men who had fallen into, or been driven into, a life of crime was Clark's most abiding concern, and his work in this field was one of his greatest achievements as Attorney General. Although Clark's interest in this subject, like most of his interests, had a humanitarian cast to it, his practical interest as the nation's chief law-enforcement officer was the overriding one, for he was convinced that sound rehabilitation was the best way to reduce the burgeoning crime rate. Although Attorney General Mitchell was far too busy attending to White House business to pay full attention to the details of the Department's various bureaus, services, and offices, he was prepared to back up the corrections policies devised by the previous Administration as fully as Clark had. Moreover, there seemed to be a good chance that his support in this area would be more effective than Clark's had been, because there was little chance that when the new Attorney General went before Congress to ask for more money for research into criminal behavior and experimental centers for criminal rehabilitation he would be looked on as an impractical do-gooder.

Mitchell's attitude toward rehabilitation struck some career officials in the Department as an unexpected departure from his otherwise hard-line views on law enforcement. But one official who had more political experience than the others considered it merely another part of Mitchell's over-all political strategy. "Although it would probably break the Treasury to do a really adequate job of rehabilitating criminals in this country, the level of expenditure on corrections now is very low," this man said. "Mitchell couldn't help but see that Ramsey was absolutely right in claiming that corrections was the one demonstrable way that you can lessen crime. So if the new Administration continues the old policies but pours more money into them—not enough to bother the economic puritans in the White House or in Congress—it's bound to have a positive effect. And if that effect is a noticeable decrease in the crime rate, no matter how small, more and more money will be spent on corrections. At the end of four years, there might even be a significant reduction in the crime rate. Now, *that* would be a real feather in Nixon's cap, and everyone would forget where these policies had come from."

Of course, if the results of Mitchell's support for Clark's policy were good, the political side of it was irrelevant. But there was also the danger, the same man pointed out, that if anything went wrong politically the new policy would be dropped at once. "If several inmates escape from one of these open institutions that are being tried out and commit some particularly atrocious crimes, the whole approach will probably be dumped, and the Administration will go back to the old human-warehouse kind of prison," he explained. "Or if some political demagogue gets the public stirred up about 'coddling criminals,' that will probably end it, too. But right now it's cheap and it looks humane, so it's good politics."

When Attorney General Mitchell appeared before the Senate Appropriations subcommittee headed by Senator McClellan to ask, among other things, that the cuts made in the House on funds for rehabilitation be restored, he did not ask that the cuts made in the budgets of the Civil Rights Division and the Community Relations

Service be similarly restored. These proposed expenditures, while even more humane, were expensive and apparently not good politics.

Three weeks after the new Administration took office, Deputy Attorney General Kleindienst announced that the Department of Justice was making an unparalleled effort to hire Negro lawyers in order to improve on the "dismal" record of the Democrats. "After all of the liberal breast-beating of the Democratic Administration, they hired only seventy Negro lawyers—and forty of those were in United States Attorneys' offices across the country," he said. (Actually, the proportion of Negro lawyers on the Department's legal staff was twice as high as the proportion of Negro students currently enrolled in law schools around the country.) Kleindienst also announced that he was looking for a Negro recruiter to fill a twenty-thousand-dollar-a-year post in the Department but so far he hadn't found a man for the job.

"The new people don't have the faintest idea of how to talk to black men," Wilkins said not long after he took a post with the Ford Foundation, which gave him an opportunity to carry on the same kind of work he had done in government service. "That's why they can't find anyone for top posts in the Administration who would suit both them and the black community. Kleindienst, Finch, and Moynihan all told me I could stay on—at the same level I had been at for three years. I'm sure they would say now they really tried hard to persuade me. But they gave me the impression they thought they were doing me a big favor. Any Negro who had the drive to get through college and law school and now has to choose between making money and helping his people faces the kind of choice that white men rarely have to make. A black man who'd made it that far would be crazy to take a job in a place where all the signs point to more repression for his people, not more justice."

In view of Kleindienst's claim, it was difficult to explain his decision to fire Homer L. Benson, one of the few Negroes who had risen through the bureaucracy of the Department to reach a high appointive post—as a member of the United States Board of Parole. Benson was fired not because there was any evidence that he had failed to do his job well—in fact, he was known to be exceedingly capable and hard-working—but because the Administration, for political reasons, chose to placate Senator McClellan, who wanted his own man on the board. The Administration's willingness to appease an ultra-conservative like McClellan, which the former Administration had refused to do even though he was a member of its own party, may have been effective in winning over some political forces that it hoped to be able to deal with on other issues. But it did little to encourage Negroes to join or remain in the Department when they saw one of their people who had tried to operate within the system dispatched without justification because, as in the case of United States Attorney Poole out in California, some white reactionary did not care for him.

In President Nixon's first press conference, on January 27th, he discussed what the Administration hoped to do about crime in general, and then went on to acknowledge that he had made "a major commitment in the campaign" to do something specifically about crime in the District of Columbia. "Consequently," he said, "I have on an urgent basis instructed the Attorney General to present to me a program to deal with crime in the District of Columbia, and an announcement as to that program, and also an announcement as to what we will ask the Congress to do, in addition to what we will do administratively, will be made at the end of this week." A hint of what this program would probably contain turned up the following day, when Kleindienst announced that the Administration would ask Congress for ten to fifteen more federal judges and a thousand to two thousand more policemen for the District. Any request for additional policemen was largely meaningless, since in 1968 Congress had authorized the District police department to increase its force by a thousand men, but it was still nine hundred men short because qualified applicants could not be found.

Several members of the City Council felt that the Administration was placing undue emphasis on this part of the District's law-enforcement needs. John Hechinger, the Council chairman, mentioned the unfilled authorization and said, "I think . . . more money now must be spent in other areas of law enforcement, on preventive measures, the courts, the parole system, and bail procedure." And the Washington *Daily News* observed, in an editorial on this subject, "When we consider that, statistically, the greatest single threat . . . to life and property here today is probably a fifteen-year-old boy with a sense of abject failure and an urge for instant self-gratification, then we'll begin to realize that one thousand additional policemen are not really going to be the answer."

As the President had promised, the Administration issued its Message on Crime in the District of Columbia at the end of that week, on January 31st. And, as the Attorney General had implied, the program contained a proposal for preventive detention. (The measure would apply to all federal courts, but would have the greatest effect in Washington, since all criminal cases come under federal jurisdiction there.) The message stated that since defendants on bail often commit crimes while waiting to be tried on the pending charge, "this requires that a new provision be made in the law, whereby dangerous hard-core recidivists could be held in pre-trial detention when they have been charged with crimes and when their continued pre-trial release presents a clear danger to the community." The message did not explain how such hard-core recidivists were to be identified or how the clear danger was to be determined. The preventive-detention section was new, of course, but most of the other proposals were straight out of material left behind by the old Administration, which had repeatedly failed to get them through Congress.

Among them was a thorough reorganization of courts in the District to set up a single municipal court—the District of Columbia Court of General Jurisdiction—where all cases involving local criminal violations would be conducted. The present Juvenile Court, which had been woefully understaffed, would be merged with the new court to provide young offenders with expanded family services and probational assistance. The proposal also authorized the thousand additional policemen that no one could find, along with ten more judges, twenty more Assistant United States Attorneys (that is, prosecutors), and enough courthouse personnel to serve the expanded system adequately. In addition, the Administration recommended an expansion of court and jail facilities, along with more manpower for the public-defender system. And, finally, it called for a larger role for the Federal Bureau of Narcotics and Dangerous Drugs in the District, where, it was believed, three-fourths of all crimes were committed by addicts.

"Except for the preventive-detention part, it's a terribly enlightened, bold, expensive syllabus," Freed said shortly before he left the Office of Criminal Justice to join the faculty at the Yale Law School. "But the problem will be twofold—drafting the actual legislation properly and then getting these proposals, most of which we recommended time and again, through Congress."

Ordinarily, an Administration follows up a Presidential message with specific legislative recommendations to implement it within a matter of days, or a few weeks at the most, but this time it was to be several months before the Administration sent an anti-crime bill to the Hill. In the meantime, President Nixon was widely complimented and widely condemned for his proposal on preventive detention. The steep rise in violent crimes committed in Washington (most of them by uneducated and unskilled Negroes who had fled the South), coupled with the perennial readiness of Congress (dominated by Southerners) to impose the most severe punishment on wrongdoers in its federal domain, led some observers to conclude, with Tom Wicker, that "Mr. Nixon's proposals were far more restrained than might have been expected."

In the scrimmage over the issue, however, the participants' jerseys became so muddied that it was difficult for spectators to tell who was on which team. Many liberals in Congress normally would have been expected to oppose anything of such dubious Constitutionality as preventive detention. But many liberals in Congress represented large cities where the proportion of Negroes and the rate of crime were both high, and a surprising number of them came out in favor of the idea. Some were said to believe that if they didn't line up behind the proposal their white constituents would pay them back at election time, whereas if they did line up behind it their black constituents probably wouldn't realize the meaning of their stand. Others agreed, or claimed to agree, with the rationale expressed by Senator Joseph D. Tydings, Democrat of Maryland, who led the liberal forces for preventive detention in the Senate. "I don't believe we can improve the environment for the disenfranchised and the disaffected until we have cut down on fear in the streets and parks of our cities," he said. "If progressive-minded people don't take the lead, extremists will." That was a curious position to take, for it amounted to an appeal to progressives to infringe the Constitution before extremists did. Further, if the lead was provided, extremists could be expected to take it over and move even more rapidly to the right.

While most conservatives also came out for the new proposal, some of their leaders, chiefly Senator Ervin, strongly opposed it. "In a free society, you have to take some risks," he said. "If you lock everybody up, or even if you lock up everybody you think might commit a crime, you'll be pretty safe. But you won't be free."

For a time, most of the Negro opposition to the plan was confined to Negro leaders, both moderate and radical. Ordinary black citizens suffered from a more extreme fear of crime than their white neighbors, since most crime was committed not only by Negroes but upon Negroes. "The biggest single thing [President Nixon] has going for him right now is that black Washingtonians are as alarmed and disgusted as whites at the increased frequency, audacity, and viciousness of local crime," wrote William Raspberry, a Negro columnist for the Washington *Post*. "That is exactly the kind of support the President needs if his war on crime is to bear palatable fruit. But he needs to tread carefully lest his war on crime become a bigger threat than crime itself to certain parts of the community."

To many radicals, preventive detention constituted just such a threat. After the plan was announced, the Student Nonviolent Coordinating Committee, the National Black Antiwar Antidraft Union, the Students for a Democratic Society, and the National Mobilization Committee to End the War in Vietnam issued a joint statement charging that the proposal was "another in the long bag of tricks to harass and intimidate poor and black people in the name of law and order," and then added, "We must understand that American fascism will be unique to this country. There will be no storm troopers, swastikas, or brown shirts. The slogan for fascism in the United States will be 'law and order,' and that is what preventive-detention laws are all about."

And even as moderate a man as Whitney M. Young, Jr., head of the Urban League, expressed concern about the "mood of repression" that seemed to be gathering momentum under the law-and-order slogan, which, he said, "could lead to a system of oppressive racial commitment at some future, crisis-ridden time." Preventive detention was not new, he added; the same approach had been used against another group of people because of their race—the Japanese-Americans in the country who had been locked up in concentration camps during the Second World War.

The immediate practical effect that a preventive-detention law was likely to have on the District of Columbia was demonstrated, shortly after the White House sent its Crime Message to Congress, in a report submitted to the mayor of Washington by a special committee that he had set up to look into allegations of misconduct on the part of guards at the Lorton Reformatory, which serves as the District's municipal prison. According to the report, white guards at the reformatory, some of whom were the sons and grandsons of Lorton guards, had taken advantage of a rumor about an inmate uprising, which proved to be groundless, to conduct a "guard riot" in "a mood of celebration" against the prisoners. As it happened, ninety per cent of those prisoners were Negroes, some of whom were reported to have been savagely beaten for earlier displays of contempt for certain guards. The report concluded that "a major segment of the Negro inmate population has become more hostile" than ever to whites. The result of that hostility once the prisoners were released was not hard to predict. Under these circumstances, any system of preventive detention could easily turn out to be causative detention.

In Attorney General Mitchell's first major speech after he took office —before the Conference on Crime and the Urban Crisis, sponsored by the National Emergency Committee of the National Council on Crime and Delinquency, which was held in San Francisco at the beginning of February—he outlined a program for a new approach called the United Anti-Crime Fund. In sum, this was to be a national volunteer organization that would give financial support to local volunteers who wanted to combat crime in their own way. After citing a poll showing that "at least ten per cent of the public would be interested in serving as volunteer workers in juvenile programs, in helping to get jobs for ex-prisoners, and in working on citizen committees on organized crime," the Attorney General pointed out that there were more than a million independent volunteer organizations of all kinds in the United States and that their sixty-odd million members could contribute as much as a total of two hundred and forty-five million man-hours a week.

Since the Administration was pledged "to encourage and to co-operate with the private sector," he went on, it now proposed the creation of "local crime-coördinating councils"—to be composed of representatives from local law-enforcement, court, and corrections agencies, along with spokesmen for social-welfare, professional, volunteer, and business groups—and suggested that these councils could collect and collate crime data as well as "establish over-all plans, eliminate duplication, aid in providing staff and funding, and integrate the efforts of each group in terms of the total local crime situation." In conclusion, he turned Nixon's campaign attacks on Clark for failing to deal with crime into an attack on him for having tried to, and told the audience, "We are not, as were past Administrations, interested in concentrating crime programs in the federal government."

While there was merit in the proposal that local citizens might help former prison inmates find their way back into society in a more productive manner than the one by which they had left it, the Attorney General's over-all program was believed by experts in the field to be more likely to hinder effective crime-control efforts than anything except possibly ignoring the problem altogether. Most of his listeners, who had wide experience in preventive and corrective law-enforcement methods, were in agreement that the primary necessities were to raise police training and pay to professional levels, to modernize archaic court and probation systems, and to revise penal institutions so that they cured rather than created criminal habits. It was difficult to see how local volunteers could achieve any of these ends—unless they volunteered to pay higher taxes to up-grade their law-enforcement agencies.

One of Mitchell's most outspoken critics at the conference was

McGeorge Bundy, who, as president of the Ford Foundation, was an expert on what local initiative and voluntary contributions could accomplish. "It would be a dangerous mistake for any of us to think that actions of citizens' groups can take the place of the massive reinforcement of every section of our public system of criminal justice which will surely be required before we can expect to arrest, let alone to turn downward, the statistics of remorselessly increasing crime," he told the audience after Mitchell had spoken. "Nothing could be a more cruel self-deception than for any public official—or any private group—to believe that volunteers can take the place of taxes in this field."

Despite Mitchell's persistent return to old campaign themes, he must have known that the federal government's chief means of dealing with crime on the local level was by providing local law-enforcement authorities with a model and by giving them guidance and money when they wanted to set up their own crime-control programs. And federal aid of this sort, which was the opposite of the centralized control he accused Clark of favoring, was a recent and wholly bipartisan innovation that had been carried out under Clark's personal supervision. This new approach—setting up the Law Enforcement Assistance Administration, which was authorized to spend three hundred million dollars a year for the next few years to modernize police departments, courts, and correctional systems—had one grievous flaw. That was the so-called "block-grant" provision, which Nixon had strongly supported during the Presidential campaign, and which compelled the government to give money directly to the states to spend, more or less as they pleased, on anti-crime programs of their own making.

As perilous as this move was, the Republicans had made the block-grant issue strict party policy—the first example of what President Nixon was later to call "the new federalism," which could be more accurately described as the old states' rights with new federal financing. "The federal government may be clumsy, because it's too big," one senator who opposed block grants in any guise said not long ago. "But, generally speaking, it isn't crooked and it isn't incompetent, like all too many state governments. As far as I can see, the new federalism just means more snouts in the public trough."

Others feared that block grants would ultimately be used as anti-black grants, or for repressive measures against anyone who opposed the existing system. In all likelihood, these critics pointed out, federal taxes paid by white civil-rights supporters in high-income sections of the North would be used by the police to intimidate black people in the low-income sections of the South. Under the new law, federal funds could also be used to subsidize the purchase of more advanced weapons for, say, the Chicago police force.

In the fall of 1968, President Johnson named three widely experienced and determinedly non-political men to fill the top posts of administrator and co-administrators in the new Law Enforcement Assistance Administration, under the Department of Justice. But Senator McClellan blocked the nominations, which were subject to confirmation by the Senate, in the Judiciary Committee. To get the L.E.A.A. on its feet and the money that was appropriated for it flowing out to the cities where it was so desperately needed, President Johnson gave the three administrators recess appointments and then renominated them when the Senate convened early in January. In deference to Senator McClellan, President Nixon withdrew the three nominations at the same time that, in deference to Senator Dirksen, he withdrew the nominations for the five judgeships. Then, on Attorney General Mitchell's advice, the White House announced that the date for the first funds to be spent on anti-crime programs under the new agency would be moved from June 1, 1969, back to April 1, 1969. That was clearly an attempt to make it appear that the new Administration was moving vigorously to combat crime. How a speeded-up operation was going to be conducted with new and inexperienced men at the top was not explained.

A career official in the Department of Justice who had helped draw up the plans for the L.E.A.A. was appalled that the President had chosen to fling the agency onto the political football field. "He got rid of the administrators not because they weren't capable, since they clearly were, and not because he wanted to hand out more patronage, since there's enough of that around," this man said later. "He got rid of them because he wanted to appease people like McClellan and Thurmond, so that he could maintain his hold on the newly strengthened conservative coalition between Southern Democrats and Northern Republicans. But the cost to the L.E.A.A.'s operations may be disastrously high."

Two months after President Nixon entered the White House, the National League of Cities and the United States Conference of Mayors jointly charged that the L.E.A.A. would have little effect in the cities, because, as critics of the block-grant approach had warned, most of the initial funds—called "planning grants," which were supposed to set up programs that would be supported by later "action grants"—were being siphoned off to low-crime rural areas. For example, Pennsylvania got eight hundred and eighty thousand dollars, and gave sixty-two thousand dollars of it to Philadelphia; Massachusetts got four hundred and sixty-four thousand dollars, and gave twenty thousand dollars of it to Boston; Oklahoma got two hundred and sixty-seven thousand dollars, and gave twelve thousand dollars of it to Tulsa. The National League of Cities also pointed out that most of the nineteen million dollars allotted in planning grants so far had been used to set up a new level of bureaucracy; twenty-four of the states had created two hundred and eleven regional crime offices. One outcome of this was that some governors, state legislators, and political leaders were turning the money into a new source of patronage, often to hire people with no known qualifications for the posts they were to fill. Another was that people who *were* qualified and had demonstrated as much through their work in urban

law-enforcement agencies were being lured away to higher-paying
but less effective jobs in the new bureaucracy.

Studies made by the league also revealed that elected officials and
minority spokesmen were invariably left off local planning boards,
which were dominated by police officers. As feared, they spent most
of the money provided under the program not to upgrade their skills
and their standards but to buy new equipment and armament. The
L.E.A.A.'s first annual report, published on August 31st of last year,
revealed that of the total action grants given to the states three and
a half per cent was spent on crime research, slightly over four per
cent on community-police relations, five and a half per cent on upgrading courts, slightly under eight and a half per cent on rehabilitation, nearly thirty per cent on police departments, and twenty-two
and a half per cent on riot control, most of which, of course, also
went to the police.

In Pittsburgh, the police department wanted to spend thirty-five
thousand dollars of its action grant on one armored rescue vehicle.
Officials promised that it would not be used for riot duty, but they
were unable to describe any other reason for having it. "I can just
see that thing clanking up Homewood Avenue," a Negro resident
of the area said. "If the police get that armored vehicle and use it
as a show of strength—even in a minor situation—anything can
happen."

In the spring of 1968, Congress passed a law stating that "whoever
travels in interstate or foreign commerce or uses any facility of interstate or foreign commerce . . . to aid or abet any person in inciting
or participating in or carrying on a riot or committing any act of
violence in furtherance of a riot" could be sent to prison for five
years and fined ten thousand dollars. The measure defined a riot as

"an act or acts of violence" by anyone in "an assemblage of three or more persons" that endangered or damaged any person or any property. The effect of the statute was to discourage the holding of any sort of large demonstration. Under the law, anyone who crossed a state line to participate in a demonstration and got caught in a fight involving at least three people—even a fight started and participated in by policemen or *agents provocateurs*—was liable to arrest. And although intent is a difficult charge to prove in court, it is an easy charge to bring, and a charge by itself is often as effective as the likelihood of conviction in persuading people not to get involved, because legal defense can be harrowingly costly and time-consuming. When the measure was enacted, its opponents were confident that the Supreme Court would strike it down as a clear-cut violation of the right of free speech and assembly. Like everyone else, however, they did not consider that within a year a liberal majority on the Court might be changed to a conservative majority. Nor did they consider the course that a conservative Republican Administration might take.

After the riot at the Democratic National Convention in Chicago, Attorney General Clark managed to get a federal grand jury there to consider whether criminal action should be taken against any Chicago policemen who might have been guilty of unnecessary brutality toward demonstrators and bystanders at the time of the Convention. Although police brutality is ordinarily a matter for local authorities to prosecute under local laws, it was clear that Mayor Daley would not support the prosecution of men whom he had encouraged to act as they did. Accordingly, Clark, who was responsible for protecting the Constitutional rights of the nation's citizens, invoked a Reconstruction law, enacted in 1866, that prohibited local officials from punishing suspects without due process, and took steps to present the case to a grand jury. Compared to the 1968 anti-riot law, which had so far never been used, this statute's penalties were mild—a maximum of a year in prison, instead of five years, and a

thousand-dollar fine, instead of a ten-thousand-dollar fine. Despite
the pressure on him to drop the case against the police and start one
against the demonstrators—extreme pressure, in fact, from the White
House, Daley, and members of Congress—Clark refused. However,
he did order his staff to examine the question of whether the demonstrators could legally be prosecuted. After a thorough review of
the law and of the evidence gathered by the F.B.I. and the half-
dozen or so observers whom Clark had sent to Chicago to keep an
eye on things, the staff reported that there was no ground for
a prosecution.

Nevertheless, shortly after taking office Attorney General Mitchell
asked the federal grand jury that was considering the charges against
the Chicago policemen to also consider charges against the leaders
of the demonstrations under the 1968 anti-riot law. On March 20th,
the grand jury returned indictments against eight policemen—seven
of them on the charge that they had violated the 1866 law and one
on the charge that he had committed perjury before the grand jury
in denying that he had beaten anyone; at the same time, it returned
indictments against eight civilians—on the charge that they had
violated the anti-riot law. The chief judge of the federal court in
that district, William J. Campbell, who was a friend of Mayor
Daley's, announced after the indictments were returned that the
grand jury would also issue a report on its findings. It was unusual
for a judge to act as a grand jury's spokesman, and it was practically
unheard of for a grand jury to put out such a report. This struck
some observers as a clear attempt to influence public opinion, including the opinions of those who would ultimately serve on the
juries hearing the cases.

"Politics, pure and simple," Clark said when asked later about the
indictments. "The eight-to-eight balance makes that clear. Also, the
same lawyers in the Department who reported to me that proceedings against the demonstrators could not be justified must have reported the same thing to Mitchell. But with the same information

he reached a different conclusion. It wasn't an attempt to exonerate Daley, of course, because the Republicans are convinced that he stole the Presidential election from them in 1960, but to exonerate the police. That's a very, very bad sign. If the police are allowed to break the law, who will be left to enforce it?"

In the first trial of the policemen completed so far, three officers were accused of beating a reporter for the Chicago *Daily News* after he shouted an obscenity at them when he saw that they were clubbing two girls and a boy in a convertible that had become stalled in the traffic jam caused by the riot. The reporter admitted that he had used the obscenity, but the government prosecutor emphasized, and the defense's only witness, the deputy chief of police, agreed, that the use of "mere words" did not justify the resort to force. Still, it was clear that in the minds of the jurors—and, for that matter, in the mind of the judge—the case turned on the obscenity. The jury found the three policemen innocent.

Afterward, Judge Joseph Sam Perry congratulated it on the decision, and said of the reporter, "He charged some of these officers with incest with their mothers. It was so provocative any red-blooded American would have flared up." Joseph LeFevour, president of the Chicago lodge of the Fraternal Order of Police, expressed his delight over the acquittal and his understanding of the ideals of justice (not to mention its symbol) when he said that the verdict "proves to us beyond the shadow of a doubt that the lady of justice is not blindfolded." And George B. Crowley, the defense counsel, said, "This will give the Chicago Police Department assurance that in the performance of their duty they will not be exposed to federal prosecutions such as this."

Around that time, the Commission on the Causes and Prevention of Violence, which had been set up by President Johnson following the assassination of Senator Robert F. Kennedy, issued a general report on violence in the United States, which asserted, in part, "A democratic society cannot depend upon force as its recurrent answer to long-standing and legitimate grievances. This nation cannot have it both ways: either it will carry through a firm commitment to massive and widespread political and social reform, or it will develop into a society of garrison cities where order is enforced without due process of law and without the consent of the governed."

In view of the generally moderate makeup of the commission, which was headed by Dr. Milton S. Eisenhower, that was a rather alarming appraisal. But a number of signs showed that there was reason for it. Among them was the opening of a new headquarters for the Civil Disturbance Directorate, an arm of the Department of Defense, beneath the parking lot in front of the Pentagon where the march on that establishment took place the year before. The Directorate, which was to prepare plans to put down riots in the nation's major cities, had received an appropriation several times larger than the appropriation for the Justice Department's Community Relations Service, which was set up to prevent riots from ever starting. Considering Kleindienst's readiness to use federal troops at the first sign of public disorder and the military's traditional eagerness to put into practice whatever plans it has devised, the chances that a new wave of riots would end up in bloody repression, bloodier response, and still bloodier repression were clearly increasing.

Other preparations were being made by the country's police, who, the Violence Commission reported, had begun to emerge as an "independent political power" that "rivals even duly elected officials in influence." In a survey of five major cities, the commission found that the police were "coming to see themselves as the political force by which radicalism, student demonstrations, and black power can be blocked." Continuing, the report asserted that because policemen had become "increasingly frustrated, alienated, and angry," their "response to mass protest has resulted in steady escalation of conflict, hostility, and violence." According to the report, many police riots in addition to the one in Chicago had been fully documented. And, according to a survey of members of the Chicago police department, most of those who were asked about the Walker Report on the police riot during the Convention were convinced that it had been written either by Communists or by the Supreme Court.

The commission laid a major part of the responsibility for violent reaction on the part of the police to public disorder directly on J. Edgar Hoover. He had testified before the commission in September, 1968, and said, "Communists are in the forefront of civil-rights, anti-war, and student demonstrations, many of which ultimately become disorderly and erupt into violence." The evidence Hoover cited was the claim that Bettina Aptheker Kurzweil, a member of the Communist National Committee, had been a "leading organizer" of the free-speech demonstrations at Berkeley in 1964. However, the commission went on, an investigating committee appointed by the regents of the University of California—scarcely a radical collection—had found "no evidence that the free-speech movement was organized by the Communist Party, the Progressive Labor Movement, or any other outside group." On this point, the commission observed, "Mr. Hoover's statement is significant not only because he is our nation's highest and most renowned law-enforcement official, but also because his views are reflected and disseminated throughout the nation—by publicity in the local media and by F.B.I. seminars, briefings, and training for local policemen." The transmission of Hoover's views throughout the law-enforcement network, the commission continued, had led the police to "view students, the anti-war protesters, and blacks as a danger to our political system," and the last of these were looked upon as a particular danger, because "racial prejudice pervades the police attitudes and actions." In conclusion, the report stated, "No government institution appears so deficient in its understanding of the constructive role of dissent in a Constitutional democracy as the police."

The frustration, alienation, and anger of the police had been repeatedly displayed in violent responses to comparatively mild provocation. One of the most shocking examples of this occurred during Attorney General Clark's time in office, early in February, 1968, when Negro students at South Carolina State College, in Orangeburg, demonstrated for three days against a segregated bowling alley near the campus. The protest was conducted peacefully at the outset, but as time wore on sporadic violence broke out, and finally state troopers fired into the crowd, killing three boys and wounding twenty-seven others. A grand jury refused to indict the troopers. Clark felt that the case constituted willful murder without provocation and was especially concerned about the effect of it on the Negroes in the area. To demonstrate the government's determination to obtain justice for black men as well as white, in the South as well as in the North, he resorted to the unusual legal device of pressing the case even without a grand-jury indictment. Nine of the troopers were charged under a Reconstruction statute that prohibited punishment of citizens by policemen without due process of law—a statute that had been enacted specifically to protect newly freed slaves from abuse by police acting under "color of the law."

In the trial the troopers' defense was that the students had fired on them first, but there was no evidence—such as bullet casings, slugs, or holes—to sustain this. Warren Koon, a reporter for the Charleston *Evening Post*, testified that he had been standing in front of the demonstrators at the time the troopers fired and that "the first shots I heard were those fired by the troopers." The defendants also claimed that they had not fired until the students charged them en masse, but the two doctors who examined the bodies of the dead boys testified that one of them had been shot once in the back, one had been shot five times in the back and side, and one had been shot six times in the back and side and once above the heart; of those who were wounded or killed, twenty-eight had been shot in the back or side, or both. The nine troopers were acquitted.

JUSTICE

"The maximum number of students present, according to testimony before the grand jury, was four hundred," Clark said later. "Well, there were a hundred and fifty state and local police and two companies of the National Guard standing not more than two hundred yards away. If the kids were breaking the law, why weren't they arrested? Surely there was enough armed force there to gather up the whole bunch and lock them up without firing a shot. Compare that situation to the one at the University of Mississippi when James Meredith enrolled there as the first Negro student. Our force was made up largely of U.S. marshals. They were mostly old men, they were inexperienced in law-enforcement techniques, they were in alien surroundings at night, they were confronted by a huge, howling mob that had already killed three people and was spraying bullets all over the place, and they were scared out of their wits. They called the Department and asked if they could fire back when fired on, and Bob Kennedy said no. Then they called back a little later and asked if they could at least take their pistols out of their holsters as a show of force, and Bob said no. Well, those men didn't fire a single shot. If they had, there would have been a real bloodbath, because the other side was just spoiling for a fight. Scores of people would have been killed, and nobody down there would ever have forgotten it." As it was, the mob finally quieted down when its fire was not returned, and no one else was shot.

Stern repressive measures were by no means unpopular, however, and state and local legislators as well as members of Congress were coming under increasing pressure to do something about civil unrest. During the spring and summer of 1969, more than a hundred bills dealing with riots on campus and off were introduced by state legislators across the country. In West Virginia, the state legislature enacted one of the first of these bills to be passed; it absolved police officers in advance of any legal responsibility if they killed someone during a riot, and it provided that all civilians who were involved

196

in a riot were equally responsible for the death of any police officer that occurred during it. If the country had not yet become a police state, West Virginia was well on the way.

Six weeks after Attorney General Mitchell took office, he announced that he intended to prosecute "hard-line militants" who crossed state lines to incite riots on college campuses. "A great deal of evidence has been collected on this aspect of campus disorders," he stated. "I would say this is a very serious component." The F.B.I., which had collected the evidence, thought so, too. A few days later, Assistant Attorney General Jerris Leonard stated publicly that he was prepared to prosecute such militants under the 1968 anti-riot law. These statements, on top of a promise by Deputy Attorney General Kleindienst to go after "radical, revolutionary, anarchistic kids," suggested that the Department now fully shared Hoover's conviction that most of the trouble in the country was caused by a few radicals and that if they were locked up everything would be fine again.

A couple of weeks after Leonard's statement, a poll conducted by the Louis Harris organization showed that the public strongly opposed student protests that employed any form of violence, and that it also opposed, by fifty-two per cent to thirty-eight per cent, even peaceful demonstrations by students. As usual, a position supported by more than half the people, even if it meant denying rights guaranteed under the First Amendment to some seven million citizens who happened to be students, was enough for Congress, and a move to impose strict federal penalties on students and teachers who disrupted college activities quickly gathered momentum in both houses. Reportedly, Mitchell tried to persuade the President to take a strong stand, at least verbally, against campus discord, but for the moment the President preferred to leave that problem up to local authorities.

JUSTICE

Not long afterward, some local authorities—National Guardsmen and state and local policemen in Berkeley, California—demonstrated how they meant to deal with campus outbursts by gassing, shooting, and beating young men and women who were attempting to demonstrate in favor of turning a small piece of real estate into a People's Park. As in Chicago, innocent, unarmed, and unresisting people, including bystanders, were clubbed senseless, and then clubbed some more. The incident led some to ask what police and military authorities might sanction if there was a real threat to the public safety. It also led *Newsweek* to devote an entire page to an openly outraged account by one of its reporters, who had been present, and who wrote, in part:

> In Berkeley, under cover of Governor Reagan's three-month-old "state of extreme emergency," police have also gone on a riot, displaying a lawless brutality equal to that of Chicago, along with weapons and techniques that even the authorities in Chicago did not dare employ; the firing of buckshot at fleeing crowds and unarmed bystanders, and the gassing—at times for no reason at all—of entire streets and portions of a college campus. . . . Beyond the smoke and confusion of last week's tragic events in Berkeley are some broader questions. When youthful citizens can be wantonly gassed and beaten, all because of a small, unauthorized park, what has happened to America? What has happened to our sense of perspective, our tradition of tolerance, our view of armed force as a last—never a first—resort?

Subsequently, President Nixon, in a speech at General Beadle State College, in South Dakota, urged students around the country to exercise self-restraint in striving for their goals, and promised that if they didn't "we have the power to strike back if need be, and to prevail." The federal government also had the power, and the legal justification, to prosecute those guardsmen and police officers who had violated the civil rights of the demonstrators in Berkeley. But when Attorney General Mitchell was asked, five months later, if he intended to file suits against these officials, he answered, "No."

While the clash in Berkeley was going on, the House of Representatives passed, by a vote of three hundred and twenty-nine to sixty-one, an amendment to the appropriations bill forbidding the federal government to give money to colleges that did not comply with the law. So far, the only applicable law was one enacted by Congress the year before stipulating that if a student or a teacher who was convicted in a local court of rioting was also found, by way of a hearing conducted by the college, to have disrupted the school's activities through that rioting, any federal aid to that student or teacher had to be cut off for two years. Since there was no evidence that the law had ever been used—chiefly because college administrators were reluctant to cut off a student's financial support and thereby force him out of school, perhaps into the Army and off to Vietnam—the new amendment looked like an attempt to get it enforced. It also looked like an attempt to compel colleges to carry out the intent of Congress in any law it might pass later on. Shortly afterward, a coalition of Republicans and Conservative Democrats in the House who appeared to have a majority proposed a measure to require every college to adopt an approved code of conduct for its students and teachers before it or they would be eligible for federal aid. In short, Congress would cut off money to any college, any student, or any teacher not behaving in a manner that Congress deemed appropriate.

The chief sponsor of this bill, Representative Edith Green, a moderate Democrat from Oregon who was chairman of the subcommittee the bill was pending before, argued that it was the only way to stave off far more punitive legislation. There was plenty of that lying around, such as a bill to withdraw federal aid from any college where a major disturbance occurred—a measure that would have unintentionally handed radical students a club that no college administrator would dare to stand up to. Support for Mrs. Green's bill, or something worse, was so strong that it appeared certain to prevail. "Few members of Congress can afford to go home and say we didn't do anything," Representative John N. Erlenborn, a conservative Republican from Illinois, explained in defense of the mood in the House. While the statement was tantamount to a sheriff's saying that he had joined a lynch mob because it represented the will of the majority, it went unchallenged. The President sent emissaries to the Republican leadership in the House urging that passage of the bill be blocked. But publicly he also yielded to the political pressure from *his* constituency, and instead of reminding angry citizens that they stood to lose, too, when anyone's rights were denied, he delivered the speech at General Beadle State College.

That led one disgruntled Republican senator to say in private, "He's about the followingest leader we've had in a long time."

The likelihood that Congress would enact legislation to control colleges if stronger voices were not raised against it at once led the Violence Commission to release in June a report on student unrest that it had intended to hold until the fall. "The members of this Commission, along with most Americans, are deeply disturbed by the violence and disorder that have swept the nation's campuses," the report began, and added, "We are equally disturbed, however, by the direction of much public reaction to campus unrest." Then the Commission described the prevailing attitudes it had found on campuses around the country:

Today's intelligent, idealistic students see a nation which has achieved the physical ability to provide food, shelter, and education for all, but has not yet devised social institutions that do so. They see a society, built on the principle that all men are created equal, that has not yet assured equal opportunity in life. They see a world of nations—states with the technical brilliance to harness the ultimate energy but without the common sense to agree on methods of preventing mutual destruction.

With the fresh energy and idealism of the young, they are impatient with the progress that has been made but seems to them to be indefensibly slow. At a time when students are eager to attack these and other key problems, they face the prospect of being compelled to fight in a war most of them believe is unjustified. This traumatic experience has precipitated an unprecedented mass tension and frustration.

The report went on to point out that most students "accept as valid the basic structure of our democratic system" and hoped to bring about the changes they felt were essential by operating within that system, and that although many adults were outraged by the form of many student protests, "which are often of a bizarre nature," they had to remember that the expression of even disturbing or revolting ideas was guaranteed by the Constitution. Going on to the "small but determined minority" that hoped to destroy rather than reform the nation's institutions, the Commission warned that any restrictive legislation against students and colleges in general would inevitably play into the radicals' hands if it denied the moderates the right to express their dissatisfaction with society's inequities. "By dramatic tactics of terror, [radicals] have focused widespread public attention upon themselves and have often induced university authorities either to surrender or to meet force with force," the report stated. "When they have managed on occasion to provoke counterforce to an excessive degree, they have succeeded in enlisting the sympathies of the more moderate campus majority." Of course, once the government—or the reactionary elements in Congress—took over the role of college administrator, the results were not hard to predict. As the report concluded, "If aid is withdrawn from even a few students in a manner that the campus views as unjust, the result may be to radicalize a much larger number by convincing them that existing governmental institutions are as inhumane as the revolutionaries claim."

While the Green amendment was pending before Congress,

twenty-two young Republican members of the House, whose political views ranged from moderate to ultra-conservative, returned to Washington after spending a couple of weeks visiting some of the nation's colleges. Their findings, which they reported directly to President Nixon, paralleled those of the Violence Commission in most respects, but here and there the emphasis was different. For example, to the congressmen's unanimous surprise, they discovered that students' paramount concern was not the war in Vietnam but rather this country's general preoccupation with getting and spending and its general disregard for the thirty or more million people who were ill-fed, ill-clad, ill-housed, ill-educated, ill-paid, and ill-treated. Above all, the students refused to accept their elders' covert or open hostility toward Negroes, and were determined to expose what they regarded as the gaping difference between the principle of equality enunciated in the Declaration of Independence and the practice of adult society as the supreme hypocrisy.

All in all, the congressmen found students "decent" and "intelligent" youngsters who were convinced that injustice could be rooted out and that their protests were the only means they had to persuade society to look at itself and reform. As unlikely as that outcome might have seemed to hardened politicians, one member of the group, Representative William A. Steiger, Republican of Wisconsin, warned his colleagues that the students' discontent was far more widely shared and their determination was far deeper than members of Congress imagined. And the great numbers of youngsters who were discontented with society and determined to change it, he added, "will not be coerced, they will not be cowed by the threat of punishment or the application of overwhelming force."

The reports submitted by the Violence Commission and the Republican congressmen generated the opposition to the Green bill that the Administration had failed, or neglected, to muster, and consideration of the measure was put off for the time being. But members of the House who wanted to crack down on student dissidents expressed their own determination to continue the fight they had started, and vowed that if they lost it they would eliminate federal aid to students altogether. Finally, the House approved a compromise measure that denied federal grants or scholarships to students or teachers who participated in campus disturbances. Then a Senate committee did the House one better by empowering the Secretary of H.E.W. to cut off federal grants to any college that had two disturbances and did not punish the students who participated in them. However, when this bill reached the Senate floor, opponents defeated that section, by the narrow vote of forty-nine to forty-three, and in the end the House went along with the change when the bill got to conference. Despite this defeat for the right, its members were confident that they would be able to muster a majority if there were serious violence on campuses during the next session. And they were equally confident that there would be such violence.

During the Presidential campaign, Nixon repeatedly told Southern audiences that although the Civil Rights Act of 1964 prohibited segregation in schools, it did not require positive action to further integration, and this was widely interpreted as a promise that if he became President he would relax federal enforcement of that law. In the spring of 1965, the Johnson Administration issued the first school-desegregation guidelines provided for in the 1964 act; these directed all school districts receiving federal aid to begin integrating their schools during the 1965-66 school year and to complete the job in all twelve grades by the end of the 1967-68 school year. Title VI of the law directed the Secretary of Health, Education, and Welfare to cut off federal funds to districts that failed, after a hearing, to meet the desegregation standards. This tactic proved to be more effective than any other school-desegregation device employed so far; when the law went into effect in 1964, one per cent of black students were attending integrated schools in the South, but by the end of 1968 the figure had risen to twenty per cent. It was twenty per cent instead of a hundred per cent, as ordered, because Southern school boards persistently came up with new delaying tactics that had to be considered in an orderly fashion by the courts or the executive branch, and because some districts preferred to give up federal aid altogether rather than integrate their schools. As a result of these delays, the Johnson Administration ordered, in mid-1968, that the dual school system, with a few exceptions, be eliminated in the South by the beginning of the next school year, in September, 1969.

It had been a constant and wearying struggle for the federal government. Each time a school district came up with a new way out of the commitment it had made to abide by the guidelines, the government had to take legal action against it at once. "It is very important to enforce the law immediately to show that compliance is necessary and that no one is going to be allowed to get by without it," Pollak, head of the Civil Rights Division under Clark, explained during the transition. "This will face the new Administration as soon as it comes in. If it doesn't act in these cases, then the word will go around the South that compliance isn't necessary. In the end, the vital question is whether the South is going to be forced to close down its dual school system. That is, will suits continue to be presented to the Attorney General for action, and if they are will he take it?"

Throughout the transition period, a large number of Southern school districts put off carrying out federal orders to desegregate, in the conviction that the orders would be withdrawn when the new Administration took over. To their intense disappointment, the Civil Rights Division continued after the inauguration to perform as if there had been no change in the White House. A month after President Nixon was sworn in, Nathan Lewin, a non-political career

official who had served as Pollak's second assistant and was kept on
for a time by Leonard, said, "The Southerners expected it all to be
different, but it's clear now that it won't be. I haven't seen even
minor, let alone major, shifts in civil-rights policies here. A new
Administration couldn't turn things around here even if it wanted
to. In a place like this, the self-perpetuating mechanism of the law
makes any basic change unlikely." It seemed that Leonard agreed
with this view, for in his first month in office the division filed nine
civil-rights suits. And it seemed that Mitchell did, too, for under the
law each case required his signature before it could be filed in court.

As events were to demonstrate before long, however, the Administration's failure to change the civil-rights policies of its predecessors
was due primarily to a delay caused by a debate within the highest
councils of government over whether they were to be dispensed
with altogether or were to be merely weakened in a way that would
please the South and not unduly antagonize the rest of the country.
The debate was protracted and, according to some reports, often
extremely bitter. The few hints of it that leaked out, then and later,
put Attorney General Mitchell down as the leader of those who
believed the President should widen his base by going after the Wallace vote, both in the South and elsewhere in the country.

"The fantastic part of it all is that it would never occur to a man
like Mitchell that this made him as much a racist as the worst of
them," one Negro who held a high post in the Johnson Administration said not long ago. "He'd be indignant as hell at such a suggestion. As he sees things, if something is good politics it's good. He's
so out of touch that he doesn't call us 'blacks' or 'Negroes'—he calls
us 'colored people.' From what I've heard, neither Mitchell, the President, nor anyone else high up in the White House has any real
understanding of what's going on among black men in our society."
The member of the Administration who appeared to have the clearest understanding of the problem was Secretary of Health, Education, and Welfare Finch, who appeared to often be standing alone

during the debate as he contended that Negro demands for equal rights had to be supported if the nation was to survive.

At the heart of the debate lay a single question: Was the federal government going to enforce and obey federal law? The question was so large and so alarming in its implications that it had never occurred to men like Lewin, who viewed the rule of law as the most inviolable principle underlying our form of democracy. But the President and the Attorney General appeared to view the subject essentially in political terms. According to Deputy Attorney General Kleindienst, "Mr. Nixon and Mr. Mitchell are pragmatists. They aren't interested in anything except how problems can be solved." "Pragmatism" is one of the most honored and least meaningful terms in the political lexicon, for the word implies nothing about ends, or even about the sort of means that might be used. In all likelihood, when the Republican candidate and his campaign manager set out during the Presidential campaign to capture the South, they did not fully consider the problems their policy would later create for them. There is no reason to believe that both men would not have preferred to press for equality for all citizens as the most decent and constructive course for the nation to follow. But if political considerations were to be paramount, then the pragmatic way—a political means to a political end—was fairly clear.

Not the least of the influences that were brought to bear on the President as he made his way toward a decision on this matter was a meeting held in the capital in mid-February, which was attended by the Republican party chairmen of the eleven states of the Old Confederacy. Designated by its participants as an "emergency session," the meeting was supposed to be secret, but, as usual in such cases, it wasn't secret for long. It soon became openly known in Washington that the unanimous conclusion of those who had attended it was that if the Presidential election were to be held then, President Nixon wouldn't win a single Southern state. And before another month was out, reports were coming in to the White House that the

South was practically in open revolt against the President, who was widely and publicly being charged with having deliberately misled white voters there during the campaign and with willfully betraying them now that he was in the White House.

In mid-April, Secretary Finch said that "no change is contemplated now in the existing guidelines." Apparently, he was speaking for himself, because other high officials in the government were all for rolling the guidelines so far back that they would be invisible. Aside from Mitchell, there were reportedly two principal advocates of this course—Harry S. Dent, a former aide to Senator Thurmond and Republican party chairman in South Carolina, which he delivered in the election, who had recently been installed in the White House as the President's chief political adviser, and Robert C. Mardian, an arch-conservative Californian who had been appointed, at Kleindienst's insistence, general counsel to the Department of Health, Education, and Welfare. The President was reported to be convinced that opponents who charged him with bowing to the South to curry votes did not understand the mood of the country as well as he did, and that the mood was deeply conservative, deeply apprehensive about Negro crime and Negro riots, deeply resentful about "handouts" to Negroes, and deeply opposed to more rapid integration. The "solid majority" of conservative citizens who made up the "new coalition" that Nixon had spoken of during the campaign—what he now calls "the silent majority"—was apparently thought to be as reactionary as the old coalition of Southern Democrats and Northern Republicans which for so long had blocked civil-rights legislation in Congress, and it was to these conservatives, not just in the South but throughout the nation, that the President was clearly prepared to look for his support. In line with this interpretation of contemporary politics, Mitchell, Dent, and Mardian proposed that the desegregation accomplished so far be reëxamined, that the deadlines set down by the former Administration be postponed indefinitely, and that the President avoid committing himself in any way to integration in the future.

When word of this proposal leaked out—as opponents within the Administration made sure it did—liberal members of Congress, buttressed by civil-rights leaders around the country, threatened to take the issue to the people and to mount a last-ditch fight against such a move, and a large number of aides on the civil-rights staff at H.E.W. threatened to resign immediately and noisily. That blocked any sudden leap to the extreme right, and for several more weeks the struggle over how big a step should be taken dragged on. Then, at the end of June, Finch, asked if reports that the guidelines would be radically changed were true, replied that there would be "no softening or modifying" of them but that they were being reëvaluated to provide "a more realistic time approach."

This sounded ominous to civil-rights workers, who had spent fifteen years listening to Southerners' pleas for more time and feared that if some school districts were allowed to postpone desegregation deadlines others would be quick to demand that they be given the same latitude. Finally, on July 3rd, the Administration issued a joint statement signed by Mitchell and Finch. It declared that the government meant to hold Southern school districts to the September, 1969, deadline set by the Johnson Administration unless they had "bona fide educational and administrative problems," and added, "It is not our purpose here to lay down a single arbitrary date by which the desegregation process should be completed in all districts, or to lay down a single arbitrary system by which it should be achieved."

Some H.E.W. aides were despondent over the statement (which had gone through a dozen drafts before it met with the President's approval) and described it as a watered-down version of Mitchell's original position but still a victory for his side. Others claimed that the statement was a victory for the civil-rights forces—presumably because they hadn't lost the war altogether—and promised that it would soon be followed by strict enforcement of the guidelines. The leader of this group, Leon E. Panetta, who was head of H.E.W.'s Civil Rights Office, announced shortly afterward that he had ordered a letter sent out to all schoolboard officials in the country informing them that the old guidelines would have to be observed. Ten days later, the H.E.W. public-information office announced that Secretary Finch saw no need for such a letter and that it wouldn't be sent after all.

Whatever claims and orders, counter-claims and counter-orders may have been issued within H.E.W., civil-rights supporters outside the Department put the joint statement of Finch and Mitchell down as an open invitation to segregationists to do their worst. One former official of H.E.W. pointed out that it provided Southerners with a pretext to claim that they lacked proper facilities, and that now they could easily delay matters—for instance, by calling for new bond issues for school construction and then covertly making certain that they were rejected by the voters. Wilbur Cohen, Secretary of H.E.W. under President Johnson, called the move "a political decision" and "an unfortunate departure that the Administration will regret." Roy Wilkins, head of the N.A.A.C.P., accused the government of "breaking the law." And Charles Evers, the N.A.A.C.P. field secretary in Mississippi, said, "I wonder what Mr. Nixon will say to Mr. Wilkins and to myself when the young Negroes tell us, 'I told you it wouldn't work. I told you that the American way of legislation won't work for black people.'" M. Hayes Mizell, a member of the South Carolina advisory committee to the United States Commission on Civil Rights, resigned by way of a letter to the President accusing him of having "broken faith with millions of people" in taking an action that "dehumanizes black citizens of this country, because its effect will be to make them feel that their rights are subject to the whims and manipulations of your Administration."

Over in the Department of Justice, Mitchell's aides assured civil-rights groups that the joint statement meant there would continue to be vigorous enforcement of the guidelines, and then disproved it by adding that there would also be less pressure to meet deadlines for compliance with them. Inside of a week, the Department filed eight desegregation suits, which it pointed to as evidence of its determination to proceed with dispatch under the law. However, some skeptics pointed out that the eight cases could have been announced so close together only because they had been held up pending the Administration's policy decision, that most of them had been started by the previous Administration, and that this brought the total number of desegregation actions filed by the Department during its first six months in office to fifteen, which was far below the number of new actions filed under Attorney General Clark during the same period the year before.

About this time, it became known that the Department of Justice intended to institute desegregation suits against whole states by way of court action, and that emphasis would be shifted from the guidelines to this method. In the Administration's first court action against a state board of education, the Department of Justice directed Georgia to abolish its racially dual school system. In announcing this action, the Department put out a press release that was full of statistical inaccuracies and factual distortions conveying the impression that court action would be far more effective and far quicker than administrative action such as cutting off funds. People at H.E.W. tried to correct the release, but most newspapers ignored their efforts. A main point in the Department of Justice's release was that the Administration was increasingly concerned about the damage done by cutoffs in funds. Though that strategy was undeniably effective, the release stated, Negro students were usually hurt most of all, because Southern school officials reduced services in Negro schools first when federal aid was withdrawn.

The release did not mention that while Negro children might be deprived of some educational funds during the few months it ordinarily took to convince a given school district that its money would be cut off if it didn't obey the guidelines, most Negro children were likely to be deprived of any hope of attending integrated schools for several years before judicial action had any effect under the Administration's plan; and since a number of judges on the federal bench in the South were unreconstructed segregationists, there was no assurance that judicial action would ever work. Further, once the federal court in Atlanta issued a statewide desegregation order under the new suit, federal law required that the government immediately restore funds to those districts that had lost them through failure to comply with the guidelines. In Georgia, this meant that thirty-six school districts that had lost federal aid got it back at once; moreover, in thirty-three other districts where federal aid was in the process of being withdrawn the government, upon the filing of the suit, continued subsidizing dual school systems.

The chief benefit expected to accrue to the Administration from this strategy was that it would mollify the South for the time being and assure that if the courts forced it to integrate later they, and not the President, would be blamed. The chief drawback was that black children were certain to learn, wherever they went to school, that their government had tried to weaken a law that worked in their favor.

Not merely an ideal of justice was at stake. Because of oppression like this over the years, millions of black families had moved North to swell the ranks of the uneducated and unskilled in Northern slums, where there was perhaps a little more hope and a little more opportunity. With additional oppression on the way, additional millions could be expected to make the same journey, and with the arrival of each of them there would be less hope and less opportunity. In the South the chief difference between a white man and a black man has always been that one is a master and the other is a servant. But in the North the difference is broader and starker than that, because there few black men have white men who are as degraded and poor as they are living next door. In the North black inequality and black poverty are largely concentrated in the great urban centers, surrounded by white opportunity and white affluence. That contrast accounts for much of the crime committed in Northern cities and for the riots that convulsed so many of them in recent years. Of course, adding to the contrast by driving more Negroes out of the South would inevitably lay the ground for more, and worse, outbursts in the future.

During the transition, civil-rights advocates in and out of the government looked forward with some apprehension to the new Administration's attitude toward the most effective piece of civil-rights legislation on the books—the Voting Rights Act of 1965. This law, which was due to expire in August, 1970, suspended literacy tests and other devices used to keep Negroes from registering to vote in any state or county where such devices were being used on November 1, 1964, and where less than fifty per cent of the voting-age population was registered on that date or voted in the Presidential election that year—meaning, in effect, counties in seven states in the Deep South. The law also empowered the Attorney General to send federal registrars and poll-watchers into any county that fit the legal formula. Under this act, Negro voter registration in the seven Southern states the measure was aimed at rose from thirty per cent to more than sixty per cent of eligible voters; the direct result was that twice as many Negroes went to the polls in 1968 than had in 1964, and the indirect result was that they put nearly five hundred Negroes in public office during that period.

In order to forestall a filibuster, the members of Congress who fought for the bill in 1965 had reluctantly agreed to a Southern move to limit its life to five years—a sufficiently long time, most of them felt, to give Southern Negroes a foothold that could never be dislodged—but by the end of 1968 it was clear that if the law was allowed to expire Southern Negroes would be back almost where they started. It was also clear that the Nixon Administration would have to move in the First Session of the Ninety-first Congress if the act was to be extended; ordinarily, a controversial measure—particularly a civil-rights measure—takes a year or more to push through Congress, and it was widely believed that if the new President did not act soon after taking office Southerners in Congress would delay the bill until the date for its expiration came closer and then filibuster it to death.

Throughout the winter, spring, and early summer of 1969, the Administration avoided taking any position on the act. In fact, although Mitchell accepted invitations to testify on the subject before a subcommittee of the House Judiciary Committee six times, each time he asked for a postponement at the last minute. Once again the Administration was locked in contention over a major issue, and once again the President was apparently unable to make up his mind. On June 25th, Senator Dirksen told reporters that one reason for the delay was that a study was being made in the White House to determine whether the President had "made something of a promise" on the subject during the campaign. The findings of the study were never revealed, but the following day Attorney General Mitchell finally appeared before the House Judiciary subcommittee. He testified that the Administration was not prepared to support an outright extension of the Voting Rights Act, which the majority of the subcommittee's members wanted. Instead, it preferred to submit its own bill, since, he explained, "I cannot support what amounts to regional legislation."

What he could support was a gutting of the 1965 act. Under that measure, any proposed change in local election laws—aimed, say, at introducing new subterfuges to prevent Negroes from voting—had to be cleared either with the Attorney General or with the federal District Courts in Washington before being used. Under Mitchell's proposal, the clearance procedure was abandoned and the Department of Justice was required to keep an eye on every move made to amend election laws in every legal jurisdiction in the country, and if one was found to be discriminatory the Department could then apply for an injunction in a federal court in the district where the law was passed—that is, the bill left it up to judges in the South to determine the validity of civil-rights actions. And, finally, the provisions of the law Mitchell proposed would apply to the entire country, not just to the region where by far the most voting discrimination was practiced, thereby diverting the government's attention from areas where it was most needed.

The only other witness at the hearing that day was Clarence Mitchell, director of the Washington bureau of the N.A.A.C.P., who warned that if Congress delayed renewal of the Voting Rights Act by adopting such an obstructive measure, "then would come again the cross-burning and the slaying of the Negro who has no other desire than to vote." He also spoke of "a sophisticated, calculated, incredible effort on the part of the chief lawyer of the United States government to make it impossible to continue on the constructive efforts we have followed." He was about the only person outside the Administration who considered the Attorney General's proposal sophisticated. "It's the most blatantly racist appeal to George Wallace's constituency since George Wallace's campaign for the Presidency," one Democratic member of the subcommittee said privately afterward. "The move to make the Attorney General keep track of every tiny amendment to election laws across the country and then the requirement that he fight amendments discriminating against black voters through the courts would either tie up the entire Department or force it to drop the whole thing."

Representative Emanuel Celler, Democrat of New York and chairman of the full Judiciary Committee, told Mitchell during the hearings that the proposal amounted to nothing more than "a delaying action." Offstage, a couple of other Democrats suggested that since the measure would obviously be unenforceable, it could not have been meant seriously. Like many other members of Congress, they considered it a signal to conservatives in the South that the President was doing his best to restore the old ways there, while at the same time it was a signal to moderates and liberals in the North that the whole affair was a mere political gesture. "In other words, the Administration is betraying both sides," one of these men said. "That is not just politically foolish, it is base." When a reporter asked Senator Hugh Scott, Republican of Pennsylvania, who was then the Minority Whip, how much more in the way of reactionary steps the Administration would have to take before liberal Republicans bolted, he answered, "Not very much."

In the House, the leading critic of the Administration's bill was Representative William McCulloch, of Ohio, who was the ranking Republican on the Judiciary Committee and a leading civil-rights advocate. Pointing out that the latest issue was not a partisan matter, since eighty-two per cent of the Republican members in the House had supported the Voting Rights Act of 1965, he told the committee, "As I understand the provisions of the Administration's bill which pertain to the heart of this controversy, they sweep broadly into those areas where the need is the least and retreat from those areas where the need is greatest. We are asked to extend the Section 4 ban on literacy tests or devices outside the South into fourteen other states from which the Department of Justice and the N.A.A.C.P. have never to this day received a complaint alleging the discriminatory use of literacy tests or devices. We are asked to repeal the Section 5 requirement that the covered states must clear their new voting laws and practices with the Attorney General or the District Court for the District of Columbia in the face of spellbinding evidence of unflagging Southern dedication to the cause of creating an ever more sophisticated legal machinery for discriminating against the black voter. In short, the Administration creates a remedy for which there is no wrong and leaves grievous wrongs without adequate remedy. I ask you, what kind of a civil-rights bill is that?"

Negroes around the country were asking the same question, and the most temperate of their leaders feared that if they hadn't already lost whatever influence they once had in trying to persuade black radicals to work within the system, they soon would. One Negro who expressed this opinion was Roger Wilkins, the former head of the Justice Department's Community Relations Service, where by this time ten of the dozen key men had resigned out of disagreement with the new Administration. (Their new boss, Ben Holman, a Negro television reporter and producer, stated publicly, at a time when the Administration's school-integration policy in the South was being sharply questioned, that he did "not believe integration is a valid practical goal for the masses of poor blacks.") Wilkins had turned down an offer from Secretary Finch to be general counsel to H.E.W., and for a time after he left the government, he wondered if perhaps he should have stayed on to do what he could to slow down the Administration's move to the right. But as events unfolded, he realized that he would have been forced to resign anyway.

One of the few high-ranking Negroes in the government was James Farmer, former director of CORE, who had been made an Assistant Secretary of H.E.W., and Wilkins said he agreed with former Attorney General Clark's description of Farmer in his current role: "He's like a man trying to build a Boulder Dam with a toothpick, and while you might admire his determination and pity his bloody knuckles, the fact is that you can't build a Boulder Dam with a toothpick." After the Administration weakened the school guidelines, shifted its civil-rights work to the courts, and unveiled its voting "rights" law, Wilkins sat down and wrote a letter to Finch, which said, in part:

These events . . . demonstrate to me a clear disregard for the aspirations and the anguish of black people in this society and a clear over-regard for the forces of primitive conservatism and for political indebtedness.

Since I have been out of the government, I have been able to talk to militant young blacks to whom I did not have access when I worked in the Department of Justice. These young Americans seriously doubt the will and the capacity of the American system to deal with their anguish. Without anything else, it would be difficult for moderate or even radical reformers to dispel the romantic revolutionary notions held by some of these young people. The task of urging radical reform within the system has now been made impossible. The Administration has not only left the reformers with no answers, it has now begun to radicalize us. When even so moderate and elegant a man as Roy Wilkins is quoted as saying of [the guidelines] decision by the Administration, '. . . it almost makes me want to vomit,' the Administration ought to take note. . . .

These comments are intended in no sense to be partisan. They are the very restrained observations of a citizen concerned about his people and troubled about his country. As a serious student of American race relations, I am trying to tell you that I believe the course on which the Administration is embarked, even if it doesn't result in disaster, is at least, in my judgment, seriously misguided. So far, the Administration's policies do not take into account black anger and black anguish. They must.

Secretary Finch did not answer the letter. For his own part, Wilkins later conceded that the restraint he had asserted when he wrote it was far greater than he had suggested. "A year ago, I figured that a black rebellion was out of the question, because black leaders— even the most militant of them—knew that all they would accomplish was to get themselves and their followers killed," he said. "But I think that the despair is far deeper now. You just can't go on seeing how white men live, the opportunity they have, listening to all the promises they make and realizing how little they have delivered, without having to fight an almost ungovernable rage within yourself. Some black children in this country have to eat dog food or go hungry. No man can go on watching his children grow up in hunger and misery like that, with wealth and comfort on every side of him, and continue to regard himself as a man. I think that there are black men who have enough pride now so that they would rather die than go on living the way they have to live. And I think that most of us moderates would have difficulty arguing with them. The other day, an old friend of mine, a black man who has spent his life trying to work things out for his people within the system, said to me, 'Roger, I'm going to get a gun. I can't help it.'"

About the time that Wilkins wrote to Finch, a group of Negro civil-rights workers came up from the South to protest the weakening of the guidelines and revision of the Voting Rights Act to Mitchell in person. When they arrived at the Attorney General's office, on the fifth floor of the Department, they were told that he could not see them. At that, they immediately sat down—on the couch and chairs and floor of the reception room—and vowed to stay there until he did see them. Informed of the sit-in, Mitchell summoned Assistant Attorney General Leonard, who reached his office by way of a private entrance. After a brief conference, Leonard appeared in the reception room, and when he saw that a white woman was in the otherwise all-Negro group he went directly up to her and said, "Let's talk this thing over." She shook her head. "I'm not one of them," she said. "I'm just a friend. Talk to *them*." Leonard did, angrily telling them that although they were "extremely presumptuous," the Attorney General would speak with them at four o'clock in the Department's auditorium, and that if they didn't leave the reception room immediately they would be dragged out.

Leo M. Pellerzi, the Assistant Attorney General for Administration, happened to be on hand and quickly moved in to remind the group that it was five minutes to four already and that if they didn't get to the auditorium soon their long trip would be to no purpose.

That modest gesture to their dignity was all that was needed, and they rose quietly and made their way to the auditorium. Shortly afterward, Mitchell arrived and listened to their grievances. When the list was completed, he assured them that the Administration was firmly committed to their cause. Then, in what must stand as the most astonishing admission of high-level duplicity in government history, he said, "You will be better advised to watch what we do instead of what we say."

The first opportunity his audience had to take this advice came a few days later, when the House Judiciary subcommittee met in executive session to consider the Voting Rights Act. The Administration exerted no pressure on Republican members of the subcommittee to approve its version, and, in fact, that measure wasn't even submitted for a vote. And in the end the subcommittee, with only one dissenting vote, agreed to recommend that the House approve a simple five-year extension of the Voting Rights Act. That seemed to confirm the suspicion that the Administration had been grandstanding over its own bill. Whatever benefit the original gesture may have left the President and Attorney General with in the South, it also left them with the prospect of an exceedingly awkward dilemma when renewal of the act came to the floor of the House for a vote. If they launched a serious effort to defeat or at least modify it to meet Southern demands, they would antagonize the greater number of their own party's representatives who supported the law. And if they made another obvious play for the grandstand, Southerners in the House, who were masters at the game, would be almost certain to do some anti-Administration grandstanding of their own for the edification of their constituents. A Republican congressman who watched the Administration laboriously construct a box around itself shook his head and said, "If this is pragmatism, I'll take a couple of wide-eyed theorists any time."

The bill to extend the Voting Rights Act was approved in the full House Judiciary Committee on July 17th by a substantial majority.

From there, it was sent to the House Committee on Rules, whose chairman, William M. Colmer, an ultra-conservative Democrat from Mississippi, blocked it for months, despite Celler's pleas that the House be allowed to vote on it. Colmer finally let the bill go to the floor, but only with the proviso that it would be open to amendment, the chief amendment that everyone expected being the Administration's measure. However, no Northern Republican could be found to sponsor that, so in the end Minority Leader Ford was obliged to offer and defend it.

At the time, civil-rights forces were confident that they had the bill beaten by at least twenty votes. But, overconfident and disorganized, they fell down on the task of keeping their supporters in line and pressuring those who might be wavering to join them. White House and Department of Justice aides, on the other hand, tirelessly went about buttonholing Northern Republicans and demanding their allegiance to party policy. "They covered this place like a carpet," one Democratic congressman who opposed the bill said later. "And our people didn't realize what was happening until it was too late." In the end, the Administration's bill was approved by a vote of two hundred and eight to two hundred and three, with a hundred and twenty-nine Republicans and seventy-nine Democrats making up the winning side. All but three of the Democrats were from the South, and if those three—Edith Green and Al Ullman, both of Oregon, and James Delaney, of New York—had switched their votes, the Administration's anti-voting-rights bill would have lost.

Still, it was the Republicans who were responsible—ninety-nine of those voting for the bill were from the North, most from districts with few Negro voters. Although none of them had been willing to sponsor a measure that deprived Southern Negroes of their elementary right to vote, all of them had been willing to vote for such a bill. Of course, when the Fourth of July came around, they could be expected, to a man, to make the usual patriotic speeches about this great land of ours. When an aide to a Republican representative who refused to blindly follow party policy on this issue was asked after the vote, "What has happened to the party of Lincoln?" he replied, "It has put on a Confederate uniform."

The Administration's measure, Congressman Celler said afterward, "gives inordinate permanent power to the Attorney General in every nook and cranny of the country. Knowing the political proclivities of the Department of Justice, I know they're going to use it for political purposes. There's going to be lots of trouble." The trouble promised to be explosive once black people across the country learned that not only were they not going to be given the same rights as white people but that the rights they had recently gained were going to be withdrawn. "Although touted by Republican leadership as 'more comprehensive and equitable,' the substitute bill is a sham," the *Times* stated in an editorial the following day. "It is more comprehensive in that it indiscriminately squanders the efforts and the personnel required for the law's enforcement. It is more equitable in that it assumes that those who are not violating the law need as much policing as those who are."

When Congress finally adjourned, on December 23rd, the House-passed bill was locked in the Senate Judiciary Committee, the graveyard of civil-rights legislation on Capitol Hill. But a band of civil-rights warriors in the Senate, led by Philip Hart, Democrat of Michigan, had some hope that they could devise a compromise that would preserve the heart of the legislation already on the books. Still, there was grave danger that action on the bill would be delayed until expiration of the original Voting Rights Act came up the following August. Senator Birch Bayh, Democrat of Indiana and a member of the band, predicted "a big, hairy filibuster one way or another." He also predicted that, as in the Haynsworth battle, the Administration would go "well beyond the pale of reason" and that a similar "death struggle" would ensue.

Late in July, the House Appropriations Committee, which had been haggling for months over federal aid to education, unexpectedly approved an amendment to an appropriations bill it was considering. The amendment, offered by Representative Jamie L. Whitten, Democrat of Mississippi, and approved by a voice vote without a recorded lineup (a parliamentary device dear to political cowards on both sides of the aisle), barred the federal government from withholding or threatening to withhold education funds, as it now could under Title VI of the Civil Rights Act of 1964, as a means of compelling parents to accept busing of their children, compelling school boards to close down segregated schools, or compelling students to attend schools that their parents didn't want them to attend. Although the amendment did not abolish Title VI outright, it went a fair way toward accomplishing that end and was a severe setback for the civil-rights cause. In effect, it required federal officials to accept freedom-of-choice desegregation plans, which amounted to freedom for white parents to refuse to allow their children to attend schools with black children. That flew directly in the face of a decision by the Supreme Court in the spring of 1968 that such plans were insufficient evidence of desegregation unless they could be shown "realistically to work" and, moreover, "to work now."

Only a few days elapsed between the time the appropriations bill came out of committee and the time it reached the floor of the House for a vote. During that period, Secretary Finch was on the West Coast attending a conference of the nation's governors, and his chief liaison with H.E.W.'s Civil Rights Office was there with him. By accident, or prearrangement, both men were unavailable, even by telephone, to other officials of H.E.W. or to members of Congress during the critical period before the Whitten amendment came up for a vote. That left Panetta, head of the Civil Rights Office in H.E.W., more or less on his own, so he immediately moved to block the amendment by drawing up a detailed memorandum showing just how bad it was, which he circulated among civil-rights leaders in both parties in the House. Congressman McCulloch suggested to Panetta that he get in touch with the dozen or so influential Republican members of the House who could always be relied on to muster votes for a good civil-rights bill or against a bad one. Panetta did, but then suddenly H.E.W.'s efforts dropped off sharply, until the civil-rights staff there was doing nothing more than giving out information on the measure when asked. Still, civil-rights forces in the House were confident that they had the votes to defeat the amendment easily if, as they fully expected, the Administration backed them up.

On the morning the debate on the bill was to open, Minority Leader Gerald Ford, of Michigan, called a meeting of the Republican leadership in the House. Eight men were there besides Ford, including Representative John B. Anderson, of Illinois, the chairman of the Republican Conference in the House; Bryce N. Harlow, then the White House liaison with Congress; Creed C. Black, H.E.W.'s Assistant Secretary for Legislation; and Attorney General Mitchell. One of the participants was very surprised to see Mitchell. "Since the lion's share of the appropriation was to be spent by H.E.W., why wasn't a top official from that department present?" he asked later. "Why was the Attorney General there? What did the bill have to do with his department?" He soon learned why Mitchell was there—to inform the assemblage that the Administration did not oppose the Whitten amendment. He did not say that the Administration supported it, but everyone in the room realized that the refusal to take a stand on this issue amounted to an endorsement.

The Attorney General's justification for the Administration's position was that President Nixon believed court action, not executive action, was the proper procedure to follow. Congressman Anderson vehemently disagreed with this view, because, for one thing, he said, cutting off federal funds for any government-assisted program where discrimination was practiced had been demonstrated to be the most effective weapon against segregation in Southern schools. For another thing, he said, the President's position ignored the fact that under existing law court action was already a key part of government procedures in trying to achieve equal educational opportunity for all children. Ultimately, Anderson refused to go along with the Administration and warned that he would oppose the amendment when it came time for a vote on the floor.

Ford tried to calm him down by pointing out that the Senate would undoubtedly reject the amendment when it got over there. Anderson was not at all certain that the Senate would, or that if it did, the House conferees would accede to its wishes when the bill came to conference. Also, he said that he would not abdicate his responsibility as a member of the House by passing the buck to the Senate. And, finally, he refused to be a party to an action that, in effect, amounted to a public pronouncement that one body of Congress had told Negroes to go to hell.

When the issue came to the floor, it turned out that the Administration's protective neutrality drew off the support that was needed to defeat the amendment, which was passed by a vote of one hundred and fifty-eight to one hundred and forty-one. That action was taken by way of another hallowed tradition of political cowardice—a teller vote, in which members file down to the well of the House, where their votes, but not their names, are recorded.

"What worries me most is the tendency among my colleagues to believe that there has been a fundamental switch in the mood of the country toward Negroes," Representative Anderson said afterward. "Whatever the mood of the white people in this country actually is, that view ignores the simple fact that there are twenty to thirty million black Americans who are bitterly angry and determined that their children aren't going to spend lives of frustration and pain the way they have. What white Americans feel isn't going to change *that*. If something isn't done, and done soon, to ease the discontent and offer hope, we are in for some very bad trouble."

Although Anderson did not say it, his appraisal of his colleagues' outlook applied with equal pertinency to what appeared to be the outlook in the White House. He had no certain information on the President's own views, he went on, but he had speculated from time to time on what they might be. "The essential reasons behind this deliberate decision to change course on this issue may lie in the President's belief that the country is sick of big government," he explained. "And perhaps Mitchell, as a trained lawyer, looks at this whole picture and sees a clearer advantage and a cleaner method by going through the courts instead of increasing the power of the federal monster. It may be that this is a part of a general move toward decentralization—what the President calls 'the new federalism.'" If this was indeed what the President and the Attorney General had in mind, the question remained whether the Administration's decision would not convince Negroes, once and for all, that they could not expect equal justice under the law and that they would have to return to the streets and fight for their rights outside the law. When Anderson was asked about this, he nodded grimly and answered, "That's what I'm afraid of."

On Capitol Hill, Democrats and Republicans alike looked on the Administration's latest change in civil-rights policy as still another attempt to placate the forces led by Senator Thurmond. And in the House moderate and liberal Republicans angrily talked among themselves about the shame the House had brought on itself by allowing the Administration to use it to pay off a campaign debt. "Gerry Ford is the one who is most to blame for this," a leading Republican there said after the vote on the Whitten amendment. "I don't believe he has ever committed a non-political act in his life." As he went on to explain, Ford's position on the amendment undoubtedly stemmed indirectly from the fight he had waged a few years before to replace Charles Halleck, Republican of Indiana, as Minority Leader. Ford won that contest by a very narrow margin. Subsequently, when the issue of open housing was before the House, in the late winter and early spring of 1968, the principal leaders of the Republican Party—former Vice-President Nixon, Governor Nelson Rockefeller, and Governor George Romney—individually telephoned Ford and told him that the Party had to have the open-housing issue behind it, with strong Party support for the measure on the record, before the Presidential election. In the end, the House approved the open-housing act and Ford voted against it. In opposing all the top leaders of his party, one of whom he knew was likely to be President within a few months, he demonstrated, as fully as anything can ever be demonstrated in politics, that he had paid for the support of the reactionary wing of his party in the leadership fight by pledging to support it on crucial issues. Of course, civil rights was the most crucial issue of all, for opposition to it was the cement that kept the conservative coalition together.

Although Finch appeared to be willing to let it seem that Mitchell had outmaneuvered him during his absence from Washington, H.E.W.'s failure to fight the Whitten amendment with the considerable force it had to command seemed to confirm a widespread suspicion that Finch had intentionally made himself unavailable during the critical period of the battle, and that, however much he might have disapproved of the Administration's decision, he had been privy to it well in advance and went along with it. The kindest view taken of his role was that he had avoided defending a hopeless cause in order to save himself for future fights against moves to weaken civil-rights work within his department. As it turned out, he did testify against the Whitten amendment in hearings conducted by a Senate subcommittee on appropriations. However, the subcommittee approved the amendment, and so did the full Appropriations Committee, despite telegrams to all its members from Finch opposing the provision. But when the bill got to the floor of the Senate,

Minority Leader Scott proposed that the amendment be modified by the insertion of the words "except as required by the Constitution"—enough to nullify the Whitten amendment, its opponents held, and the motion carried. When the bill got to the House, Representative Anderson informed his colleagues that H.E.W. supported the Scott amendment and that this represented the Administration's position. Apparently, this was the battle that Finch had saved himself for, and apparently the President was unwilling to sacrifice him again, especially after the victory of the Voting Rights Act.

Many people in H.E.W. and the Civil Rights Division of the Department of Justice have become more and more concerned about Secretary Finch's diminishing influence and Attorney General Mitchell's growing influence with the President. "At least Finch has some concept of what society should be like," one of them said last summer, shortly after the Administration had ordered a broad retreat on civil rights. "Mitchell, on the other hand, doesn't have the faintest idea of the needs of society, and neither do most of the men over in the White House. People who go there to talk things over are stunned by the lack of philosophy on the top level. A lot of these incredibly important decisions are made, or at least implemented, by those advertising and public-relations men that Nixon brought into the White House with him. Oh, they think they're being clever and devious as hell, but to everyone around here with any political experience they're unbelievably blatant. What's more, there is no realistic appraisal on their part of what these policies will do to the nation. Like Mitchell, all those guys think about is getting President Nixon reëlected. If they go on this way, he may be reëlected, but it will only be to preside over the wreckage of democracy."

In this official's opinion, a realistic appraisal of the Administration's civil-rights policies would demonstrate that their social consequences were almost certain to be disastrous. "We were well on the way to solving the civil-rights problem in Southern schools," he explained. "Most of the men in the South who count in matters like this—governors, mayors, school-board heads, leading business-men—had got to the point where they realized that further resistance was futile. Of course, they reached that conclusion only with the greatest reluctance after years of fighting us every step of the way. But once they reached it, they were ready to go along with us. Now the whole issue of civil rights in this country has been reopened, because President Nixon has as much as stated publicly that obstructionism will work again. Since everyone in the South knows from the headlines in local newspapers that the national government has said they can slow down, they'll run any school official who attempts to work with us right out of town. What all this adds up to is a signal from the Administration that it believes a nation of laws is no longer workable."

Another result of the new Administration's shift in policy was that most of the Justice Department's Civil Rights Division man-power was now tied down again on school-desegregation work and had no time to carry out what the former Administration had planned on—a broad push to enforce the equal-employment-oppor-tunity laws. In sum, the right to a decent education, to vote, and to earn a fair living all stood in jeopardy for Negroes. Moreover, the Department of Justice soon announced that it was expanding its civil-rights efforts to the North. While there was surely much to be done for black citizens there, the move was widely considered, inside the division and out, as being prompted by Southern politicians. Their hope, it was said, was that they could press the government to take widespread action in the North, with insufficient staff and hastily drawn plans, in a manner that would antagonize local citizens there and create pressure on Northern politicians to become allies of the Southerners on this issue.

Despite the obvious importance of the Administration's new policies, the change in course went largely unnoticed at the time by the general public. "The Administration is getting away with all this because the press has fallen down on the job terribly," the same man said. "The bare facts are usually reported—at least, the most unavoidable facts are—but there's been damned little in the way of any attempt to show what they add up to." That failure could largely be put down to the press's traditional observance of a "honeymoon" for any new President, whatever the cost to the public and to history.

The honeymoon finally ended around mid-summer, when the press resumed its duty of telling the public what was happening in the government and what it all meant. Apparently, high members of the Administration had imagined that they were not to be subjected to close scrutiny or criticism, for once the newspapers and news magazines again met their responsibilities, many officials began acting as if there was suddenly a conspiracy against the President. In a moment of high dudgeon, Mitchell called some members of the press "bastards" for their treatment of the Haynsworth case, and in a moment of calmer reflection he said, "The press in the large cities has not been sympathetic to us." Perhaps it had not, but then perhaps it had found little to be sympathetic about. Later, when the President addressed the people over television on the war in Vietnam, he seemed to be attempting to polarize the nation by appealing to "the silent majority" to stand up against the "small minority" that had expressed its opposition to the war during the Moratorium appeals of mid-October. What was left unsaid in that speech was soon said by Vice-President Agnew in his intemperate attacks on those millions who had demonstrated across the nation for peace. And when a few television commentators and their guests on panel discussions following the President's speech questioned it, Agnew—reportedly with the assistance of Attorney General Mitchell and Dean Burch, formerly a high adviser to Barry Goldwater in the 1964 Presidential race and now head of the Federal Communications Commission—set out to intimidate them in a way that had not been attempted since the days of Senator Joseph McCarthy. Dissent, it appeared, was to be stifled not just on the streets but in the mind.

Although the joint policy statement issued by Attorney General Mitchell and Secretary Finch early in July promised, in effect, that the guidelines on school desegregation would be relaxed under some circumstances, it was not until late August that the Administration showed how far it meant to go in specific cases. The first of these concerned school desegregation in Mississippi, the most doggedly resistant state in the South to integration. Like other Southern states, Mississippi had tried to circumvent government directives through freedom-of-choice plans. On July 3, 1969, the federal Court of Appeals for the Fifth Circuit, which covers much of the Old Confederacy, approved a motion filed earlier to reject these plans, and ordered that thirty-three Mississippi school boards involved formulate new plans in coöperation with H.E.W. for submission to the United States District Court for the Southern District of Mississippi by August 11th. H.E.W.'s Office of Education drafted plans, which were much the same as more than a hundred similar plans it had drawn up in recent months for other Southern school districts, and which, like the rest, were drafted with the aid of school officials from the districts involved. The District Court was scheduled to hold hearings on the matter on August 21st, and the final plans were to be put into effect no later than August 25th.

Things were proceeding much the same as they had in hundreds of other desegregation cases during the previous four years, until, on August 19th, Secretary Finch suddenly announced that he was withdrawing H.E.W.'s plans—affecting two hundred and twenty-two schools attended by a hundred and thirty-five thousand white and black youngsters—and that he had asked the court to allow Mississippi to postpone integration in the thirty-three school districts until December. In justification of this step, he said that "the administrative and logistical difficulties which must be encountered and met in the terribly short space of time remaining must surely, in my judgment, produce chaos, confusion, and a catastrophic educational setback." This was news to the people in H.E.W.'s Office of Education who had prepared the plans, to Dr. Gregory Anrig, who supervised their work, and to the lawyers in the Justice Department who were preparing to defend the plans in court; none of them had uncovered any major flaws. When Anrig submitted the plans to the District Court, he wrote that they were "educationally and administratively sound, both in terms of substance and in terms of timing."

The move was unprecedented, and so were several of the reactions to it. For fifteen years—ever since the Supreme Court's landmark decision in Brown v. Board of Education, which ordered the desegregation of all dual public-school systems—the federal government had been assisted in its efforts to carry out this order by the N.A.A.C.P. and its affiliate, the Legal Defense and Educational Fund, Inc., which had provided much of the money, the legal assistance, and the investigative work that were necessary to wage the fight on the scattered fronts that Southern tacticians periodically opened up. When the government, in the person of Assistant Attorney General Leonard, appeared before two of the three judges of the District Court, in Jackson, on August 25th to argue the case for Finch's motion, representatives of the Fund were there, too. One of them, Melvyn R. Leventhal, who represented several of the Negro plaintiffs in the case, rose and said to the two judges on the bench, "The United States government for the first time has demonstrated that it no longer seeks to represent the rights of Negro children." He then requested that the government be changed from plaintiff to defendant alongside the recalcitrant school boards. As expected, the motion was denied, but the break was on the record. Robert Moore, a Department of Justice lawyer who had spent years fighting for the civil-rights cause, sat slumped in a chair, and when Leonard asked the court to grant Finch's request Moore buried his face in his hands. Across the courtroom, lawyers for the school boards grinned delightedly at the rupture between their chief adversaries, and court attendants treated the Fund's spokesmen—particularly Norman Amaker, a Negro and its senior lawyer—with open contempt.

"Almost everyone agrees that this is the most crucial year in the long struggle over school desegregation," the *Times* observed in a lengthy and detailed news story on the Mississippi case at the time. Most other newspapers around the country, however, failed to report the matter fully, let alone take a stand on the spectacle of front-line troops in the civil-rights war being fired on by their own commanders. This led to another unprecedented action. On the day that Leonard was arguing the government's motion in Jackson, a lawyer in the Civil Rights Division back in the Department of Justice who realized that no public outcry was going to be raised outside the government circulated a note among the lawyers in the division stating that "recent events have caused some of us to question the future course of law enforcement and civil rights" and inviting all the lawyers below the supervisory level to attend a meeting the following night to decide "what action, if appropriate, we should take."

Because of the Department's entire case load—some sixty thousand suits pending every year—most of the lawyers in the Department were overworked. But few of them were as overworked, and as willingly overworked, as members of the Civil Rights Division. When Leonard first took office, he confessed that he couldn't believe that a hundred and six attorneys had been able to accomplish the astonishing amount of work the division had to its credit. Pollak, his predecessor, has explained that they accomplished it because of their deep commitment to civil rights and their willingness to work twelve- and fourteen-hour days for months on end to fulfill it. Of course, in private practice the same hours, even without the same dedication, could have brought these men two or three times the salaries they were getting. If the cause they were dedicated to was removed, they would have little reason to stay on and no reason at all to continue at the same exhausting pace.

These factors contributed to a remarkable response to the note. At quitting time the next afternoon, forty lawyers in the division—more than half the total number of lawyers below the supervisory level, and some were not in town that day—made their way to the apartment of one of their colleagues who lived in an integrated housing development in downtown Washington. When the meeting got under way, some of those present pleaded for mass resignations to protest the Administration's policies and bring the issue to the public's attention. But others argued that while this would certainly publicize the issue, it was a rather complicated one to explain to the ordinary citizen, and that in the end the revolt might hit the headlines for a few days and then be forgotten. If that happened, they went on, their resignations would bring the division's operations to a virtual halt and play into the hands of the segregationists. Finally, the group decided to draw up a list of their grievances and to present copies of it to Leonard, Mitchell, and the President. But most of the evening was devoted to discussions of a persistent rumor all of them had heard—that the Administration's backdown on civil rights had been a political concession to the South, and particularly to one of its leaders in the Senate, John Stennis, Democrat of Mississippi. Since he had led the fight for the Administration over the ABM program, some of those who attended the meeting wondered if the Department's action in Mississippi was, as former Attorney General Clark later suggested, a case of "Stennis cashing in his ABM chips."

JUSTICE

When Leonard returned from Mississippi and learned about the rebellion, he summoned his six section chiefs and explained to them that the decision in the civil-rights case there had indeed been made on the ground of political necessity. That undoubtedly would have been ample justification for a political figure, but, unlike Leonard, most of the lawyers in the division were not impressed by political justification for what they regarded as an illegal move by their government. That was the main factor but not the only one. According to Gary J. Greenberg, a senior trial attorney in the division who was later forced out because of his part in the affair and who wrote about it in the *Washington Monthly*,

> Certain other irritants played a part in creating an attitude among the attorneys which made "revolt" possible. There was Mr. Leonard himself, a politician from Wisconsin with no background in civil rights. . . . He was insensitive to the problems of black citizens and other minority-group victims of discrimination. . . . In marked contrast to the distinguished lawyers who preceded him in his job, Mr. Leonard lacks the intellectual equipment to deal with the legal problems that come across his desk.

In any event, the dissidents proceeded with their plan and drew up a four-hundred-word declaration, which was signed by sixty-five of the seventy-four non-supervisory lawyers in the division, and delivered copies to both Leonard and Mitchell on September 8th. "It is our fear that a policy which dictates that clear legal mandates are to be sacrificed to other considerations will seriously impair the ability of the Civil Rights Division, and ultimately the Judiciary, to attend to the faithful execution of the federal civil-rights statutes," the key paragraph in the statement asserted. "Such an impairment, by eroding public faith in our Constitutional institutions, is likely to damage the capacity of those institutions to accommodate conflicting interests and insure the full enjoyment of fundamental rights for all."

234

To this day, Mitchell has not responded, but ten days after receiving the statement, Leonard replied with one of his own, and warned that it was a final expression of official policy and that anyone who disagreed with it would have to resign. The dissidents fully disagreed with it and adamantly refused to resign. Leonard's reply was a fuzzy outline of how the Administration intended to desegregate public schools, and then it went on to admit that political pressure had indeed played a role in the Mississippi case and that in the future civil-rights actions would be taken not on the basis of the law but on the basis of "soundness." While that was a novel doctrine for the chief law-enforcement agency in the nation, it was scarcely one calculated to appeal to men who had devoted their lives to the law. No one, Greenberg observed, had questioned the Attorney General's right to choose between policy alternatives. "But in the matter of enforcing Constitutionally required school desegregation in Mississippi, the Attorney General had no discretion," he added. "He was bound to uphold the dictates of the law, an obligation that could not be squared with the decision to seek delay."

A week later, the rebels delivered to Leonard and Mitchell a new statement pointing out that the Attorney General obviously meant to continue the kind of policy that had been followed in the Mississippi case, "which, in our view, is inconsistent with clearly defined legal mandates." The following day, Mitchell testily told reporters that policy would be made by the Department, "not by a group of lawyers in the Civil Rights Division," and at a press conference after that Leonard warned that the revolt had to be ended at once. Then Leonard summoned Greenberg to his office, told him that it was the duty of the division's lawyers to defend the Department's Mississippi action in other courts, and demanded to know whether he would conduct himself accordingly.

"I said that I could not and would not," Greenberg recounted, and went on to tell how he had explained to Leonard that his responsibility was to enforce the law.

At that, Leonard demanded his resignation, saying, "Around here the Attorney General is the law."

While the revolt in the Department of Justice was going on, the Administration was suddenly attacked from another unexpected quarter—by the United States Commission on Civil Rights. That body was established by Congress in 1957 as an independent, bipartisan agency directed to advise the executive and legislative branches on civil-rights matters and to serve as a kind of clearing house for civil-rights information; it has no enforcement powers, except the indirect power stemming from its moral authority. Shortly after taking office, President Nixon selected Father Theodore M. Hesburgh, president of the University of Notre Dame, who had come to his attention, and received his public commendation, after taking a strong stand on campus disorder.

In a hundred-and-five-page report issued on September 12th, the Commission lashed out at the Administration on several fronts. "For the first time since the Supreme Court ordered schools desegregated, the federal government has requested in court a slowdown in the pace of desegregation," the Commission said. "Certainly those who have placed their faith in the processes of law cannot be encouraged." Among the Commission's specific findings were that "the new procedures and recent actions involving federal efforts to bring about school desegregation appear to be a major retreat in the struggle to achieve meaningful school desegregation"; that "the statistics purporting to show the present extent of school desegregation, which were contained in the July 3 joint statement of the Attorney General and the Secretary of the Department of Health, Education, and Welfare, give an overly optimistic, misleading, and inaccurate picture of the scope of desegregation actually achieved"; that "a number of federal judges in the South have been unsympathetic to the necessity of eliminating racial segregation in elementary and secondary schools . . . and have by their direct actions and tolerance of the actions of others significantly retarded the pace of school desegregation in the cases before their courts"; and that "emphasis upon court orders rather than administrative proceedings as the vehicle of federal efforts to desegregate schools can be expected to slow the pace of school desegregation." In conclusion, the Commission stated,

If this nation truly respected the rule of law, if it truly cherished each of its children, the last vestiges of segregated education would have disappeared years ago. Instead, segregation continues as the pattern, and not the exception, of education in many states. . . . While progress has been slow, the motion has been forward, and this is certainly no time to create the impression that we are turning back, but a time for pressing forward with vigor. This is certainly no time for giving aid and comfort, even unintentionally, to the laggards while penalizing those who have made commendable efforts to follow the law, even while disagreeing with it. If anything, this is the time to say that time is running out on us as a nation.

In a word, what we need most at this juncture of our history is a great positive statement regarding this central and crucial national problem, where once and for all our actions clearly would match the promises of our Constitution and Bill of Rights.

The Legal Defense and Educational Fund appealed the Mississippi case to the Supreme Court. While the decision was pending, Leonard stated, "If the Court were to order instant integration, nothing would change. Somebody would have to enforce that order." His explanation of why the order would not be enforced was that "there just are not enough bodies" in the Civil Rights Division. That rationale astonished former members of the division, who pointed out that there never had been enough people there to enforce every part of every law but that what could be enforced had to be enforced if the legal system was to have any meaning. In the end, the Supreme Court ordered exactly what Leonard had mentioned and had expected least of all—integration "at once"—by a unanimous vote.

The decision, which one paper called "a stinging setback for the Nixon Administration," was possibly a political blessing for it, since now Southerners would have to blame the Court, not the Administration, which could justifiably claim that it had done its best to slow down the course of integration. That conclusion seemed inescapable when Leonard responded to an appeal for advice—from the Court of Appeals for the Fifth Circuit—by asking that the school districts involved, not H.E.W., be allowed to draw up desegregation plans and the timetable for carrying them out. Pollak, the former head of the Civil Rights Division, said, "That can only be interpreted as another slowdown."

For its own part, the Circuit Court was willing to accept the government's move for a slowdown, and set the fall of 1970 as the date for carrying out the Supreme Court's order. However, several parents of children attending schools in the area concerned appealed to the Supreme Court. The Department of Justice opposed them and defended the lower court's decision. Twelve days later, the Supreme Court unanimously reversed the Circuit Court and set February 1, 1970, as the deadline for "complete student desegregation."

A couple of days later, Cary H. Hall, a native of Georgia whom President Nixon had made Southern director of H.E.W. a month earlier, publicly stated that "the courts, not the government" had demanded desegregation. Charles Morgan, Jr., the Southern director of the American Civil Liberties Union, found the remark distressingly funny. "After fifteen years, he should have an understanding of what the law is," Morgan said. "In this country, at least up until this point in time, the federal courts have been considered a part of the government."

It was apparent that the Nixon Administration would have to rely on men, like Leonard and Hall, who were insensitive to social and legal problems to carry out its policies. It was also apparent that the Administration had concluded it not only had the support of a strong majority of white Americans but that black Americans either would not take to the streets again in protest or that, if they did, they could be restrained or forcibly put down. During the fall of 1969, members of the Administration repeatedly stated in public that the corner had been turned and that, as White House aide Moynihan confidently asserted, black riots were now a thing of the past. Those who shared this view took comfort from the way the summer had passed with no serious outbursts in urban slums. But others who looked at the persistent lack of equality between whites and blacks in education, housing, jobs, health care, nutrition, and police treatment, at the continuing resistance of white citizens to a fair share of abundance for black citizens, and at the likelihood that the threat of a Wallace candidacy in 1972 would drive President Nixon further and further to the right were not so optimistic. "The cool new situation may . . . seem encouraging to whites, but it can hardly seem so to blacks," Reston observed in the *Times* as the summer ended. "And the real lesson of the years of violence is that the black ten per cent of our population neither intends nor has to let the majority rest on token achievement, congratulate itself on loud intentions, or proceed at the snail's pace of white moderation. So those who may be tempted to think one cooler summer means the corner has been turned and the need for action is past are flirting tragically with something worse than the fire next time."

By this point, Mitchell's behavior began to suggest that he may have been out for far bigger game than a few million Southern votes for President Nixon in 1972. The appointment of a conservative to be Chief Justice and the choice of a Southern conservative to be Associate Justice of the Supreme Court seemed like sufficient payment to the South for its electoral favors in 1968. Softening the guidelines, introducing a revision of the Voting Rights Act, and switching the

government's action on school desegregation from effective withdrawal of federal funds to ineffective court procedures amounted to
the kind of overpayment that indicated the President and the Attorney General perhaps had another goal in mind—the most managed revision of American political alliances in our time or any
other. Since the South had voted Republican for a President, it followed that the South might well vote Republican for other officeholders. Of course, that would sooner or later compel Southern
Democrats in Congress to switch parties, as the leading Republican
in the South, Senator Thurmond, had already done. If the rewards
were great enough—large numbers of patronage jobs and large sums
of money in the form of new government installations and new
government defense contracts in the South—some of them might be
persuaded to make the switch before the congressional elections in
1970 and 1972. And if the rewards were even greater—suspension
of the seniority system in Congress to allow Democrats-turned-
Republican to retain their seniority and thus their committee chairmanships—the Republican Party could gain control of both the
Senate and the House.

To be sure, the seniority system is a deeply entrenched tradition,
but it is only a tradition, and a caucus of Republican members in
each house could choose to suspend it, at least as far as their party
was concerned, by deciding to make the length of time one has
served in Congress the basis for seniority, not, as now, the length of
time one has served in a given party in Congress. While that would
deprive some Republicans who had accumulated seniority within
the Party of certain chairmanships, which would be retained by
former Democrats with longer service, many Republicans might well
be willing to make such a deal in order to take over powerful sub-
committees that they could not hope to gain control of as long as the
Democrats ran Congress. Although Southern Democrats are probably not sufficiently threatened by Republican opponents to defect
right now, the Republicans might easily pick up a few Senate seats

in the next election, and then the switch of only a handful of Democratic senators—headed, say, by a couple of Southern leaders who shared the President's views and were convinced that the only way to save the country was for them to join him—could give the Republicans the votes to organize the Senate. And once that happened, the House would surely follow. If this was the Administration's strategy, and if it worked, the Republican Party—by then an implacably conservative majority—might keep control of Congress indefinitely.

On July 6, 1969, Senator Tydings rose on the floor of the Senate to remind his colleagues that the President had issued his Message on Crime in the District of Columbia soon after taking office, and that he had promised an immediate legislative prescription to cure the infectious spread of crime in Washington. "Now, nearly half a year later, Congress has not received a single local crime bill from the Administration," Tydings said, and added, "We have had no bill on narcotics, no bill on the courts, no bill on tightening bail procedures."

Once again, the action promised by the Administration had not been forthcoming because, once again, it was divided over the course it should follow. Lower-echelon members of the Department of Justice who had long wanted to employ stern measures to counter crime had had little say in policy matters under previous Administrations, but Mitchell and Kleindienst were said to be listening to them more and more. At the start of the new Administration's deliberations on this subject, the role of the Office of Criminal Justice had somewhat balanced the role of those who were known as "hardliners." As it functioned under the Democrats, that office represented all law-enforcement viewpoints—those of the prosecutor, the defense attorney, the judge, the policeman, the probation and parole officer, the Constitutional expert, the academic specialist, and the bureaucrat—in the hope that the tug and pull among these factions would create a new outlook that would be as vigilant in safeguarding a defendant's rights as in prosecuting his wrongs.

The new Administration announced when it came into office that it was going to upgrade and expand this effort, and to accomplish that the office was placed under the personal supervision of Associate Deputy Attorney General Santarelli. Within a few months, not a single person who had been associated with the office at the time of the inauguration was still around, and the principal emphasis of the office as it was reconstituted represented a single viewpoint—the prosecutor's.

Shortly after Tydings' attack, the Administration finally sent to Congress the anti-crime package it had settled on after nearly six months. The first item in the package was a bill that called for an overhaul of the federal court system in the District, including an enlarged budget and staff for the legal-aid agency serving poor defendants, an expanded bail agency, and more job counselling and supervision for offenders on parole or probation—most of which had repeatedly been recommended by the previous Administration, and by the Administration before it. But some of the proposals were new, including one that allowed a federal judge to impose a life sentence on anyone convicted of three felonies, one that allowed a policeman with a search warrant to enter any premises unannounced, one that imposed a mandatory five-year prison sentence and a five-thousand-dollar fine on anyone who jumped bail, and one that called for preventive detention. Although this last proposal was expected, some of its details came as a surprise. The preventive-detention measure stated that any defendant who was a narcotics addict charged with a violent crime, or who was charged with, but not necessarily convicted of, committing two or more violent crimes, or who was charged with committing a "dangerous" crime like robbing a bank

or selling drugs could be sent to jail for up to sixty days. This could
be done after a hearing, to be held within five days of arrest, if the
defendant gave the presiding judge the impression that there was
"substantial probability" he was guilty as charged and would be a
danger to the community if released.

Senator Ervin, the Senate's leading Constitutional expert, said
that since the measure suspended the traditional presumption of innocence it was "un-Constitutional and smacks of a police state," but
Attorney General Mitchell said that the high rate of crime among
defendants out on bail made such legislation imperative.

The proposal was questionable on several grounds. For one, the
best statistics available indicated that defendants out on bail committed only six per cent of the total crimes reported. Furthermore,
the premise that judges could determine by way of a hearing
whether a defendant was a danger to the community was not supported by any evidence. Extensive studies of the parole system have
demonstrated that even when a parole is granted on the basis of a
thorough investigation of an inmate's background and character by
trained parole specialists—a far more detailed investigation to base a
decision on, of course, than anything a hearing could provide on a
defendant five days after his arrest—there is no way of knowing
whether the parolee will go out and commit another crime.

Studies have shown that the longer a defendant is out on bail the
greater is the likelihood that he will commit another crime, with the
highest incidence of criminal behavior beginning sixty days after
release. Under the proposed law, the longest a person could be preventively detained was sixty days, and yet the average delay between arrest and trial in the District of Columbia was more than
three hundred days. On this point, Senator Ervin later observed, "The
need for preventive-detention legislation concededly rests on the inability to provide speedy trials for criminal suspects. It is an attempt
to compensate for a progressive breakdown in our law-enforcement
structure and especially our overburdened courts. . . . The required

full adversary hearing and the need to make informed decisions on predictability would, in many instances, take as much time as would actual trial of the principal case. . . . Court congestion would get worse. Delays in criminal trials, now running ten to twelve months, would increase. . . . Thus, we have the curious situation where our failure to give defendants and the public their Constitutional right to speedy trial has spawned legislation which will further burden the judges and make speedy trials even less likely than at present."

While the bill incorporated various procedures that had to be followed before a defendant could be jailed, apparently as a means of demonstrating that care had been taken to observe due process, the reliance upon a judge's determination that there was "substantial probability" that the person committed the offense he was charged with constituted the greatest violation of due process conceivable, since its effect was to convict a person without a trial. The bill also set down a formula to enable a judge to decide whether some intermediate form of detention—such as freedom during the day to hold down a job and imprisonment during the night to keep temptation out of reach—would prevent someone from criminally preying on society. At the same time, however, the bill made this impracticable by failing to provide staff and funds so that partial restraint of this sort would be possible.

The Administration's proposal was also open to question, this time by Republicans, in terms of the political philosophy it suggested, for it set out to do what Republicans had always attacked Democrats for trying to do—that is, it attempted to reform one part of society by changing one part of the social system instead of allowing the play of contending forces to work things out; moreover, the part of the system that the Administration wanted to change was the Constitution, which even the wildest reformers on the liberal side had never contemplated. Finally, the measure was almost certain to ultimately defeat the aim that the Attorney General and his staff had in mind when they drafted the bill. Under the Bail Reform Act, defendants in federal non-capital cases could not be denied bail unless the presiding judge had reason to believe that they would not show up for trial. Many federal judges obeyed the law conscientiously, but many others, concerned about letting dangerous-looking defendants loose, chose to set high bail on the pretext that they were unlikely to appear in court voluntarily. Such a move was difficult to test on appeal, because it was difficult, if not impossible, to demonstrate what a given judge's motives had been. And if a case of this sort was appealed, a decision on it was bound to be limited to that case alone. However, once a preventive-detention statute was enacted, it would immediately present a Constitutional issue and would ultimately lead to a Constitutional ruling. And, whatever the makeup of the Supreme Court, it was widely believed that the law would be found un-Constitutional. In the end, then, the authors of the measure would be worse off than if they had let federal judges go on imposing high bail, pretext or no pretext, to keep felons and likely felons off the streets.

Four days after the Department of Justice sent the court-reorganization and preventive-detention bills to Congress, it tossed a new narcotics-control bill into the legislative hopper, thus meeting the rest of Senator Tydings' demand. The measure, which was largely a codification of existing laws covering drugs, was somewhat more punitive than the ones already on the books. Although it asked Congress for more funds to finance research into methods of preventing and curing drug addiction, its over-all emphasis was on punishment. The outcry against the bill was immediate and intense on the part of experts who felt that the experience of the past thirty years had been utterly ignored by the Administration when the bill was drafted.

Dr. Melvin H. Weinswig, director of the Drug Abuse Institute at Butler University, commented, "This type of legislation is fine for letting the politicians make a lot of noise, but it will not reduce the drug-abuse problem." And Dr. Vincent P. Dole, of Rockefeller University, said, "This is the simplistic approach. It's the attitude that when a system is not working you just stiffen the penalties." The objections to the bill were not confined to outsiders. H.E.W.'s senior health officers and experts on the effects of drugs were told generally what the bill would contain, but they were not allowed to see it before it was announced publicly. Once they did, most of them came out against it, and one of them sent Secretary Finch a confidential memorandum urging the Department to officially oppose the measure. But it had been approved by the President, and Finch was obliged to ignore their objections. As it later emerged, the emphasis on punishment had been insisted on by top White House aides, without consultation with any specialists in the field, apparently because, one disgruntled H.E.W. official said, it was "all part of the law-and-order theme."

It was also another example of the pragmatists being at odds with reality where the welfare of the nation was concerned. According to a study made by the New York State Narcotics Addiction Control Commission, juries across the country convicted less than one per cent of those who were arrested for possessing or using drugs because the penalties were already too harsh. "This bill may seem like smart politics to those public-relations operators in the White House," an attorney in the Department of Justice said at the time. "But, of course, they didn't stop to consider the effect that a law like this would have on our society in general—especially on young people, whose respect for the law is so vital right now. Once you openly invite them to flout one important law, you invite them to flout all laws. And once the law goes, everything else goes with it."

Subsequently, the Administration suggested modifications of the most stringent penalties in its proposal. Attorney General Mitchell said not long ago that this had been contemplated from the outset, pending further study, and blamed "the press" and "a bunch of kookie doctors" in H.E.W. for misrepresenting the situation, which, he added, had been clearly set forth in his letter of transmittal accompanying the original bill. To be sure, the letter asked Congress to "devote special attention" to the sentences proposed. But at the same time it concluded, "Legislation such as this is long overdue. We recommend its prompt enactment."

A few days after the Department of Justice sent the last of its anti-crime bills to Congress, Santarelli testified before the Senate Subcommittee to Investigate Juvenile Delinquency on another crime issue—the control of firearms. The subcommittee, which had led the fight in Congress to place some sensible control on the ownership and use of guns, was considering a bill that would require gun owners to register their guns by obtaining a federal license, which would cost nothing and would be good for five years. Most of the evidence available indicated that probably no other single law would do more to cut down the commission of serious crimes than a law of this kind. For example, the chief counsel for Toledo testified before the subcommittee that since his city made permits for handguns mandatory the homicide rate there had fallen by nearly two-thirds. But, at the same time, probably no other single law would cause such political repercussions from millions of citizens who had been persuaded that *any* control of firearms was merely the first step in a conspiracy to disarm them altogether. When Congress was considering a comparatively modest gun-control bill following the assassinations of Dr. King and Senator Kennedy, Nixon was privately asked to support it and publicly refused. Now he refused to support the broader proposal, because, Santarelli told the subcommittee, it "would constitute an unwarranted invasion into the province of state and local governments" and would be too expensive to administer.

Four days later, the government's own Violence Commission released a report on firearms in the United States. "Firearms are a primary instrument of injury and death in American crime," the report stated, and then described in detail how primary they were. For example, two out of three homicides were committed with guns, and although the number of non-firearms murders had risen by ten per cent since 1963, the number of firearms murders had risen by nearly fifty per cent. Moreover, in 1963, thirteen per cent of all serious assaults had been committed with guns, whereas by 1968 the figure had risen to twenty-three per cent. One out of three robberies involved guns, and in that one-third the fatality rate for victims was four times as high as it was in robberies where other weapons were used. Only a quarter of the ninety million guns privately owned in the country were handguns, but they were used in half of all homicides committed by any means, and in three-fourths of all homicides in which guns of one kind or another figured. And in the case of assaults and robberies committed in large cities, if any gun was used it was invariably a handgun.

A popular belief among gun-lovers was that firearms were essential to one's self-defense at home—a belief that was endlessly played on by the weapons industry's leading lobbyist, the National Rifle Association, which ran a monthly column in its periodical, the *American Rifleman* (devoted equally to handguns and long guns) on cases where homeowners and store proprietors fought it out with intruders. The magazine never pointed out, as the Commission proceeded to, that while exceedingly few home robberies or burglaries resulted in injury or death to the occupants, whether they were armed or unarmed, the chances of being injured or killed were a good deal higher if one appeared with a gun. Nor did the N.R.A. mention that in only two per cent of such intrusions were householders able to scare away or capture criminals in the home by the use of guns. It also failed to point out the comparison between the opportunities for self-defense and the opportunities for accidental death and murder when guns were kept in the home. A large percentage of the country's twenty-three thousand accidental deaths by firearms each year occurred in the home, and over eighty per cent of all murders committed with guns were committed within families or among acquaintances, often in the home. Then the Commission stated,

Half of the nation's 60 million households possess at least one gun, and the number of guns owned by private citizens is rising rapidly. During the first half of this century, about 10 million firearms were added to the civilian firearms supply in each decade. In the decade since 1958, however, nearly 30 million guns have been added to the civilian stockpile. Moreover, the sharpest increases have occurred in the last five years—a period of urban riots and sharply increasing crime rates. Annual rifle and shotgun sales have doubled since 1963. Annual handgun sales have quadrupled. . . . After the 1967 Detroit riots, for example, gun sales skyrocketed: Detroit issued four times as many handgun permits in 1968 as it did in 1965, and a nearby predominantly white suburb issued five times as many permits.

Lending impetus to the arms buildup are the exhortations of extremist groups, both black and white. In their speeches and publications, leaders of these groups urge their members to buy firearms and be prepared to use them against the "enemy." Neighborhood protective associations have proliferated and have sometimes come to share the fears of the right-wing paramilitary groups, with the result that firearms are now being stockpiled in homes as well as "in the hills." A new wave of American vigilanteism could result from these activities. Further, black extremist organizations urge their members to obtain firearms for neighborhood and home defense, and sometimes for guerrilla warfare and terrorist activities as well. Ironically, extremist groups, regardless of race, are remarkably alike in their attitudes toward firearms and their opposition to firearms control.

On June 13, 1966, Chief Justice Earl Warren delivered the Supreme Court's five-to-four decision in the case of Miranda v. Arizona.

Speaking for the majority, he said, "When an individual is taken into custody or otherwise deprived of his freedom by the authorities and is subjected to questioning, the privilege against self-incrimination is jeopardized," and, to guarantee protection for the privilege, the Court had decided that any suspect who met these conditions "must be warned prior to any questioning that he has the right to remain silent, that anything he says can be used against him in a court of law, that he has the right to the presence of an attorney, and that if he cannot afford an attorney one will be appointed for him prior to any questioning if he so desires." Actually, all the Miranda decision did was assure to the uninformed and the poor the same rights that reasonably knowledgeable and prosperous citizens had asserted all along. But bitter and persistent attacks—originated in large measure by policemen and prosecutors who had failed to do their jobs properly in the first place, and then taken up by the right wing as a handy weapon to belabor the "Warren Court" with for a number of its decisions—finally convinced most conservatives and even many moderates that the Court had done something wildly radical.

Finally, resentment against the Court reached such inflated proportions that Congress, under the leadership of Senator McClellan, passed a law overturning the Miranda ruling. Since 1803, when the Court decided Marbury v. Madison, the Supreme Court had been accepted as the final arbiter of what the Constitution meant, and it had been assumed from that point on that Congress could not legislatively overturn any of its rulings. It was also assumed that Congress's attempt to do that in the Miranda case would be rejected by the Court as un-Constitutional and a usurpation of the judiciary's rights. On this assumption, which was widely shared by legal experts, Attorney General Clark refused to allow the McClellan law to be used by the Department of Justice. Fearing that if it was followed hundreds of convictions obtained by the Department would later be thrown out by the Court, he ordered all government agents and prosecutors to continue using the Miranda rule.

For several months after the new Administration took over, Clark's order was allowed to stand. Then, on June 11th, Assistant Attorney General Wilson, the head of the Criminal Division, sent a memorandum to all the lawyers in the Department informing them that while the Miranda rule should continue to be observed, if someone in the Department happened to violate it unintentionally the case involved would still be prosecuted. When the time came for a test before the Supreme Court, he went on, the Department would try to convince it that the McClellan doctrine was Constitutional and that the Court should reverse itself on this issue. To the astonishment of both Wilson's and Mitchell's predecessors, this order was reportedly given without the approval of the Attorney General, and without even consulting him. Mitchell was so preoccupied with White House business that he had instructed his subordinates to bother him only with matters that they could not handle on their own. Apparently, Wilson decided that his move—a high-policy matter, by any measure—was not important enough to bother the Attorney General with and proceeded on his own.

Although Mitchell was reported to have been surprised as much by Wilson's initiative as by his new policy, he defended the latter shortly afterward when he appeared as a witness before the House Select Committee on Crime. The Department no longer felt bound by the Miranda ruling, he testified, and added, "If a federal official inadvertently fails to give a full warning, the Department of Justice now believes that the confession may still be a voluntary confession and should be presented to the court as evidence." That position, which was akin to claiming that ignorance of the law *was* an excuse, constituted an astonishing legal doctrine, for it made inadvertency the test of whether someone's Constitutional rights had been observed. And, quite practically, it meant that any officer who was too lazy or too incompetent to do his job properly could now fall back on age-old techniques of eliciting a confession from a suspect and then say that he had inadvertently neglected to give the Miranda warning.

Another witness before the House Committee, James Vorenberg, who had been the first head of the Office of Criminal Justice and later director of the Crime Commission under President Johnson, was outraged by the Attorney General's testimony, and after listening to it he took the witness stand and pointed out that the Miranda rule affected less than one per cent of all criminal activity, adding, "It is simply a hoax that is being perpetrated on people to say that if you will fiddle with the Bill of Rights you will change crime." Like the preventive-detention and narcotics-control proposals, which, he added, were "easy, cheap solutions," the latest move was a "diversionary sideshow that is undermining the drive for real change in our system of justice." And Vorenberg went on to say, "At the local level, everything this Administration has said is being interpreted to mean 'Don't bother about prevention or research into the real causes of crime. Don't bother about improving the bail system when you can have preventive detention. Don't bother with any of the real—and difficult—solutions.'"

Far and away the most ambitious attempt to fiddle with the Bill of Rights under the stewardship of any Attorney General had been undertaken secretly in the Department earlier that year—in the form of a study to determine whether that document, and especially the Fifth Amendment's guarantee that "no person . . . shall be compelled in any criminal case to be a witness against himself," should be amended. This guarantee, which dates back to the time of Charles II, lies at the heart of the difference between the inquisitorial system of justice used by totalitarian governments and the accusatorial system of justice used by democratic governments. If the Fifth Amendment could be altered—or, as some would prefer, abolished altogether—the safeguards laid down by the Supreme Court in recent years to protect the rights of defendants in criminal

actions would, of course, be eliminated at a single stroke. But somewhere along the way during the spring the study was, as Attorney
General Mitchell said recently, "put on the back burner." According to one lawyer who has left the Department, the decision to put
it there was apparently made at about the time Warren Earl Burger
was chosen as Chief Justice. That choice, which James Reston described as "probably the most obvious indication of the turn to the
right" by the Administration, was made on the recommendation of
Attorney General Mitchell, who had turned down the President's
suggestion that he take the job himself.

The Attorney General had ample opportunity to learn where Burger stood on the crime issue, for Judge Burger had repeatedly and
publicly condemned his own court—the District of Columbia Court
of Appeals—for its decisions on rules of evidence and on the Fourth
and Fifth Amendments and for "coddling" criminals. In a symposium held the year before at the Center for the Study of Democratic
Institutions, in Santa Barbara, California, Judge Burger had questioned the inviolability of the presumption of innocence, trial by
jury, and the privilege against self-incrimination. On the last point,
he told the members of the symposium, "Certainly you have heard
—and judges have said—that one should not convict a man out of his
own mouth. The fact is that we establish responsibility and liability
and we convict in all the areas of *civil* litigation out of the mouth of
the defendant." The statement ignored a couple of points—for one,
that most civil litigation is between citizens, not between one citizen
with limited resources and a government with comparatively un-
limited resources, and, for another, that no one who loses a civil
suit faces imprisonment or execution.

"With Burger heading the Court, there may not be any need to
cut down the Fifth Amendment," the lawyer who revealed the secret
study said afterward. "Now it may be allowed to atrophy."

Of course, Chief Justice Burger would have only one vote, but that could be enough to change the five-to-four liberal majority on the Court to a five-to-four conservative majority. And the additional vote of a "strict constructionist" like Haynsworth—that is, one who construes the law, if not ethics, strictly in favor of the status quo— to fill Fortas's seat—would give the conservatives a six-to-three edge. Even if a couple of justices, such as Byron R. White, who usually sided with the conservatives moved somewhat to the left to preserve judicial balance, President Nixon was apt to have two more places on the bench to fill before he left office—those now occupied by Justices William O. Douglas and Hugo L. Black, both of whom are old and increasingly infirm—and there was no reason to doubt that he would find suitably conservative men for them. If this, along with the Southern strategy for taking over Congress, worked out, the government would be turned overnight into an unshakable monolith of conservatism.

When Congress approved McClellan's proposal to legislatively reverse the Miranda decision—by passing the Omnibus Crime Control and Safe Streets Act of 1968—it also approved his proposal to permit federal, state, and local prosecutors, with the permission of judges in their jurisdictions, to plant taps and bugs on anyone who had committed, was committing, or was about to commit crimes punishable by a year or more in prison, or on anyone who was even remotely connected with such suspects. Legal authorities were almost unanimous in their opposition to the new law, as well as in their belief that the Supreme Court would promptly strike it down. Again, however, that belief was based on the assumption that President Johnson would appoint the new Chief Justice, and it did not take into account Justice Fortas's resignation after President Nixon's inauguration.

Quite apart from the debate over the Constitutionality of the new law, many top law-enforcement people felt that it was an ineffectual weapon to add to the war on crime, because the manpower it required could be far better used to augment more ordinary efforts to combat crime. Many police officers, on the other hand, claimed that surveillance of this kind was the only way they would ever get at members of organized-crime rings, but others pointed out that state and local police and prosecutors had covertly been tapping and bugging gangsters for years without very remarkable success. Fred Vinson, head of the Criminal Division under Clark, suggested that if these proponents of electronic surveillance really wanted to break up organized crime they would start with the four hundred thousand men who manned their police forces. "Of course, most policemen on the beat know who the minor drug peddlers are, know who's running the numbers, and know who the guys on the lower rungs of the mob are," he explained. "If city officials seriously wanted to wipe out syndicated crime, they would look to their police departments."

A month after Attorney General Mitchell told members of the Senate Judiciary Committee during his confirmation hearings that he meant to use wiretapping, he announced that for the first time in the history of the Department of Justice taps had been placed (legally, that is) on telephones used by members of La Cosa Nostra. No one was surprised by that, but a lot of people were surprised some time later when it emerged that in the course of the F.B.I.'s routine tapping of foreign embassies (one of the worst-kept secrets in Washington) agents had overheard and recorded conversations between embassy officials and several men who were appealing federal convictions—among them Cassius Clay, who had been convicted of violating the selective-service laws. Since these taps had been used before McClellan got the system legalized, Clay's lawyers demanded that they be permitted to see the transcripts of the taps to determine whether any evidence against their client had been obtained by illegal means.

On March 10th, the Supreme Court, in a five-to-three decision, ruled in another case that the government had to let anyone under indictment for, or anyone convicted of, committing a federal crime have access to transcripts obtained from illegal taps. From this, the Department of Justice hastily concluded that it was faced with the choice of either dropping the case against Clay (and, it later emerged, against the Chicago demonstrators as well) or admitting that it had tapped foreign embassies' telephones. The Department asked the Court for a rehearing on the matter. "We're not worried about what's in the law—it's the fact that they [the taps] were there," Assistant Attorney General Wilson told Fred Graham, of the *Times*. Then, apparently with a perfectly straight face, Wilson added, "We don't want the Communists to know we had them tapped." On March 24th, the Supreme Court rejected the Department's motion for a rehearing, and stated that it had ruled only on illegal eavesdropping in ordinary criminal cases but had never taken a position on whether taps in the name of national security were illegal. In a tart opinion, Justice Potter Stewart wrote, "One might suppose that all of this should be entirely clear to any careful reader of the Court's opinion."

But the problem of illegal wiretapping came up again early in June, during a hearing on Clay's appeal, when an F.B.I. agent testified that while he was assigned to the bureau's Atlanta office he had been in charge of a tap on Dr. Martin Luther King, Jr. The agent stated that he had conducted the surveillance until May, 1965, when he was transferred from his post in Atlanta, and that he understood it had been continued by the F.B.I. after that—in fact, until a few days before King was assassinated. The agent did not know why the taps were used, but could only say that they had been installed shortly after King attacked the F.B.I. for assigning Southern, rather than Northern, agents to civil-rights cases in the South.

When this testimony was published, former Attorney General
Clark immediately announced that he had never authorized the
F.B.I. to conduct such surveillance, and added, "The implication
that people [in the Department] thought Dr. King was a security
threat is outrageous." Since President Johnson had issued an executive order on June 30, 1965, forbidding all federal wiretapping and
bugging except in national-security cases, and then only with the
express approval of the Attorney General, and since Clark had been
Attorney General during much of the period King had been tapped
and yet had not given anyone permission to tap him, it appeared
that the F.B.I. had willfully violated a Presidential directive.

The F.B.I. refused at first to comment on the matter, except to
refer reporters to Hoover's testimony before the House subcommittee
on appropriations for the Department of Justice between 1965 and
1968. In each of those years, he informed the subcommittee about
the precise number of taps conducted by the F.B.I., all of which,
he stated, were "in the internal-security category," and all of which
were authorized in writing beforehand by the Attorney General.
Someone had to be lying.

In a column in the Washington *Evening Star* entitled "It Is Time
for J. Edgar Hoover to Go," Carl Rowan supported Clark's version
of the story. The next day, Clyde A. Tolson, the associate director
of the F.B.I. and Hoover's putative heir, wrote the *Star* to complain
about the "malicious article" and to reveal that the tap on Dr. King
had been authorized by Attorney General Kennedy. The day after
the letter appeared, the *Star* also published an exclusive interview
with Hoover, who said that Kennedy had proposed tapping King to
see if he was a Communist or a Marxist, and that he had two memoranda in his office to prove it. This story seemed extremely dubious
to many observers, and Katzenbach, who had been Attorney General
Kennedy's deputy and his successor, told the press that Hoover's account was misleading in a number of important respects. Several
people who were close to Kennedy during that period explained

that Hoover had begun to importune him for permission to place taps on King two weeks after Kennedy took office, and had continued with these requests persistently for two years. Finally, Kennedy, in exasperation over Hoover's conspiratorial belief that everyone who attacked the existing system was a Communist, let him go ahead with the taps to show him, once and for all, that he was wrong about King.

"But to say or imply that this tap was the original conception of Robert Kennedy—that he was the moving force in this situation—or that he had any doubt whatsoever about Dr. King's integrity or loyalty is false," Katzenbach said. That left hanging the question of Attorney General Kennedy's integrity if he had permitted a wiretap to be placed on a man he believed to be above suspicion.

In any event, former Attorney General Clark described Hoover's insistence that he had been a reluctant eavesdropper on Dr. King as "deceptive," and added, "He repeatedly requested me to authorize an F.B.I. tap on Dr. King while I was Attorney General. The last of these requests, none of which was granted, came two days before the murder of Dr. King."

A couple of days after the *Star* interview with Hoover was published, President Nixon was asked about the affair during a press conference, and he answered that he had personally asked Hoover if he had ever placed a tap without authority. "I found that it had always been approved by the Attorney General, as Mr. Hoover testified in 1964 and 1965," the President said. He did not say anything about 1966, 1967, and 1968—when, according to the F.B.I.'s own agent, a tap had been used on Dr. King and when, according to the Attorney General during that period, there had been no current authorization for such a tap. Unaccountably, none of the reporters present asked him about those years. The F.B.I. director, President Nixon said, had his "complete confidence."

At the height of the contention over the F.B.I.'s taps on Dr. King, the Justice Department revealed that taps had been installed by the

F.B.I. on the Chicago demonstrators who had been indicted for conspiring to incite a riot during the Convention. To head off a demand by the defendants' attorneys that the Department release the transcripts of the taps so that they could determine whether any evidence detrimental to their clients had been obtained by illegal means, the Department filed a brief with the federal court in Chicago. It was one of the most unusual documents in the history of American law. In it, the Attorney General asserted that the government did not have to abide by the restrictions laid down in the new wiretapping law—principally, that a federal judge had to approve a tap or bug placed by a federal agent—if there was reason to believe that the subject intended to "attack and subvert the government by unlawful means." (Presumably, the "unlawful means" meant the charge that the demonstrators had conspired to incite a riot in Chicago, which violated the 1968 anti-riot statute, but that law, though it had not yet been tested in the courts, was widely believed to be unlawful itself.) He also asserted that the government had this power despite the Fourth Amendment's prohibition against "unlawful search and seizure," because it was the President's overriding duty to protect the nation's security. Nothing was said about the President's oath to "preserve, protect, and defend the Constitution of the United States." Of course, the Attorney General's claim that the particular interests of a particular President at a particular time were paramount to the law was another way of saying that the country would henceforth be ruled by men, not laws.

The lawyers for the demonstrators immediately demanded Mitchell's resignation, arguing, "For the first time in American history, a member of the President's Cabinet has publicly—and proudly—stated that he has, in open violation of his oath of office, taken the law into his own hands." And the American Civil Liberties Union filed a suit in the United States District Court for the District of Columbia asking for an injunction against electronic surveillance of political demonstrators and for criminal prosecution of Hoover and Mitchell. In its brief, the A.C.L.U. stated, "By announcing a policy of unfettered executive power to determine possible danger presented to the nation by dissenting persons or groups, they have assumed judicial, penal, and other regulatory authority over the [Constitutionally] protected activities of all dissenting Americans."

The alarm expressed by moderates and liberals over Attorney General Mitchell's policies—especially by moderate and liberal lawyers, who were more aware than most citizens of the importance to society of the legal safeguards that these policies threatened—finally led him to respond publicly to what he called "the most virulent criticism." He chose the annual convention of the American Bar Association, held in Dallas in mid-August, as his forum. After thanking the association for giving him the "opportunity to reflect upon and evaluate our recent progress," the Attorney General observed that while it was "undeniable that some of our new concepts have areas of error which ought to be corrected," such "minor adjustments do not imply an abandonment of a principle but, rather, a dedication to making that principle work." These adjustments were his responsibility, he went on, and in making them he intended to follow "the ancient common-law guide of the 'reasonable man,' whom our forefathers established as the enlightened compromiser in a pluralistic society," which would enable him "to negotiate a practical, middle-of-the-road solution." But, he hastened to warn, the job would be especially difficult because of "the misrepresentation, the posturing, and the extravagant rhetoric of the last few years."

Aware that members of the audience were most concerned about the Administration's wiretapping, preventive-detention, and civil-rights policies, the Attorney General devoted the rest of his speech to those topics. In the case of wiretapping, he said, "the basic Constitutional and moral controversy stems from the conflict between the individual citizen's right to privacy in his home and in his office versus the individual citizen's right to demand that his government properly investigate those persons whose criminal activities pose a substantial danger to the general welfare and thus to the personal security of each citizen." The key words were "versus" and "properly." The first assumed that the government was unable to assure its citizens' personal security unless it was free to invade their privacy with devices that, unlike search warrants, did not simply permit the collection of criminal evidence but recorded *all* of their conversations, whether or not they were pertinent to an investigation. Critics of secret surveillance by the government, as Mitchell certainly knew, had long maintained that there was no evidence to sustain this conclusion, and that individual privacy was such a precious part of freedom that a pervasive invasion of that privacy could be countenanced only if overwhelming evidence of its need and its efficacy was demonstrated. In their opinion, neither need nor efficacy had even been presented, let alone proved. And the Attorney General's use of the word "properly" assumed that it was possible, given man's weaknesses, to conduct these secret investigations ethically, which the government's own misuse of taps on Dr. King, the Chicago demonstrators, and only God and Hoover knew who else flatly disproved.

Continuing, the Attorney General pointed out that although the Fourth Amendment protected citizens "against unreasonable searches and seizures," that protection had never been considered absolute. To define its limits, he went back to the Constitution's declaration that its authors' purpose was to "promote the general welfare and secure the blessings of liberty." Then he said, "It is undeniable that organized crime presents a substantial threat to our 'general welfare.'" Of course, with equal logic, he could have concluded that government wiretapping and bugging presented a substantial

261

threat to our general welfare and that it certainly presented more than a substantial threat to the blessings of liberty.

To buttress his defense, Mitchell cited Congress's approval of wiretapping and bugging to catch members of organized-crime syndicates, but he did not mention that the law had been so loosely drafted that such devices could be used to listen in on just about anybody in the country. Then he added that he had "insisted—and continued to insist—that each application and full supporting papers [for authorization to tap or bug] be personally presented to me for my evaluation." That assurance ignored two points. For one, his record of using taps in federal prosecutions did not inspire unbridled confidence; for another, his decision to use these devices would encourage state and local prosecutors and policemen, who had the same rights he had under the law, to use them, too—in all likelihood, if experience was any guide, in a far more reckless manner. Moreover, he did not say—perhaps because he did not know it—that the F.B.I. often circumvented the government's pre-1969 prohibition on the use of tapping and bugging by persuading state and local law-enforcement agents to do its spying for it, which made approval by the Attorney General irrelevant.

In his defense of the Administration's policy in this area, Mitchell said, "As one could have predicted, the Department has been criticized by both sides—by those who want massive wiretapping on the five thousand known members of organized crime, and by oversensitive civil-libertarians who claim that any wiretapping is an invasion of privacy." With that, he asked the audience to decide for itself "whether our middle-of-the-road position—although not compatible with either extreme—is not 'order with progress.'"

Some people who had closely followed Mitchell's career as Attorney General felt that this statement solved a puzzle they had been troubled by all along—how he could continue to describe himself as a moderate. "Apparently, he just puts himself down as being in the center, and then places everyone else to the left and right," a lawyer who had attended the A.B.A. meeting said later. "In the case of wiretapping and bugging, most of the men I know who oppose it are moderates and old-fashioned conservatives. They're the ones who stand to lose the most if any radical change, like this one, is made in the status quo."

On the question of preventive detention, or, as the Attorney General preferred to call it, "pre-trial detention," he claimed again that he had taken a stand halfway between extremes. After outlining the history of the "money bail" system, under which prisoners of the court bought temporary freedom, he got to the subject of whether or not preventive detention punished presumably innocent people without due process. This objection was not really valid, he said, since "even under the money-bail system presumably innocent persons were denied their freedom." Of course, that was one reason that the Bail Reform Act of 1966 was enacted. Continuing, the Attorney General asserted that he was "establishing a much more careful method of determining who should not be released" than had been used when money bail was allowed. Since preventive detention was supposed to improve the Bail Reform Act, not the law that it had replaced, it was difficult to see how the inequities of a rejected system were a defense for the inequities of a proposed one. And Mitchell's promise that the government's means of deciding who should be preventively detained would be based on "the most overwhelming evidence" did little to convince the judges, prosecutors, and defense lawyers in the audience, who knew that such evidence was impossible to come by. In conclusion on this point, the Attorney General said, "I know that there are those who argue that no arrested man should be denied his freedom until he is convicted, and I know that there are those who argue for more extensive pre-trial detention on the grounds that society needs even more protection than we have proposed. But we have selected a moderate course." Senator

Ervin, a conservative, thought the course was most immoderate. He called the preventive-detention measure "un-Constitutional, unwise, and deceptively appealing," and added, "Plainly it is an evil law."

When Mitchell got around to the subject of civil rights, he forthrightly took the stand that racial discrimination was morally, legally, and socially wrong and that it had to be "substantially eliminated if we are to survive as a nation of free and independent people." But he went on to say that the Department faced several difficulties in trying to eliminate discrimination in schools. One of them was that withdrawal of federal aid to Southern school districts deprived Negro children first and most of all, and another was that Southern school officials had privately told the Department that voluntary negotiations with the government under the guidelines were more difficult to justify to the voters than involuntary court orders.

The first objection, as mentioned earlier, had the effect of claiming that a few more months of deprivation for extremely deprived children was worse than several years of deprivation for them. As for the advantages of involuntary over voluntary compliance, the view that the government's job was to make life easier for Southern school-board officials was a novel, if hardly a relevant, one. Moreover, voluntary compliance—voluntary in the sense that school boards had to accept desegregation plans if they wanted federal money—had clear psychological advantages, whereas compliance under court order amounted to simple compulsion. In fact, a survey made by H.E.W. in the South at about that time revealed that nine out of ten people who had any experience with integrated schools said things were going better than they had expected.

"We live in difficult times, where moderation is frequently rejected—where the practical and progressive reasonable man, seeking a common-sense solution, is drowned out by the cries of extremism," Attorney General Mitchell said at the close of his address. "But if the reasonable men of this nation do not come together now in a

sincere attempt to heal our differences and improve our institutions
—both in the law and in other areas—I feel that we may be headed
for even more tragic times."

Nearly a year after the 1968 Presidential campaign ended, Mitchell
was still waging it. During a speech he delivered, in October, 1969,
before the Annual United Press International Editors & Publishers
Conference, held in Bermuda, he said, "When this Administration
took office eight months ago, we decided that the time had come to
stop talking, to stop offering excuses, and to start acting—*now*." The
main difficulty, he went on, was that Congress had failed to enact
the legislation recommended to it, and then he added, "It seems to
me that the members of the press would do well to tell the people
of this nation how the Administration has put forth a program for
the nation's capital, and how this program is being stymied by in-
action on Capitol Hill."

His request came at just about the time the Administration's long
honeymoon with the press was coming to an end, and while some
of those on hand might have been willing to heed his appeal a few
weeks earlier, most of them now listened with fresh skepticism. For
one thing, many members of the press in the audience knew that
it had taken the Administration six months to prepare its "anti-
crime package," and perhaps they felt it was somewhat unseemly for
the man in charge of that preparation to attack Congress for not
hastily approving it within three months. For another, they also
knew that the Attorney General's preventive-detention and
narcotics-control proposals were highly controversial and required
extensive study and debate before they were acted on. And, finally,
they were aware that most of what remained in the package—
chiefly the revision of the District court system—had repeatedly been

proposed by prior Administrations and that Congress was unlikely to suddenly look on it now with a sense of urgency.

In another speech delivered around the same time—this one before a convention of the International Association of Chiefs of Police, in Miami Beach—Attorney General Mitchell repeated his claim about "acting *now*" verbatim. Then he told the police chiefs, "I think that you will find that this Administration is sympathetic to law enforcement and that, in areas of doubt, we tend to put our faith in the good intentions of the police, rather than to rely on the bad intentions of criminals." The implication, of course, was that his predecessor was unsympathetic to law-enforcement officials and had somehow put his trust in malevolently inclined criminals, whatever that could have meant. As the record demonstrated, Clark had tried to encourage the good intentions of the police and control their bad intentions. "Let me give you some examples of how we have exercised our federal leadership, how we have resolved areas of doubt in favor of law enforcement," Mitchell continued, and then listed the use of wiretapping, the preventive-detention proposal, and the Department's policy reversal of adherence to the Supreme Court's Miranda ruling. If anything ever relied on the bad intentions of criminals, it was these three courses. Mitchell also told his audience that he had "proposed legislation which would correct some of the technical barriers that now unnecessarily tie up criminal trials and exclude otherwise reliable evidence of guilt." The technical barriers appeared to be those set up by the Bill of Rights, for he seemed to be referring to an Administration proposal that witnesses be compelled to testify once they were promised immunity from prosecution—in short, that they be deprived of their rights under the Fifth Amendment.

On November 20, 1968, the *Times* published an advertisement paid for by the International Committee to Defend Eldridge Cleaver, the Black Panther leader who was then appealing a decision by the California Court of Appeals to send him back to prison for allegedly violating parole. A week after the advertisement appeared, Cleaver, who believed that he would be murdered if he went back to prison, fled the country. (Since twenty-eight members, chiefly local leaders, of the Black Panther Party were killed by policemen around the country in the two-year period ending January 1, 1970, his fear was far from unfounded.) Almost a year after his flight, the Department of Justice subpoenaed two officials of the defense committee to appear before a grand jury sitting in Philadelphia and ordered them to bring along all committee records, including a list of donors and of those who had signed the advertisement. The two officials were Miss Sandra Levinson, a professor of political science at the Brooklyn Polytechnic Institute and an editor of *Ramparts* magazine, and Nathan H. Schwerner, a New York wig manufacturer and father of Michael Schwerner, who was murdered in 1964 while engaged in civil-rights work in Mississippi.

The subpoena contended that the two had possibly violated the federal mail-fraud laws, but their lawyer, Henry W. Sawyer III, in an appeal before the United States Court of Appeals for the Third Circuit charged that no showing of probable cause had been offered and that "what the government is up to" was nothing less than a campaign to intimidate dissenters from dissenting, since anyone would think several times about joining a cause if that might subject him to the trouble and expense of retaining a lawyer and traveling to another city to defend himself. A hundred and forty people had signed the advertisement, including many leading members of the liberal establishment. Leonard B. Boudin, a lawyer representing several of them, filed an *amicus curiae* with the Court of Appeals, in which he stated, "The present drive against dissent and the role of the Department of Justice in this area naturally causes concern that a new era of McCarthyism may lie shortly ahead."

As the contention over the nomination of Judge Haynsworth to the Supreme Court raged throughout the summer and fall of 1969, the principal claim made by President Nixon and Attorney General

Mitchell on his behalf was that he had done no wrong and was eminently qualified to sit on the Court. The principal public claim made by his opponents in the Senate was that he was, at the least, insensitive to judicial ethics, while the principal private claim there was that he was an utter mediocrity and unfit for a place on the highest court. But the basic issue, underlying all the claims and counter claims, was whether the President was serving his own political interest or the public interest. Probably the best answer to this question came not from anyone in the government but from Frank Askin, a professor of law at Rutgers University, who observed, "The issue is not whether Justice Haynsworth will decide cases in a fair and equitable manner. The tragedy is that the very act of his nomination by the President suggests the possibility that the nation may once again renege on its promise of freedom to its black citizens. This prospect is incompatible with the social compact by which Americans bind themselves to live together under law."

Most commentators in Washington concluded that the President had been pushed into a monumental blunder by his Attorney General, who had recommended Haynsworth and who should have known beforehand about the judge's possible conflict of interest between his financial speculation and his role on the federal bench in South Carolina. To a degree, it was a blunder because the President should never have been put in the position of having to defend someone when he didn't know about his past activities. When the Senate rejected Haynsworth's nomination by a vote of fifty-five to forty-five, on November 21st, an editorial in the *Times* called the action "a political setback of stunning proportions" for the President. As far as the Senate was concerned, it certainly was. But as far as the Administration's over-all strategy was concerned, the entire episode was a political victory for the White House. Every day that the battle over the nomination continued, the President picked up support where he most wanted it—among Southerners in general and Wallaceites in particular. And the defeat itself was the greatest vic-

tory of all, since it both created overwhelming sentiment on behalf
of the President in the South, and it opened the way for him to get
still more credit there by naming another Southern conservative
in Haynsworth's place. Politically speaking, that was almost as good
as if he had actually sent two Southern conservatives to the Court.

Although Mitchell could not have had these political advantages
in mind when he first recommended Haynsworth, in all likelihood
he saw the opportunity presented by the opposition to the nomination and persuaded the President to stand by Haynsworth, since
either his approval or rejection by the Senate would be a big victory
for the White House. The President may have had this in mind
when he publicly announced that he would not withdraw Haynsworth's name even if Haynsworth asked him to. Of course, the
benefit to the Administration was attained at some cost to Haynsworth, who could have salvaged part of his reputation if he had
been allowed to withdraw rather than to go down in history as the
first nominee to the Supreme Court to be rejected in forty years.

On December 6, 1969, Attorney General Mitchell and his wife
went to Boca Raton, Florida, where he attended the annual conference of the Investment Bankers Association of America, as he had
for many years while practicing on Wall Street. Mitchell was there
unofficially and was not scheduled to speak at the affair, but on
December 10th he addressed the meeting and in the course of his
speech he announced that in an unnamed state "there is going to
be a massive indictment of public officials on the local level" within
a week or ten days. Officials in the Department of Justice confessed
that they had been taken by surprise by the statement but would say
nothing more than that the state involved was New Jersey, where
one of the Department's Strike Forces had been at work for several
months and had presented the evidence it had collected to a federal
grand jury there.

Former officials of the Department and legal experts were shocked
by the Attorney General's announcement, which, as far as anyone

could recall, was unprecedented. Matters before federal grand juries are normally guarded with the grimmest kind of secrecy, both to assure that the jurors' deliberations are protected from outside influence and to encourage witnesses to come forward, as they might be unwilling to in the glare of publicity. "This kind of ballyhoo may be politically productive, but it doesn't serve the ends of justice," one high official who had served in the Clark era said after Mitchell's announcement. "So far, they've brought in around seventy indictments. In one of our Strike Force actions, we produced a hundred and twenty indictments, without publicity and without endangering the effectiveness of the grand jury. Of course, we didn't get all the credit Mitchell probably will."

Shortly after the 1968 Presidential election, a Republican task force on crime in the House of Representatives sent a special report to President-elect Nixon detailing some of the problems involved in fighting crime, particularly organized crime, and making certain recommendations. Among the latter was the unusual request—unusual for a one-party committee—that a Democratic incumbent United States Attorney be retained after the new Administration took over. The man cited was Robert M. Morgenthau, U.S. Attorney for the Southern District of New York, who had been appointed by President Kennedy in 1961 and who had been widely praised as the most vigorous U.S. Attorney in the country in combating organized crime. It is customary for U.S. Attorneys to resign when a President from the opposing party is inaugurated, but Morgenthau, whose term was supposed to run until 1971, refused to offer his resignation, saying that he had started a number of important cases and would not leave until he had finished them.

During the summer of 1969, it was widely reported that Morgenthau would soon be forced out of office and replaced by Whitney North Seymour, Jr., whose father was an influential member of the Republican Party, both in the state and nationally. But other influential Republicans—Governor Nelson Rockefeller, along with Senators Jacob Javits and Charles Goodell—rallied to Morgenthau because of the outstanding work he had done and because of his standing with the public. The struggle went on, mostly offstage, for several months, until, on December 17th, a hand-delivered letter from Attorney General Mitchell was presented to Morgenthau asking for his resignation. The letter was private, of course, but two hours later, before Morgenthau had time for an equally private reply, the Attorney General told reporters that he had asked for the resignation, and shortly afterward he told them that he had chosen Seymour to take over the post. In view of Morgenthau's accomplishments in office, Mitchell's act could only be considered as a purely partisan one. Clearly, the Administration meant to take all the credit for forthcoming prosecutions of public officials and their criminal associates in New York, including the credit for prosecutions based on groundwork that Morgenthau had already laid. There were also rumors that one particular investigation of Morgenthau's then under way—into the use of secret Swiss bank accounts by wealthy tax-dodgers and a few large banks—might land some exceedingly big fish, among them a number of generous contributors to the Republican Party. In the House, Representative Charles A. Vanik, Democrat of Ohio, rose on the floor and urged the Ways and Means Committee to subpoena Morgenthau's files on such accounts, and said, "It is incumbent upon Congress to utilize this evidence of the tax abuse before it disappears." (Neither he nor anyone else suggested that Seymour, who has been praised by members of both parties as an honorable man, would be involved in such malfeasance in any way.)

For his own part, Morgenthau refused to resign until he completed his work, but a few days later, when it became clear that he could not hope to complete it, or even continue it, without the support of the Department, he announced that he would leave office on

January 15, 1970. In making his decision public, he said, "I hope that my fight for independence will make it easier for my successor to withstand the harsh, narrow, partisan views on law enforcement currently in favor at the Department of Justice."

To no one's surprise, the Department denied that Morgenthau's cashiering was motivated by partisanship. Not long before, Attorney General Mitchell had expressed his view on matters of this nature when he said, "Today, government officials on the highest level are likely to ask not whether a certain decision is politically or legally feasible but whether it conforms to the morality of national leadership. This is particularly true in our Administration, because we are extremely sensitive to the great divisions in our society and to the necessity to heal these wounds as quickly as possible."

Perhaps the best way to judge Mitchell's stewardship of the high office he holds is by accepting his earlier suggestion: "You will be better advised to watch what we do instead of what we say." Anyone who watches with any care must be compelled to conclude that the policies of Barry Goldwater and the right wing, which the voters overwhelmingly repudiated in 1964, have become the policies of the government today. Most people no longer seem to care—if, indeed, they know—what is happening to their country. Exhausted by the demands of modern life and muddled by the fearful discord tearing at society, they seem to have turned their common fate over to their leaders in a way that would have been inconceivable five years ago, when the public rejected extremist appeals for more war in Vietnam and less justice at home. And their leaders—convinced that this abdication means agreement, and that agreement means the public interest is being served—manage the people's affairs in a way that can only divide the country further. When the people finally awaken, they may find their freedoms gone, because the abandonment of the rule of law must bring on tyranny. Since it is the majority's fear—fear of black men, fear of crime, fear of disorder, fear even of differences—that allows repression to flourish, those who succumb to their fears are as responsible as those who make political use of them. And in the end both will suffer equally. "For they have sown the wind, and they shall reap the whirlwind."

Index

Index

Index

The Author

Richard Harris, a staff writer for *The New Yorker* magazine for the past fifteen years, has written widely on the subject of politics in America. His first book, *The Real Voice*, has been acclaimed as the first fully documented account of how a piece of legislation—in this case, to establish controls on the American pharmaceutical industry—makes its way through the incredible labyrinth of Congress. His second book, *A Sacred Trust*, describes the fifty-year battle, in Congress and out, over the Medicare issue. His last book, *The Fear of Crime*, is an examination of the omnibus Crime Control and Safe Streets Act of 1968. The author's work has earned him the reputation of being one of the most thoughtful and courageous political journalists of our time.